May 3, 2018

Emily,
    Thank you for your hard
work and assistance in
preparing this chapter. May your
new endeavors bring you much
fulfillment and may we all
experience a more just +
peaceful world.
                    Clay

Migration

and

Religious Freedom

Essays on the interaction between

religious duty and migration law

edited by
Carolus Grütters &
Dario Dzananovic

Centre for Migration Law
Jean Monnet Centre of Excellence

Research Centre for State and Law
Radboud University, Nijmegen, The Netherlands

Wolf Legal Publishers - 2018

Title   **Migration and Religious Freedom**
            Essays on the interaction between religious duty and migration law

Editors   Carolus Grütters & Dario Dzananovic

            Centre for Migration law
            Jean Monnet Centre of Excellence
            Radboud University
            Nijmegen, the Netherlands

ISBN   978-94-62-404656

©   Copyrights by all individual authors

Layout   Carolus Grütters

Publisher   ᴡ   Wolf Legal Publisher, Nijmegen, the Netherlands

Printed   2018

Table of Contents

Preface

About the authors

Graziano Battistella

is the director of the Scalabrini Migration Center in the Philippines. He was previously with the Center for Migration Studies in New York and dean of studies at the Scalabrini International Migration Institute in Rome. He has a background in political science and ethics. In 1992, he founded the quarterly Asian and Pacific Migration Journal (APMJ). He has published extensively on Asian migration, the human rights of migrants and migration policies.

Jorge E. Castillo Guerra

was born in Panama and studied Theology in Chur in Switzerland, Tübingen in Germany and Nijmegen in the Netherlands. He defended his PhD thesis on the Liberation Ecclesiology of Jon Sobrino in Nijmegen. Currently he is assistant professor and researcher in the Empirical and Practical Study of Religion at the Faculty of Philosophy, Theology & Religious Studies, Radboud University Nijmegen and researcher of the program World Christianity and Migration at the Nijmegen Institute of Missiology. His research deals with theology of migration, interculturality and interreligious relations in Latin America.

Myron M. Cherry

is Managing Partner of Myron M. Cherry & Associates LLC, a well-known trial firm based in Chicago, Illinois (USA). For decades, the firm has specialized in commercial litigation throughout the U.S. involving all areas of substantive law, representing companies and individuals on a contingent fee basis. He maintains an interest in political, civic, charitable and energy and economic matters, and was appointed by President Clinton to the U.S. Holocaust Commission. Mr. Cherry is an adjunct Professor at Northwestern University School of Law and is widely sought after for his trial skills.

Dario Dzananovic

is a PhD candidate at the Centre for Migration Law at Radboud University in Nijmegen, the Netherlands. He holds a J.D. from DePaul University College of Law (Chicago, USA), and an LL.M. in human rights and migration law from Radboud University. Prior to beginning his PhD, Dario worked as a lawyer in Chicago, specializing in complex civil litigation. His PhD research lies on the intersection of migration, law, and religion. More specifically, his project aims to determine which arguments play a role when state laws and religious norms conflict in the context of migration. That is, how are these conflicts between state law and religious obligation resolved?

Carolus Grütters

is senior researcher at the Centre for Migration Law of the Faculty of Law of Radboud University in the Netherlands. After his graduation (Law at Leiden University) he did research at Radboud University on simulation models in the area of asylum law. He holds a doctoral degree awarded by Radboud University in the area of Law as well as Management Sciences. His research focuses on asylum law, distribution of asylum flows, regularisations and policy guidelines on migration. He is editor-in-chief of the Newsletter on European Migration Issues (NEMIS) and the Newsletter on European Asylum Issues (NEAIS).

Elspeth Guild

is Jean Monnet Professor *ad personam* at Radboud University in Nijmegen, the Netherlands, as well as at Queen Mary, University of London (UK). She is also partner at the London law firm, Kingsley Napley. She has published widely in the field of European free movement of persons, asylum and immigration. Professor Guild provides regular advice to the European Parliament, the European Commission, the Council of Europe and other European and international organizations (such as the UNHCR) on free movement of persons, migration and asylum. Professor Guild is also co-editor of the European Journal of Migration and of the book series Immigration and Asylum Law and Policy in Europe (published by Brill | Martinus Nijhoff).

Rev. Craig B. Mousin

has been the University Ombudsperson at DePaul University (Chicago, USA) since 2001. He received his B.S. *cum laude* from Johns Hopkins University, his J.D. with honors from the University of Illinois, and his M. Div. from Chicago Theological Seminary. He joined DePaul's College of Law faculty in 1990, and served as the Executive Director of the Center for Church/State Studies until 2003, and co-director from 2004-2007. In 1984, he founded and directed the Midwest Immigrant Rights Center, which has since become the National Immigrant Justice Center. Rev. Mousin was ordained by the United Church of Christ in 1989 at Wellington Avenue U.C.C.

Dolores Morondo Taramundi

is currently Head of Research at the Human Rights Institute of the University of Deusto (Bilbao, Spain). She has taught Human Rights and Legal Philosophy for several years at the University of Urbino (Italy) and acted as an independent expert for human rights projects of the European Commission. Her main topics of research and publication include human rights, antidiscrimination law, intersectionality and vulnerable groups. She is currently working on issues of human rights research methods and on complex forms of inequality.

Jim Murdoch

joined the School of Law of the University of Glasgow after qualifying as a solicitor. He read law as an undergraduate at Glasgow and has an LLM from the University of California at Berkeley. He was Head of the School of Law between 1996 and 2000. He has taught at the universities of Mainz, Freiburg, Hamburg and Paris Ouest, and was a *professeur stagiaire* with the Directorate of Human Rights of the Council of Europe in France. He is a regular participant in Council of Europe seminar programme visits to Central and East European states and has developed a particular interest in non-judicial human rights enforcement mechanisms. In March 2012, he was awarded the *Pro Merito* medal of the Council of Europe. The medal is the highest distinction granted by the Secretary General to individuals (or organisations) in recognition of their commitment to the Council of Europe's values and work.

Federica Sona

is an affiliated researcher at the Laboratory of Fundamental Rights (Turin, Italy) and at the Max Plank Institute for Social Anthropology. She holds a PhD in Law (London); PhD in Law and Society (Milan, Italy); MA ICLS (London, UK); PSC ICM (London, UK); Laurea in Law (Turin, Italy). Her main expertise regards Western Islām and horizontal/vertical kinship relationships. She is currently completing a manuscript on Muslim prospective parents reoccurring to fertility treatments in Italy. She is also working on the (non-)recognition of Islamic/Muslim marriages and divorces in Common Law and Civil Law jurisdictions.

Roberto Scarciglia

is Full Professor of Comparative Law, University of Trieste Italy, and Associate Member of International Academy of Comparative Law (IACL), Paris (France). He wrote many articles and some books on legal pluralism, comparative methodology, comparative law and history and global law. His most recent books are: *Islamic Symbols in European Courts*, edited with Werner Menski (Kluwer, 2014); *Metodi e comparazione giuridica* (Cedam, 2016); and *Pluralism and Religious Diversity: A Methodological Approach*, edited with Werner Menski (Kluwer, 2017).

Amaya Valcarcel

is a Spanish refugee lawyer who has worked as a Protection Officer with the UNHCR in Spain and in Kakuma refugee camp, Northern Kenya, between 1995 and 1997. In 1998, she joined the Jesuit Refugee Service (JRS) as Policy Coordinator. While working at JRS, she lectured on Refugee Law and between 2002 and 2003, she was the Coordinator of the Master's Degree on Humanitarian Aid and Development Cooperation at the Pontifical University of Comillas, Spain. She worked between 2003 and 2005 at the Arrupe Center for People with a Disability in Cambodia. Between 2006 and 2008 she was the Secretary General of the Spanish Commission for Refugees. In 2009, she again joined the Jesuit Refugee Service, where she works at present as International Advocacy Officer.

Derk Venema

is a philosopher and legal scholar (Leiden University). He wrote a PhD dissertation on the Dutch judiciary during the Nazi occupation (Radboud University Nijmegen 2007). Currently, he is assistant professor in law at Radboud University and professional ethics instructor for the Dutch judiciary training centre. He publishes on law's relations to war, ethics, language, literature, evolution, political transition and fundamental rights.

Lisbeth Zornig Andersen

is founder of the *House of Zornig*, aiming at improving the state of society's most socially vulnerable citizens. She is president of the think tank Social Innovations Forum, former Children's *Ombudmand* in Denmark, former CEO of Specialists employing people with Asperger's syndrome as IT testers and founder of the Children's IT foundation that provides computers for all Danish children in care. She graduated from the University of Copenhagen with a Masters of Economics, specializing in game theory. In 2011, she published her childhood biography *Zornig - Anger is my middle name,* which became a best-seller. In 2014, she won the radio award of the year for her portrait programs in *Zornigs Zone* on Radio 24syv. In 2015, she won the TV award of the year for the series *The burned children* on Danish TV2. Also in 2015, she published the debate book *Social commando soldiers* about children who not just survived a difficult childhood, but made it to the top.

Chapter 1   **Introduction**

Carolus Grütters & Elspeth Guild

1.1   **Background**

In Pope Francis' first address to the European Parliament in Strasbourg in November 2014, he deplored the EU's treatment of migrants. "We cannot allow the Mediterranean to become a vast graveyard", Pope Francis said, in reference to the thousands of migrants who drown as they seek to reach Southern Europe from North Africa and the Middle East.

The first trip which Pope Francis took (July 2013) was to the island of Lampedusa, the landing place of many migrants and refugees arriving in Europe after dangerous sea trips from North Africa. He met with refugees and migrants there and sought first hand experiences of people who have suffered these difficult trips and the ambivalent reception on arrival. The Pope also praised (Lutheran) Sweden in particular for its open-door policy for refugees and its acceptance of the largest number of Syrian refugees over the period of the civil war there juxtaposing the treatment of refugees in that mainly protestant country against the less generous reception of refugees of a number of primarily Catholic countries in Europe. "Sweden opens its borders, organizes language classes, gives economic assistance, and offers paths to join society", Pope Francis said.[1]

This challenge by the head of the Catholic Church to the legitimacy of the EU's border and immigration management project represents a substantial policy move at the top of the Catholic Church regarding the normative obligation of European policy makers, border guards and people to accept and respect the human dignity of non-citizens (asylum seekers, refugees, migrant workers and other migrants) both in law and practice. It is incumbent on scholars to examine this issue from the perspective of the role of churches in assisting migrants and refugees and framing the ethical imperatives of our times.

All kinds of churches, i.e. religious bodies, have played a very important role in the assistance and social insertion of migrants in Europe over the past decades. During the years of labour migration from Southern Europe to Northern Europe, churches were a central institution in providing a mechanism for migrants and refugees to find ways to understand their new environments and realise their human potential in their new homes. These churches have been central in promoting good interfaith relations, social insertion of newcomers and equality.

---

1   Report of Vatican Radio 15 February 2014.

A number of orders and denominations within the churches have been particularly active in Europe over the past 20 years in the field of migration. The Jesuit Refugee Service is perhaps the best-known example with its Charter which stresses that it accompanies refugees and forced migrants serving them as companions and advocating their cause. However, it is not the only religious body, which is engaged with the support of migrants and refugees. Such actions not only often come into tension with state policies and national, regional or federal laws but also supra-national legislation and programmes designed to manage migration by keeping some people out and allowing only some other citizens in. This challenge takes the form of a normative position that all people are deserving of dignity and that divisions on the basis of citizenship are suspect. The legitimacy of national and supranational or federal migration and border policies is questioned through many of these activities – and not just in Europe or the United States of America.

1.2   Problem of priority

There are three main ways in which churches act which privilege people over immigration and border laws.

The first is in respect of arrival. In the context of the irregular arrivals of people on small boats in the Mediterranean, many of the press releases and accounts of the saving of life include details that when the boats got into difficulties, someone on board had a mobile phone and the number of a priest in Italy to whom the distress call was sent and from there the priest alerted the authorities to the need for a search and rescue operation. In the process of embarking on a dangerous trip in inadequate conditions, the migrants and refugees leave the North African coast with knowledge that there is someone, a priest, who will dare to raise the alarm when and if they run into trouble. The challenge to EU law here is both direct in bringing international humanitarian law into a picture which EU border guards prefer to configure as a border control matter and indirect in that by assisting the irregular entry of non-EU citizens, the priest puts himself potentially in the category of persons who may be facilitating 'illegal' entry (as the EU documents describe such action) and thus potentially committing a criminal act.[2]

The second way concerns reception. In Europe, churches take an important role in providing reception facilities and shelter for destitute non-EU citizens arriving in the country. In some cases, this reception provision is supported by the state with funding being channelled through religious institutions to assist people. In this capacity of providing reception to migrants, churches or municipalities often find themselves in a position of some friction with certain parts of immigration authorities which have a policy of trying to starve foreigners into

---

2   Council Directive 2002/90/EC of 28 November 2002 defining the facilitation of unauthorised entry, transit and residence.

leaving the state – a rather unsavoury formulation of policy but one in currency today. Some churches have taken a central role in challenging the deprivation of new arrivals of reception facilities, food, housing and medical treatment. Not only through direct provisions albeit in contrast to state policies but also through supporting legal challenges such as the very important case from the European Committee on Social Rights interpreting the European Social Charter as prohibiting the destitution of people on the basis of their immigration status or manner of arrival in the state.[3]

The third way in which churches provide support to irregularly present migrants (and often asylum seekers whose applications have been refused) engages an even more immediate challenge to state authority: the use of church asylum to protect persons at risk of expulsion from state authorities. In many instances, a Church becomes the sole or last intervener on behalf of irregularly present migrants who are facing coercive action by state authorities.[4] In the USA, a comparable approach is known as 'sanctuary city' in which a city limits its cooperation with the federal government to enforce immigration law.

The normative framework of migration and border control has been much influenced by the application of human rights law. Some commentators have even gone so far as to see human rights as a 'new belief system'. However, while access to lawyers willing to argue human rights cases became the norm in many states in the 1980s, 1990s and early 2000s, the diminution in funding of legal aid has resulted in the exclusion of many migrants from legal advice (let alone legal advice and assistance of a high quality). The role of human rights as a mechanism to reframe the normative issues of non-citizens lives has become more limited in the 2010s. This may have created new dynamics for churches in respect of the humanity of migrants. The question, then, becomes which framework – state or faith – has priority and why.

1.3   This book

On 9 and 10 February 2017, experts from various backgrounds joined in a seminar *Migration and Religion* organized by the Centre for Migration Law, Jean Monnet Centre of Excellence at Radboud University, Nijmegen the Netherlands. During this seminar, the focus was on the intersection of migration, law and religion. We hoped to identify which arguments play a role in the discussions where state law and religious norms conflict in the context of

---

3   European Committee of Social Rights, 1 July 2014, Complaint 90/2013, *Conference of European Churches v. the Netherlands.*
4   For example, the work of the Jesuit Refugee Service together with a change in the judicial authority reviewing immigration detention in Germany has resulted in the sharp reduction of non-citizens kept in detention with a view to removal from the country and a possible closure of several detention facilities for foreigners.

migration. In this book, we have included the most important contributions to
this seminar thematically organised around four topics:

(1) Religious Social Thought,
(2) Application of religious freedom
(3) Comparative analysis of religious freedom laws,
     and
(4) Practitioners' views.

The first theme, *Religious Social Thought*, is examined first by Graziano Battistella. In chapter 2, he outlines the historical foundations of Catholic Social
Thought on the issue of migration and the repeated attention to date. He also
underlines that Churches recognize the tension between *love for migrants* and
love thy neighbour. Subsequently, Jorge Castillo Guerra provides a closer look
(chapter 3) at the current views of the Vatican held by Pope Francis, who offers
the view that the Church is without borders or boundaries. Migration is not a
'mere ethical issue' but rather a 'faith issue'. The third contribution on this
theme (chapter 4) is by Myron Cherry who presents the views of Talmudic law
on migration and concludes that 'Talmudic law regards immigration policy as
circumstantial and transactional'. Thus, illustrating a balance between the rights
and duties of a stranger, i.e. the migrant, and society. Although these three
narratives seem to represent equivalent ideas, there are differences as to what is
given priority.

   The second theme, *Application of religious freedom to migration laws*, is
developed by Rev. Craig Mousin (chapter 5), who demonstrates that courts (in
the United States of America) still fail to address international law under the
International Religious Freedom Act. He concludes that the government shows
a lack of sensitivity to national laws, cultures and practice that silence religious
belief and practice. Subsequently, Federica Sona (chapter 6) elaborates the
Italian case. She focuses on the right of Muslim migrants to contract a valid
marriage in Italy with civil and religious effects. Along with national legislation
and religious rules, the EU directive on family reunification is dealt with.
Dolores Morondo Taramundi (chapter 7) goes one step further and investigates
how to break the law. More in particular, she discusses cases of infringement of
legislation stemming from the Facilitation Directive.

   The third theme, religious freedom laws, is first dealt with by Jim Murdoch
(chapter 8). He shows that jurisprudence of the ECtHR on Article 9 ECHR
acknowledges the principle that diversity matters and that there may well be a
need for limits to the freedom of, among others, religious belief. However, he
proceeds in arguing that Article 9 is not necessary to protect freedom of thought,
conscience and belief in light of case law developments on Article 14 ECHR.
He suggests that discounting any element of the exercise of religious belief in
favour of the application of the principle that cases are better determined by the

simple question of which side better advances pluralism, tolerance and broad-mindedness. The second contribution in this part (chapter 9) comes from Roberto Scarciglia who discusses the legal problems related to the exercise of freedom of religion and immigration at the level of comparative administrative law. Specifically, he focuses on freedom of religion in places of immigration detention.

The fourth part of the book contains some practical experiences of offering help. Almaya Valcarcel (chapter 10) describes the hospitality offered by the Jesuit Refugee Service. The JRS has developed a *Welcome Network*, a programme for individuals and families to welcome refugees into their homes. The practical problems one runs into by 'just' offering help is exposed (chapter 11) by Lisbeth Zornig Andersen. She tells the story of how helping others brought her in (legal) problems in Denmark. Quite depressing is her conclusion that after a Danish District Court punished her for helping refugees, no higher Court came to her aid. The Danish Court of Appeal upheld the verdict of the district Court. Subsequently the Danish Supreme Court declared her case inadmissible: too little importance. Even the European Court of Human Rights did not want to touch it: inadmissible. Lastly, Derk Venema (chapter 12) illustrates the problematic character of freedom of religion describing the Church of the Flying Spaghetti Monster. Interestingly, the principle characteristic of a religion does not seem to be sincerity but seriousness.

In the concluding remarks in the postface of this book (chapter 13), Elspeth Guild expresses the competing viewpoints that have emerged from several papers regarding the propriety of assisting migrants. She does so by reference to two biblical passages: Romans 13, which commands submission to governing (worldly) authority, and Matthew 25, which commands people to help strangers or migrants.

We hope this book will clear up the arguments used in the discussions on the important issue on migration and religion.

Part 1

Religious Social Thought

Chapter 2   Do Likewise

Obligations toward migrants in Catholic Social Thought

Graziano Battistella

2.1   Introduction

It is probably a platitude, but I would still like to begin by remembering the pictures of those two boys found dead, one on the shore of the Mediterranean Sea and the other on the banks of a river between Bangladesh and Myanmar. The first, Aylan Kurdi, was a three-year-old Syrian boy who drowned on 2 September 2015 near Bodrum, Turkey, while his family was attempting to reach the island of Kos in Greece, after their application for asylum in Canada was rejected. The second, Mohammed Shohayet, was a 16-month-old Rohingya boy who drowned while the family was trying to cross the river Naf on the Bangladesh-Myanmar border on 4 January 2017. Two similar pictures, one year apart, miles apart, but pointing to the same reality: there are people in the world trying to escape violence, persecution or poverty, but there is sufficient willingness to welcome them in countries where there is security and prosperity. Should anyone feel obliged to respond to the plight of people seeking asylum and if yes, who should? The countries closer to problematic areas are the ones providing immediate solutions. But should the moral responsibility to intervene only fall on them? Is geography the main determinant for moral responsibility toward migrants and asylum seekers?

Two additional images need to be presented in this introduction. On the one hand, the image of thousands of migrants from Syria in a European country, Germany, and the image of the border of another European country, Hungary, closed with barbed wire to avoid the entry of refugees. Of course, things cannot be oversimplified and other images could be shown which lead to a different conclusion. The purpose, however, is to raise some questions. Why is there such a difference among countries with the same cultural background (insofar as being European spells cultural similarities)? And closer to our topic, why are there such differences in countries with the same Christian background? To put it differently, is it possible to share the same faith and have a different attitude toward migrants? Is such difference coherent with Catholic Social Thought (CST)?

The question hides many other concerns: among them, the relevance of CST in general, for public policies in particular and, ultimately, the possibility that people listening to CST may reach different policy conclusions. It is not our intention to resurrect the old debate about the autonomy of political mediation in governing social realities. The purpose of this chapter is much more modest. It attempts to illustrate CST in regard to migration and examine whether and what obligations toward migrants arise from that teaching. In addition, it must be specified that reference to CST is mostly limited to documents of the Holy See and it cannot be exhaustive, as documents, messages and speeches already comprise hundreds of pages.[1]

This chapter will begin with a brief illustration of the biblical foundations of the teaching on migration; it will then examine the main obligations deriving from CST; it will discuss the normative nature of CST and its convergence with or divergence from international norms on migration. It will conclude with the call for an ethic of inclusion and proximity.

2.2   Biblical foundations

Extensive writing has been devoted, particularly in recent years, to the biblical perspective on migration. This increased attention follows the attempt to propose a theology of migration, a development emerging from the growing trend of doing contextual theology.[2] Relying on migration as a *locus theologicus* and a "sign of the time", the theology of migration attempts to shed new light on the mystery of salvation using migration as a metaphor for the journey of God with his people and the aspiration of people to return to God. In this context, the many circumstances of displacement, escape, expulsion, exile, diaspora, welcoming and hospitality found in Scripture are utilized as metaphors for the unravelling of the mystery of salvation.

If careful exegesis and hermeneutics is necessary in the reading of Scripture in relation to a theology of migration, much more attention is required when using the Scriptures for ethical reflection. After centuries in which Scripture in Catholic moral theology was used mostly as proof-texts,[3] magisterial and theological contributions after Vatican II make a much more extensive reference to the Bible, also following the recommendation of *Optatam Totius* (16) which asked that moral theology "should draw more fully on the teaching of Holy Scripture". At the same time, there was no agreement among moral theologians on the method for using the Scriptures. Spohn contends that Catholics use an analogical approach between the situations in Scripture and the contemporary

---

1   See: Tassello G. & L. Favero (eds.) (1985), *Chiesa e mobilità umana. Documenti della Santa Sede dal 1883 al 1983*, Roma: Centro Studi Emigrazione; Fondazione Migrantes (2001), *Enchiridion della Chiesa per le Migrazioni. Documenti magisteriali ed ecumenici sulla pastorale della mobilità umana (1887-2000)*, Bologna, EDB; Baggio Fabio & Maurizio Pettenà (eds.) (2009), *Caring for Migrants. A Collection of church Documents on the Pastoral Care of Migrants,* Strathfield, NSW: St Pauls Publications. See for most documents of the Holy See: <www.vatican.va>.

2   Campese 2012.

3   Bowe and Nairn, 2002.

context, while Protestants prefer a dialectical approach.[4] Behind these methodological differences, however, there is agreement that more than providing specific moral rules, the narration of salvation testified in Scripture is the source for the living of discipleship.

This brief digression on the use of Scripture is necessary because a fundamentalist misuse of the Bible remains common, even in regard to migrants. Sen. Jeff Sessions of Alabama, Attorney General of the USA, claims to find support in Scripture for his political choices and indicated the decision of Nehemiah to rebuild the wall of Jerusalem as the equivalent of the wall between the US and Mexico. In ridiculing this position, Rev. Craig B. Mousin of the Chicago Theological Seminary pointed out that the whole history of salvation would have been different if a fundamentalist interpretation had been applied.[5]

The commandment: "The foreigner residing among you must be treated as your native-born. Love them as yourself, for you were foreigners in Egypt. I am the Lord your God" (Lv 19:34) is the most direct reference to normative behaviour toward migrants that we can find in Hebrew Scripture. It was observed that it is repeated more than 30 times (more than any other commandment except for the injunction to recognize the supremacy of God).[6] Exegetes rush to specify that not all foreigners were included in that commandment, but only what we would call the permanent residents (*gēr*). The visitor or temporary residents (*zar* or *nochri*) were considered strangers and were not given such attention. Perhaps what is most significant in the commandment toward the foreigner, who could be of any nationality or ethnicity, are the reasons for the protection.[7] First is the condition of legal weakness, similar to that of the orphan and the widow. The reason for the lack of protection comes from the fact that these persons do not possess the sources of protection: property or people who could provide a guarantee for them. "The Israelites should not take advantage of their condition, but should favour their survival by allowing them to glean wheat and grapes after the harvest" (Dt 24:19-21). Second is the fact that Israel was a foreigner in Egypt. Having experienced oppression in a foreign land, Israel should remember the suffering connected with it and not impose it on others. The same logic that sustains the golden (or silver) rule also informs the commandment not to oppress the foreigner, and is sanctioned by the will of God: "I am the Lord your God."

Rushing from the commandment to love foreigners to conclusions on public policy is an inappropriate shortcut. Immigration restrictionists have spared no effort to utilize Scripture in their favour[8] and it is worthwhile remembering, as pointed out by the Lutherans, that "Scriptural teaching on immigrants (…)

---

4   Spohn 1999.
5   <www.ctschicago.edu/about/blogs/challenge-response-blog>.
6   Plaut 1996.
7   Bonora 1993.
8   Edwards Jr. 2009.

cannot be directly translated into current immigration laws or policies".[9] At the same time, Scripture provides us with "an interpretive framework" and the commandment to love the foreigner cannot be ignored. It is the first obligation we have toward migrants, regardless of the form of migration in which they are involved as it would be anachronistic to utilize the biblical distinctions between foreigners and strangers and apply it to contemporary migrants.

Naturally, such a commandment must be considered an instance of the more general commandment to love one another. It is the original responsibility, considered in its semantic value as responding to the other. It is a response required from the very beginning of the history of salvation. "Then the Lord said to Cain, 'Where is your brother Abel?'" (Gen. 4:9). Levinas has provided the philosophical foundation for the understanding of the other as someone who cannot be assimilated to the self and who requires instead recognition in his "otherness," from which moral duties derive. It is the foundation of an ethics of alterity which becomes the ethics of responsibility as the other requires that I respond to his existence.

In the New Testament, alterity is redefined as proximity. The indigence of the other reveals my own indigence and requires that I reach out to him, become a neighbour, and love him like myself, because he is myself.[10] The reference to the parable of the Samaritan (Lk 10:25-37) becomes natural. It defines the ethical consequences of discipleship as an ethics of proximity. As Christ, the estranged among his own people, reaches out to wounded humanity, so the disciple is invited to become a neighbour to those in need. It is a parable that has been utilized often in regard to the concern for migrants, but which invites reinterpretation. Traditionally migrants have been identified with the man beaten up and left half dead on the side of the road and the recommendation is for Christians to act as good Samaritans, rescuing them from the abuses suffered on the migration trail. But an ethic of proximity also has a reciprocal side. It is in the encounter with the other that I discover who I am. Accepting the logic of proximity is accepting to be welcomed in the act of welcoming. Today more than ever the migrants are the ones who desire to become our neighbours, they are the Samaritans trying to approach us.[11] Legal barriers erected by migration policies and structural walls built at the borders are keeping them out. We feel secure because of those barriers and do not realize that our secure societies are in need of rescue.

With this perspective, it is easier to understand the New Testament normative injunction in reference to migrants: "I was a stranger and you invited me in" (Mt 25:35). An ethics of responsibility and proximity requires hospitality, but hospitality implies identification and recognition. Through hospitality the other is no longer a stranger but a neighbour. Differences cannot be eliminated, but can be appreciated in a relationship of mutual recognition. Hospitality is offered

---

9   The Lutheran Church, Commission on Theology and Church Relations 2012.
10   Piana 2008.
11   Battistella 2010.

gratuitously, but Jesus' identification with the stranger gives to hospitality an ethical and eschatological dimension, because "Jesus Christ is the paradigm for Christian moral life", as he said: "follow me".[12] Again, from the command of hospitality we cannot derive specific policies, but we have an interpretative framework within which to discern when policies turn against the spirit of the Gospel.

2.3   Obligations to migrants in the Church's Social Thought

In the Gospel, Jesus identifies with the foreigner without distinction as to the type of foreigner. The same universalistic approach is maintained in the early Christian community as powerfully expressed in the short writing *To Diognetus*. Diognetus has various questions about Christians and one such question is "what is the affection which they cherish among themselves?" The author answers: "They love all men, and are persecuted by all." As Burin observes, they do not just love one another, they love all, as required by the Lord (Mt 5:43-46).[13] Certainly, the early Christian tradition also contains an adversarial tone, particularly in the apologetic literature as found in the Hebrew Scripture.[14] It is also possible that the apologetic purpose leads to embellishing things, but it is still worthwhile quoting Aristides of Athens, who wrote in the *Apologia* (15:7): "And when they see a stranger, they take him in to their homes and rejoice over him as a very brother".

The universalistic framework is never lost but the progressive experience of concern for foreigners from the same Christian faith has led to directives and institutions that can be qualified more as pastoral care. When contemporary forms of migration generated by the Industrial Revolution took place, the Church developed specific teachings and action for the care of migrants. These teachings reflect the evolution of origin, direction and types of migration. From the specific concern for Italian migrants to the Americas at the time of Leo XIII the teachings re-acquired a universalistic approach after Vatican II and more specifically with the latest instruction *Erga Migrantes Caritas Christi* and have been written to address migration as a globalized phenomenon. Throughout this development, some essential obligations toward migrants can be identified. These are duties which correspond to migrants' rights.

2.3.1   Obligation to ensure that migration is not a necessity

It has been frequently stated that a comprehensive approach to migration requires addressing its root causes. While this is not the place to discuss the

---

12 Spohn 1999, 1.
13 Burin 1993.
14 Rivera-Pagàn 2013, 40.

determinants of migration,[15] it can be said in general terms that migration is remotely caused by economic, political, social and cultural disparities which force people to decide to seek a more dignified life in another country. What is considered problematic are the constraints, which are manifested in different degrees in the various forms of migration (higher for refugees, less compelling for economic migrants) but which bear consequences on the decision to migrate.

Leo XIII expressed the idea that migration is the result of compelling factors when he said in *Rerum Novarum* (47): "No one would exchange his country for a foreign land if his own afforded him the means of living a decent and happy life". *Pacem in Terris* (25), *Gaudium et Spes* (66) and *Erga Migrantes Caritas Christi* (29) reiterated and made more explicit the need to ensure that people are not constrained into migration: "Also the right of the individual not to emigrate is affirmed, that is, the right to be able to achieve his rights and satisfy his legitimate demands in his own country".

2.3.2   Obligation to admit migrants

The obligation to receive migrants derives from the fact that the Church recognizes the right to migrate as a natural right. The initial formulation of such a right is attributed to Pius XII. He looked at migration mostly as an issue of overpopulation. Migration was a way of redistributing population for the benefit of both the country of origin and the country of destination. Behind this practical reasoning was a theological argumentation, the fact that land was a resource that "God created for and prepared for the use of all".[16] In the Apostolic Constitution *Exsul Familia* he argued that the right to migrate was founded on natural law and duties toward humanity.[17] The right was expressed in clear terms in the radio message *Levate capita vestra* pronounced on Christmas Eve 1952, where he said that numerous families found obstacles to migration because of the measures imposed by migration policies and therefore "the natural right of the person not to be hindered from emigrating or immigrating is not recognized or is practically nullified under the pretext of a common good falsely understood or falsely applied, but nevertheless sanctioned and validated by legislative or administrative dispositions".[18] In those words, Pius XII affirmed the right to migrate as a natural right, but also the right of the state to regulate migration in the name of the common good of the country. However, limitations deriving from the common good cannot be falsely understood or falsely applied. In addition, even if the common good of the country would lead to restrictions, "Christian charity and the sense of human solidarity existing between all men,

---

15 From the countless publications on the determinants of migration we can suggest Massey *et al.*, 1998.
16 The Solemnity of Pentecost, 1 June 1941, AAS XXXIII, 203.
17 AAS XXXXI, 69-70.
18 AAS XXXXV 41.

children of the One Eternal God and Father, will not be forgotten."[19] Considerations deriving from membership in the common human family should temper the restrictions which the state can determine in the name of the common good of the country and invite human solidarity.

The articulation provided by Pius XII was then reiterated by his successors, mostly in the same terms, although international migration had changed. John XXIII listed the right to migrate in art. 25 of *Pacem in Terris*. Paul VI in *Octogesima Adveniens* (17) advocated an international charter for migrants "which will assure them of the right to emigrate, favor their integration, facilitate their professional advancement and give them access to decent housing where, if such is the case, their families can join them." The Instruction *Nemo Est* (1969), which replaced *Exsul Familia* as the guiding Church document on the care of migrants, reformulated the right to migrate in its essential elements in art. 7 as a right of the persons but also of the families and which should not be denied "except for grave requirements of the common good, considered objectively." John Paul II provided the clearest formulation of the right to migrate in the 2001 World Migration Day Message (WMDM), specifying "its dual aspect of the possibility to leave one's country and the possibility to enter another country to look for better conditions of life."

This brief excursus shows consistent teachings by the Church on the right to migrate, which should not be considered an absolute right since the country can regulate it, but which should be affirmed as taking precedence over regulation, since for the Church it is the state that should explain the reasons for limiting such right and the reasons can only be for the common good of the country, but a common good considered objectively. In Church teachings countries should ensure general openness to migrants and refugees. The reasons why migrants and refugees should be accepted is because they are escaping conditions which are against their human dignity (*Nemo Est* 7) and because, before belonging to specific nations, everyone belongs to the common human family.

2.3.3   Obligation to protect the migrants' families

The Church affirms the right to migrate not simply as a right of the individual but as a right of the family (*Mater et Magistra 45*; *Familiaris Consortio* 46). The right of migrants to live together as a family should be safeguarded (*Apostolicam Actuositatem* 11; *Charter of the Rights of the Family* 12,b) and the same should apply to refugees, as recommended by Benedict XVI in his 2007 *WMDM*. Obligations toward the migrants' family concern all aspects with which every family has to contend (housing, education of children, working conditions, social benefits). John Paul II reminded states that protecting the family, in particular the migrant family, was a priority duty.[20] Often, the right to

---

19   Address to the US Senators member of the Committee on Immigration, 14 March 1946. Quoted in *Exsul Familia*, note 124.
20   Pope John Paul II 1986.

live as a family is not expressly opposed, but it is frustrated by the lack of conditions to live as a family. This applies in particular to workers in temporary migration, confined in barracks or labour camps. Attention to the family left behind is recommended in documents of episcopal conferences such as the 2003 joint document of the US and Mexican bishops: *Strangers No Longer. Together On the Journey of Hope* (46). Specific obligation is required in regard to the children of migrants, the object of the 2017 *WMDM* of Pope Francis, who recommends protection, integration and long-term solutions to issues related to migrant children.

2.3.4   Obligation to ensure integration and cultural dialogue

The admission of migrants is only the first step in the migration process. Insertion into the community, with all its related aspects, constitutes the largest part of migrants' rights and, conversely, of society's duties and obligations. The Church has recommended social integration countless times, warning against the temptation to assimilate the migrant both into the society and the Church.[21] Integration begins with avoiding discrimination in all its forms.

The Church is aware that the presence of migrants increases the cultural differences within societies. John Paul II, addressing this issue in his message for the World Day of Peace (1 January 2001), observed that migration often enriched the cultural environment of the countries of destination. At other times, cultural differences remain sharp and fan ongoing tensions. The Pope was aware that there were no "magic formulas" to address differences but invited inter-cultural dialogue, the need to address both the needs of the local population as well as of the migrants, and the obligation to respect the cultural traditions of the migrants "as long as they do not contravene either the universal ethical values inherent in the natural law or fundamental human rights."

2.3.5   Obligation to respect the human rights of irregular migrants

Irregular migration is ubiquitous. There is practically no country which can claim to be without irregular migrants, and the harshest measures against them, including structural barriers, often make the process more dangerous but do not eliminate it. Irregular migration is a function of the conflict between the number of migrants intending to go abroad and migration policies limiting such possibility. Differences in the number of irregular migrants in countries depend on the geographical proximity between origin and destination, the imbalance in their living and working conditions and ultimately the usefulness of irregular migrants for the destination economy.

The Church does not advocate irregular migration. However, John Paul II warned that "His irregular legal status cannot allow the migrant to lose his dignity, since he is endowed with inalienable rights, which can neither be

---

21   Pope John Paul II 1985.

violated nor ignored".[22] Together with the respect of human rights, which are not lost because of the irregular status, the Church recommends preventive action and legislative harmonization.[23]

2.3.6 Obligation to assist victims of smuggling and trafficking

Increasingly, smuggling and trafficking of persons have received the attention of the international community, which has addressed the issues through two widely ratified protocols of the 2000 United Nations Convention against Transnational Organized Crime (CTOC). Although this phenomenon is not limited to persons involved in migration, as trafficking in particular can also happen within the national borders, it is migrants who are mostly caught in it. The Church has raised its voice several times on the subject. The EMCC defined trafficking as "a new chapter in the history of slavery" (5) and recommends speaking about it in catechetical instruction (41). Pope Francis has spoken often on the subject with the intention of raising awareness on this "modern form of slavery, which violates the God-given dignity of so many of our brothers and sisters, and constitutes a true crime against humanity."[24] He called the victims of trafficking the most vulnerable people in society and encouraged action within the Church, where several groups have already been established on the issue of trafficking, such as the Santa Marta Group (senior law enforcement chiefs and members of the Catholic Church), RENATE (Religious in Europe Networking Against Trafficking and Exploitation) and Talitha Kum (a coalition of religious congregations).

2.3.7 Obligation to avoid forced migration and to welcome refugees and asylum seekers

Forced migration is increasing, driven by conflicts and natural disasters, and comprising internally displaced persons, asylum seekers, refugees and persons of humanitarian concern. The Church has dedicated two major documents to refugees: *Refugees, A Challenge to Solidarity* (1992) and *Welcoming Christ in Refugees and Forcibly Displaced Persons: Pastoral Guidelines* (2013). The purpose of this second document is clearly stated: "Through this Document, we hope to make all Christians, pastors and faithful alike, aware of their duties as regards refugees and other forcibly displaced persons" (7). In this regard, the main direction was set by John Paul II:

> *every situation in which human persons or groups are obliged to flee their own land to seek refuge elsewhere stands out as a serious offence to God. (...) The dramatic*

---

22 Pope John Paul II 1996.
23 Blume 2003.
24 Message at the 2nd Assembly of RENATE, 7 November 2016.

*plight of refugees demands that the international community
do everything possible not only to treat the symptoms, but
first of all to go to the root of the problem: in other words,
to prevent conflicts and promote justice and solidarity in
every context of the human family" (32).*

Detailed recommendations for addressing the issues of and providing pastoral
care to refugees, asylum seekers, internally displaced persons, stateless persons,
trafficked persons, and people subject to sexual exploitation are offered.

2.3.8   Obligation to provide pastoral care

The Christian community is directly charged with the obligation to welcome
migrants within the Church, to provide them with specific pastoral care and the
possibility to participate actively within the community. The welcoming derives
from the fundamental principle expressed by John Paul II "In the Church no one
is a stranger, and the Church is not foreign to anyone, anywhere".[25] Migrants,
however, must be assured not just of welcome, but of full pastoral care (EMCC
32). This duty is weighed upon the bishops, first (CD 18), and therefore upon
the local Churches. Specific pastoral care requires the possibility to serve the
migrants in their language and culture but with a view to building communion.
The presence of migrants within the local Church serves as a sacrament for the
experience of the dimension of catholicity which characterizes the Church, but
also as a measure of it (EMCC 103). Migrants should be assured of the possibility to express their baptismal vocation as full participants within the community, overcoming a perspective which considers them outsiders and only in need
of social assistance. "They offer the Church the opportunity to realize more
concretely its identity as communion and its missionary vocation" (EMCC 103).

2.4   The nature and cogency of obligations toward migrants

After highlighting, necessarily in general terms, the obligations toward migrants
contained in CST, it is necessary to examine what is the nature of such
obligations. The dispositions provided in early documents were absorbed and
codified in the Canon Law and are normative for those involved in the care of
migrants. *Erga Migrantes Caritas Christi* also contains Juridical Pastoral
Regulations, intended to update the guidance of the Church on the pastoral care
of migrants. In reality, the innovations over the previous Instruction are few.
Among them, is the organization of the text, beginning, like *Lumen Gentium*,
with the tasks of the lay faithful and ending with the duties of Episcopal
Conferences and the now abolished Pontifical Council for the Care of Migrants
and Itinerant People. The Instruction directs itself also to migrants of Catholic

---

25   Pope John Paul II 1996.

Oriental Churches as well as to non-Catholic and non-Christian migrants. This positive openness reflects the need of the Church to reach out to the millions of non-Catholic and non-Christian migrants of the current era. At the same time, from a canonical perspective, it creates the necessity to coordinate with other dicasteries within the Roman Curia who have direct competence over those faithful. Likewise, Art. 22 confers upon the Pontifical Council the authority to issue instructions, which traditionally was reserved only to the Congregations within the Roman Curia.[26]

Outside of the juridical norms, the obligations toward migrants carry the same cogency as the entire CST. This is not the place to revisit the discussion about the various expressions utilized to refer to CST. Leo XIII spoke of "Christian philosophy" (RN 14); Pius XI used the expression "social philosophy" (QA 4). It was Pius XII who introduced the term "social doctrine,"[27] which was continued by John XXIII, but abandoned in the documents of Vatican II and by Paul VI, who emphasized the need for the Church not only to teach, but also to learn. "Social doctrine" reacquired currency with John Paul II and it is in the title of the *Compendium of the Social Doctrine of the Church*. Within theological schools, the most common term is "social thought," an expression which downplays the normative character of CST. Beyond the terminological dispute, what is essential is to capture the characteristics of CST, which should not be considered an ideology or the search for a third way between capitalism and socialism (SRS 41). It is instead a thinking which is evangelical, prophetic, critical, dialogical and pluralist.[28]

The normative nature of CST was addressed by Paul VI in *Octogesiam Adveniens* (4). The Pope acknowledged that it was not possible to provide a unified solution to all the different situations and affirmed that that was not his ambition or mission; he deferred the duty to provide practical solutions to local Christian communities. This should be done in dialogue between all stakeholders, including all persons of goodwill. Nevertheless "the forcefulness and special character of the demands made by the Gospel" should not be lost. This forcefulness consisted of the inspiration that the Gospel and Church tradition provided to advance life in society. However, no specific option should claim to exhaust the Gospel's inspiration.

From the words of Paul VI it is possible to conclude that obligations toward migrants can be articulated in a different way in different situations but also that the different articulations cannot escape the demands generated by the Gospel, enriched by the experience of Church tradition. When examining the normative character of CST obligations toward migrants we discover that it is absolute when the human dignity of the person is offended and when the human rights of migrants are violated, it is progressive when addressing the causes and consequences of migration, it is inspirational when envisioning a community

---

26 Sabbarese 2005.
27 Radio message for the 50th anniversary of *Rerum Novarum*, 1 June 1941.
28 Carrier 1996.

and society that incarnate the dynamics of the kingdom of God, which remains within the constant tension between the "already but not yet." CST has a universal dimension, it is offered to all peoples as all are responsible for the common good, but it demands much closer consideration and adherence from the disciples of Christ, as it is derived ultimately from the teaching and example of Christ.

2.5   Convergence and divergence of obligations toward migrants between CST and international norms

Although migration remains governed by national migration policies, there are many international instruments applicable to migrants and obliging the states that have ratified those instruments.[29] The covenants and conventions that constitute international humanitarian law are applicable to migrants, except when such application is specifically excluded, usually because of citizenship requirements. The same can be said of the ILO conventions. Instruments directly adopted for the protection of migrants include the International Convention on the Protection of the Rights of All Migrant Workers and Members of Their Families, and ILO Conventions 97 and 143.

Specific categories of migrants find additional protection in specific instruments, such as the ILO Convention 189 on Domestic Workers. Also, many regional instruments exist for the protection of migrants within the regional borders. CST, which is not tasked with providing specific measures for the protection of migrants, does not diverge from such a vast corpus of international law. At the same time, instruments in favour of migrants are notorious for their very limited level of ratification. Although countries might provide the same measures in their national legal system, they tend to not ratify international conventions to avoid being tied by international obligations in the regulation of migration. Furthermore, even when international norms are adopted, the national implementation often remains unsatisfactory.

Because of this complex and fragmented scenario, for the analysis of convergence and divergence it is not possible to examine the actual implementation of norms. The following considerations simply provide a general appreciation of Church teachings in relation to the accepted approach to migration within the international community.

2.5.1   Obligation to avoid migration as a necessity

While the Church affirms explicitly the right not to emigrate, there is no such terminology in international law. This, however, does not mean that the international community is not conscious of the issue. Perhaps the closest

---

29   Aleinikoff & Chetail 2003.

international statement is the 1986 Declaration on the Right to Development, reaffirmed in the 1993 Vienna Declaration, although one could argue that the right to development does not imply that such development should take place within the country and exclude migration. Countries of origin have been challenged to increase the level of development to avoid a flow of migrants which critics see as a specific strategy toward development. Some countries, like the Philippines, have established in the law[30] that migration should not be used as a strategy for national development, but legal statements might not converge with actual policies.

The closest convergence is in the first principle of action of the final report of the Global Commission on International Migration, which says: "Women, men and children should be able to realize their potential, meet their needs, exercise their human rights and fulfil their aspirations in their country of origin, and hence migrate out of choice, rather than necessity".[31] Since then, it has become common to repeat this principle as the guidance for migration policies, but coherence with other development policies is another story.

2.5.2   Obligation to admit migrants

While the Church explicitly affirms the right to migrate as a natural right and in its dual dimension (right to leave and right to enter another country) international law does not contain such a right. It simply speaks of the right to leave a country and to return to one's country.[32] One could argue that the divergence on this essential point between the Church and the international community is irrelevant, because in all instances in which the Church affirms the right to migrate, it contextually affirms also the right of the state to regulate migration. It might appear a complex and futile exercise of balance on the part of the Church, but in reality, it carries importance for the obligation toward migrants. On the one hand, the Church's recognition of the right of the state to regulate migration is always residual. Secondly, the recognition of the right of the state to regulate migration is qualified; it must be motivated by the common good of the country and the common good must be properly understood. The US and Mexican bishops have concluded that the control is not admissible "when it is exerted merely for the purpose of acquiring additional wealth".[33] In general, this divergence allows for the ethical scrutiny of migration policies in the name of duties toward the common human family and in solidarity with those most in need.

---

30   The Migrant Workers and Overseas Filipinos Act of 1995 (RA 8042), amended in 2010 by RA 10022, Sec. 2c.
31   GCIM 2005.
32   Art. 12 ICCPR 12; Art. 8 MWC.
33   USCCB and CEM 2003: 36.

2.5.3   Obligation to protect the migrants' families

The migrant's family is inherently included in the protection afforded to migrants. The fact that it is included in the title of the Migrant Workers Convention speaks loudly about it. In addition, the Convention on the Rights of the Child, the widest ratified UN Convention, considers specifically the situation of the children of migrants and recommends that states facilitate family reunification (art. 10). However, it is on family reunification that some divergence can be observed. While the Church affirms the right of family reunification,[34] international instruments only recommend that states facilitate it or not hinder it, but never acknowledge it as a right of the migrant.[35] Perhaps the above-mentioned art. 10 of the CRC comes closer to it. It is possible that, particularly in the case of migrant workers, the conditions for family life are not available and family reunification is not a recommended solution. It is also true that family reunification is sometimes abused, with migrants resorting to fake marriages to obtain admission or stay in the foreign country. But it is also true that even traditional countries of immigration have reduced admission for family reunification in favour of admissions which bring economic benefits to the country. The Church's stance reminds legislators of the duty to not deprive migrants of family life.

2.5.4   Obligation to ensure integration and cultural dialogue

Integration is differently addressed in the various migration systems. Some countries, like the US, have adopted a laissez-faire approach and leave it to the migrants to decide how to integrate. Other countries, like Canada and Australia, have adopted a specific multicultural approach. European countries have played with multiculturalism but declared it a failure. Instead, the European Union has adopted a common agenda to favour the integration of migrants.[36] Countries of temporary migration, like the Gulf Countries, do not foresee the integration of migrants, who are not allowed to acquire long-term residence rights.

The Church's recommendation to ensure the integration of migrants speaks in general terms and it is not possible to go beyond that precisely because of the variety of situations in which integration can take place.[37] As for the contentious aspect of cultural differences introduced or exacerbated by the migrants, the Church's invitation to encourage intercultural dialogue goes beyond the increasing isolationism among countries, as well as the reaction to terrorism manifested even by some bishops in Eastern Europe, and finds echoes in

---

34   *The right of reuniting families should be respected and promoted*, Compendium of the Social
     Doctrine of the Church, Pontifical Council for Justice and Peace, # 298.
35   Such right is recognized in regional contexts, such as the European Union, which has issued
     Directive 2003/86/EC on the right to family reunification.
36   COM(2005) 389.
37   For an example of a detailed discussion on migrants' integration from the Church's per-
     spective, see: Kerwin & George (2014).

UNESCO's (2009) invitation to start intercultural dialogue. Although ignored, both the Church and UNESCO's recommendations maintain their validity and require proper education to see a change in attitudes and perceptions.

2.5.5 Obligation to ensure the protection of the rights of irregular migrants

In this regard, there is wide convergence between the Church and international law. In fact, it was the ILO Convention 143 first, and the MWC later that codified the protection of the rights of irregular migrants and the Church has supported this effort. It is well known that the reference is basically to their human rights, the rights that irregular migrants have because they are human beings. Nevertheless, many countries did not ratify the MWC with the motivation that it went too far in protecting irregular migrants.[38] In addition, many countries have proceeded to declare irregular migration a crime, and therefore irregular migrants can be detained and expelled, and those who provide them with assistance are also committing a crime. This is where some divergence exists between the teachings of the Church and migration policies. When law and the duty of solidarity conflict, the Church maintains that it is necessary to go beyond the law. In the words of John Paul II: "Solidarity means taking responsibility for those in trouble. For Christians, the migrant is not merely an individual to be respected in accordance with the norms established by law, but a person whose presence challenges them and whose needs become an obligation for their responsibility. 'What have you done to your brother?' (cf. Gn 4:9). The answer should not be limited to what is imposed by law, but should be made in the manner of solidarity".[39]

2.5.6 Obligation to assist victims of smuggling and trafficking

There is wide convergence on this aspect, as the Church utilizes the Protocols of the CTOC as the general framework as well as the assistance provided by countries and international organizations to support preventive and protective initiatives toward the victims of trafficking, while leaving prosecution to the state. Partnerships established among the various stakeholders are aimed at increasing attention to this modern scourge.

2.5.7 Obligation to avoid forced migration and to welcome refugees and asylum seekers

The Church cooperates widely with the UNHCR in the protection and assistance given to refugees, particularly through its presence in refugee camps (for instance with the Jesuit Refugee Services), and through the activities of the International Catholic Migration Commission (ICMC). The Church does not

---

38 Pécoud & de Gutcheneire 2006.
39 Pope John Paul II 1996, 5.

agree with the confinement of children in refugee camps and criticizes extra-territorial asylum processing, recommending instead shared responsibilities among countries according to national capabilities. To prevent forced migration, Hollenbach has maintained that countries have negative duties, duties not to engage in actions which will lead to the displacement of many people to escape situations of conflict and violence, while they have positive duties to provide assistance to refugees.[40]

Pope Francis has shown practical concern in providing resettlement to some refugees after his visit to the island of Lesbos, but also in recommending that refugees should not just be admitted but also integrated. In the in-flight press conference while returning from Sweden, in 2017, he said that countries "must be very open to receiving refugees, but they also have to calculate how best to settle them, because refugees must not only be accepted, but also integrated." This should not be interpreted as avoiding the obligation to admit refugees, but as distributing responsibilities among countries according to their different capabilities.

2.6   Conclusion

The teachings of the Church on migration were developed over a long period of time, during which migration changed origins, destinations and dynamics. From the time of the great migration from Europe, particularly Italy, to the Americas, to the permanent and labour migration after World War II, to current global migration, the Church always saw migration as an opportunity and a challenge, but also as a "necessary evil" (LE 23). The current international scenario has become much more complex, as migration flows are increasingly mixed, forced migration is generated by international instability, traffickers and smugglers are exploiting the need of people for dignity and safety, and destination countries tend to view migration mostly as a security issue.

From the biblical framework and the constant reminder for hospitality commanded by its Founder and repeated throughout its tradition, the Church has articulated obligations first of all for the disciples of Christ but also for society in general. Obligations are founded on the fundamental commandment of love for all and on Jesus' identification with the stranger. As stated by Benedict XVI, "charity is at the heart of the Church's social doctrine" (CiV 2). They are moral obligations, which should not be ignored when the dignity and human rights of migrants are threatened, but which should also be followed when different solutions are allowed in the name of the common good if we want to build a civilization of love. In this regard, the Church's teachings often depart from the normative and political solutions prevalent within the international community and the individual countries and it must be so, as the

---

40   Hollenbach 2016.

Church is oriented toward the eschatological horizon of the full implementation of the kingdom of God. That horizon requires the constant overcoming of unjust structures, a contemporary social sin,[41] that force people to migrate and do not provide them a welcoming environment.

A few obstacles keep resurfacing and require the vigilant guidance of the teachings of the Church. Many Christians find love for migrants in conflict with love for neighbour and are challenged by the need to prioritize. It is a concern voiced also by the Lutheran Church (LC-CTCR 26): "for the immigrant is not the only neighbour Christians are called to love. There is also the neighbour citizen or resident of a nation, who may or may not be as vulnerable or needy as the immigrant neighbour in every case, but whose well-being is also a matter of concern for both the government and for Christian citizens." On a pragmatic level, research tends to indicate (although the issue remains controversial) that migrants are marginally substitutes for citizens, as they are mostly com-plementary to them.[42] Love for migrants and love for fellow citizens does not have to be in conflict, and the misinformation spread by political forces for electoral purposes should be corrected.

Increasing terrorism in the world has led to the securitization of migration and the support for restrictive migration policies, with stunning examples in the popular UK referendum that led to Brexit and the executive orders of Donald Trump, president of the US, building the wall between the US and Mexico and banning the entry of citizens from seven countries to the US.[43] Security is a fundamental good for everyone. While building walls to protect those inside against migrants, countries forget that migrants are trying to enter because they are in search of security, not because they intend to export insecurity. Security is obtained only if it is searched for together and if it is security for all. From its vantage point of a reality without borders, the Church is recommending overcoming barriers. In the words of Pope Francis: "A person who thinks only about building walls, wherever they may be, and not building bridges, is not Christian."[44]

Obligations toward migrants formulated in CST constitute an application of social ethics to the field of migration. At the same time, migration constitutes a vantage point, a sign of the times, for a hermeneutical rethinking of ethics and in particular for the call for an ethic of inclusion and proximity. In the words of the EMCC (8): "migration raises a truly ethical question: the search for a new international economic order." Ethics of inclusion and proximity require that "the dynamics of poverty creation for the defense of the welfare of few should be radically revised. It is contradictory to frustrate the attempt of the poor toward development and at the same time reject them at the borders. Borders intend to impede that the poor become our neighbours. But if we do not allow them, we

---

41   Heyer 2012.
42   Ottaviano & Peri 2007.
43   This latest decision, however, has encountered wide opposition, also by the courts.
44   Pope Francis, In-flight Press Conference from Mexico to Rome, 17 February 2016.

will just remain on the side of the street, victims of our own violence".[45] The waters lapping at our shores or flowing at our rivers should no longer return the bodies of little children with their faces in the sand. They should carry the hopes for dignity and murmur the songs of liberty.

References

Aleinikoff, T.A. & V. Chetail (2003), *Migration and International Legal Norms*, The Hague: TMC Asser Press.

Battistella, G. (2010), 'The Poor in Motion', *Asian Christian Review*, 4(2).

Blume, M.A. (2003), 'Migration and the Social Doctrine of the Church', in: G. Campese & P. Ciallella (eds.), *Migration Religious Experience and Globalization*, Staten Island (NY): Center for Migration Studies.

Bonora A. (1993), 'Lo straniero in Deuteronomio', in: *L'altro, il diverso, lo straniero*, Edizioni Dehoniane Bologna.

Bowe B.E. & T.A. Nairn (2002), 'The Bible and Moral Theology: Pitfalls and Possibilities', *New Theology Review*, February.

Burini C. (1993), 'Dall'amore reciproco all'amore verso l'altro', in: *L'altro, il diverso, lo straniero*, Edizioni Dehoniane Bologna.

Campese G. (2012), 'The Irruption of Migrants: Theology of Migration in the 21st Century', *Theological Studies* 73(1).

Carrier H. (1996), *Dottrina sociale, Nuovo approccio all'insegnamento sociale della Chiesa*, Cinisello Balsamo: San Paolo Edizioni.

Edwards Jr, J. (2009), *A Biblical Perspective on Immigration Policy*, Backgrounder, Washington DC: Center for Immigration Studies, <cis.org>.

Global Commission on International Migration (GCIM) (2005), *Migration in an interconnected world: New directions for action*, Geneva: SRO-Kundig.

Heyer K.E. (2012), *Kinship across Borders, A Christian Ethic of Immigration*, Washington DC: Georgetown University Press.

Hollenbach D. (2016), 'Borders and Duties to the Displaced: Ethical Perspectives on the Refugee Protection System', *Journal on Migration and Human Security*, 4(3), p. 148-165.

Kerwin D. & G. Breana (2014), *US Catholic Institutions and Immigrant Integration, Will the Church Rise to the Challenge?* Vatican City: Lateran University Press.

The Lutheran Church – Commission on Theology and Church Relations (2012), *Immigrants among Us, A Lutheran Framework for Addressing Immigration Issues*, Missouri Synod.

Massey Douglas *et al.*, (eds.) (1998), *Worlds in Motion, Understanding International Migration at the End of the Millennium*, Oxford: Clarendon.

---

45   Battistella 2010, 80-81.

Ottaviano G. & G. Peri (2007), 'America's Stake in Immigration: Why Almost Everybody Wins', *Milken Institute Review*, 3rd Quarter.

Pécoud A. & P. de Gutcheneire (2006), 'Migration, human rights and the United Nations, An investigation into the obstacles to the UN Convention on Migrant Workers' Rights', *Windsor Yearbook of Access to Justice*, 24(2).

Piana G. (2008), 'Un'etica delle migrazioni: valori e norme morali', *Rivista di teologia morale*, 160.

Plaut G.W. (1996), 'Jewish Ethics and International Migration', *International Migration Review*, 30.

Pope Benedict XVI (2007), *World Migration Day Message* (WMDM), Vatican.

Pope Francis (2017), *World Migration Day Message* (WMDM), Vatican.

Pope John Paul II (1985), *World Migration Day Message* (WMDM), Vatican.

Pope John Paul II (1996), *World Migration Day Message* (WMDM), Vatican.

Pope John Paul II (2001), *World Migration Day Message* (WMDM), Vatican.

Rivera-Pagàn L.N. (2013), 'Xenophilia or Xenophobia: Toward a Theology of Migration', in: E. Padilla & P.C. Phan (eds.), *Contemporary Issues of Migration and Theology*, Palgrave McMillan.

Sabbarese L. (2005), 'L'Ordinamento Giuridico Pastorale dell'Istruzione Erga Migrantes', in: G. Battistella, *La Missione viene a noi, In margine all'Istruzione Erga Migrantes Caritas Christi*, Urbaniana University Press.

Spohn W.C. (1999), *Go and Do Likewise: Jesus and Ethics*, New York: Continuum Publishing.

UNESCO (2009), *Investing in Cultural Diversity and Intercultural Dialogue.*

United States Conference of Catholic Bishops & Conferencia del Episcopado Mexicano (USCCB & CEM) (2003), *Strangers No Longer, Together on the Journey of Hope*, A Pastoral Letter Concerning Migration from the Catholic Bishops of Mexico and the United States.

Chapter 3   Proposals for a 'Better World'

Pope Francis' contributions in order to generate a 'culture of welcome' to face the current challenges of human mobility

Jorge E. Castillo Guerra

3.1   Introduction

Since the beginning of his pontificate, Francis has taken on migration as one of his main preoccupations and supports this subject with the Social Doctrine of the Catholic Church. His visit to Lampedusa, on 8 July 2013, was not a unique event in his pontificate. On the contrary, he has taken on the challenges provoked by the migrant flows as one of the main concerns of his ministry. And he seeks support in the teachings formulated to orient answers of the Catholic Church to issues concerning social justice. In fact, the interest of the Church in migratory affairs was already present in the Encyclical *Rerum Novarum* by Pope Leon XIII, who showed concern about the labour situation of migrants when he affirmed, among other things, that "no one would exchange his country for a foreign land if his own afforded him the means of living a decent and happy life" (Leo XIII 1891, no. 47). Awareness on this topic has conjured up social teaching that merits special attention and is contained in the Apostolic Constitution *Exsul familia nazarethana: On spiritual care to migrants* (Pius XII 1950), the Encyclical *Pacem in Terris* (John XXIII 1963), the instructions *De Pastorali Migratorum Cura* (Congregation for Bishops1969), and *Erga Migrantes Caritas Christi* (Pontifical Council for the Pastoral Care of Migrants and Itinerant People 2004). In these documents, there are topics that concern human mobility and instructions for the pastoral accompaniment and the defence of the rights of migrants, in addition to instructions to guide the destination nations and societies on their responsibilities to the migrants as well as the obligations of the migrants once they arrive in these destination countries.

In this chapter I reflect on the Social Teaching of Francis as related to the topic of migration from three basic questions:[1] What are his contributions, in light of the dilemmas, challenges and tensions, surrounding the boundary policies and the reactions from both the original and destination locations? Is it

---

1   An earlier version of this text appeared under the title "'A Church without Boundaries': A New Ecclesial Identity Emerging from a Mission of Welcome Reflections on the Social Magisterium of Pope Francis as related to Migration" in the *Journal of Catholic Social Thought* 2017, 14(1), p. 43-61.

possible to distinguish the various contexts towards which his message is directed? What are the repercussions for an ecclesial identity, of a mission oriented towards migrants?

In this chapter I attempt to answer these questions from the perspective of the nascent theology of migration that has, among its goals, the defence of the life and rights of migrants.[2] This theology reflects a diversity of ways through which migrants experience and express their faith in specific contexts in order to understand, through them, God's promise of liberation and universal communion.

Various studies concerned with migration, find support in the social teachings of the Catholic Church as a framework within which to analyze migration and to discern God's path through our history, as is manifested through the practices of migrants and the groups in the destination societies that are engaged in creating a convivial society.[3]

In this chapter I do not consider the perspective of the ecclesial mission that the migrants themselves develop; mainly my reflection points to the responsibility of societies and ecclesial communities in general, with regards to migration.[4] I approach this by studying Pope Francis' social teachings as he develops a motivation to welcome migrants and to answer situations that are generated by migration. I also explore how the ecclesial mission of welcoming migrants proposed by the Pope, has a bearing on the understanding of ecclesial identity.

I begin with an interdisciplinary approach to inquire into the reasons that legitimize the creation of mechanisms for border controls that endanger the lives and increase the suffering of migrants. By the same token, I study the Pope's contributions in order to generate a "culture of welcome". In the conclusions, I will highlight that migration is an issue that has to do with faith in Jesus and his Spirit, which allows the Church to recover its identity as a pilgrim Church "without boundaries".

3.2   Fear and Migration Policies

During the past two decades, the increase in human mobility has led to extremely ambiguous interpretations, according to the contexts that migrants include in their treks between countries of emigration, transit and destination.

---

2   Castillo Guerra 2004; Campese 2008; Tulud Cruz 2010; Kim 2012; Kessler 2014.
3   Blume 2003; Battistella 2003; Tassello, 2010; Baggio and Susin, 2012; Castillo Guerra 2015a.
4   In other publications, I have highlighted how migrants themselves contribute criteria to overcome the limitations of practices and theological reflections that lack a true awareness of the power relationships that tend to reduce the migrant to the category of guest. I have also reflected in this sense, on the intercultural transformation of the deaconry set forth by the migrants which when unified with koinonia generates human communion. Cf. Castillo Guerra 2010; 2011, 2013; 2015b. See also: Schroeder 2015

Within these interpretations, the one that seems to prevail is that of the destination rich countries, because of their political and economic capacity to define the rules of the game. These countries dominate the migratory process even before they are initiated by the migrant; in other words, even before the migrant crosses the borders of his or her home territory. Due to the inefficacy of border policies, there is pressure placed on the transit countries to become guardians of the external borders.[5] Transit countries, for their part, use the migrant flows as part of a political game to negotiate advantages with the destination countries. In the specific case of Europe, since the beginning of the new millennium European countries have placed more and more restrictions on visas to enter the Schengen Zone, they have militarized international borders and drawn up agreements with countries such as Morocco, Turkey, Nigeria and Senegal, in order to create new external borders to discourage migration; they have built detention and deportation centres and waged war against human trafficking networks. European frontiers garner a sense of defence and repression. Walls are built, access points are blocked and high technology instruments are employed to detect irregular migrants.

The goal of blocking the migration process is based on a deterrent strategy implemented by building walls and the increased militarization of boundary zones. Physical barriers such as oceans, rivers, deserts, tropical jungles or mountains also play an essential role in this strategy, where the risk of losing human lives is taken as a significant warning within the deterrent strategy. Frontex, a European agency that manages borders, has a central role in the implementation of this dissuading strategy. Their actions are well known both on land and at sea, where international rights are often violated, such as the right to be rescued at sea that stress the obligation to save the lives of endangered survivors in international waters, and the human right to asylum, when they apply their pushback methods or "summary removal", to obstruct refugees from asking for asylum.[6]

Migrants who are desperate, for various reasons, take on the deadly risks of these frontier policies. Those who travel in order to ensure their own lives or to improve the lives of their families have to confront new problems that arise when they move through countries that have criminal organizations and corrupt officials that assault, extort, and sequester them for trafficking or to sexually exploit them.

The deaths of migrants throughout the so-called "death routes", found on all continents, bear witness to the *modus operandi* of the frontier policies. They prevent the crossing of thousands of human beings through their frontiers because nature takes charge and punishes them with death, or because migrants lose when they attempt to cross a fence in Melilla or fall under the wheels of a

---

5   Menjívar 2014.
6   Strik 2015:52; Ferrer-Gallardo & van Houtum 2014.

train apocalyptically called "The Beast", in Mexico.[7] The routes of death acquire even more relevance; so much so that Fargues and Bonfanti state that, within the Mediterranean context, the "sea routes to Europe are increasingly lethal".[8]

How can we explain the existence of border control mechanisms that endanger the lives and increase the suffering of the migrant? How can we understand the relationship established by the Pope, between the suffering of the migrants and the attitude of indifference they face?[9] The destination countries implement control mechanisms that are determined by subjects who have been politically empowered by their own societies. The border or frontier policy answers to a public agenda where political games, pressure and international agreements enter the arena. According to Zapata-Barrero, the criteria on which to admit or exclude foreigners in the destination countries are based on three social concerns: security, wellbeing, and identity.[10]

The first concern has to do with the fear of losing security, which is linked to an *a priori* perception of the foreigner as a social danger. The fear of losing security gives way to measures of restraint as instruments of political management that serve an even more important goal, which is the security and the internal freedom of its citizens. A goal which is reached through the mechanisms that unchain vulnerability issues within their "recipients". In this way, on the other side of the border, the values that are upheld are inverted within the destination country because the security and liberty of the citizens are preserved through the insecurity and lack of liberty of mobility of the non-nationals. Therefore, the fear of loss of security protects the deterrent decrees which outside the frontiers, induce migrants to transit through the death routes and, within the frontiers produce a mindset of the migrant as a dangerous and "illegal" subject.

The fear of losing the sense of wellbeing awakens a second social concern that legitimizes the exclusion of migrants. However, regarding this concern, two ambitions are set against each other; on the one hand the "fear of losing comfort", and on the other hand the drive to increase it. These seemingly contrary elements imply that destination societies are formulated as "gated communities", because they cannot close the doors to all migrants. The oasis of wellbeing, cannot easily relinquish the cheap "illegal" labour which is necessary to reach their "targets" of economic growth and to carry out agricultural, industrial or domestic tasks that the "happy few" consider below their own level of dignity and quality of life standards.[11]

---

7   According to the International Organization for Migrations, in 2013, worldwide, at least
     2,300 emigrants lost their lives while attempting to arrive in another country (OIM 2013).
     The newspaper *El País* published that in the last two decades 25,000 migrants have died in
     the Sicilian Canal, known now as the Island of Lampedusa, including 2,700 victims during
     the Libyan conflict of 2011 (El País 2013).
8   Fargues & Bonfanti, 2014, 5.
9   Francis 2013.
10   Zapata-Barrero 2012.
11   Van Houtum & Pijpers 2007, 116.

A final concern that the topic of border control imposes on the public agenda emerges from the fear of losing "frontiers", which is not defined solely as the border or wall, to prevent the entry of intruders but rather, as a defence of national identity. New nationalistic discourses regarding identity begin to emerge that tend to homogenize ethnic characteristics, dialects or religions, among other aspects. Myths also arise regarding an epic of evolution and historical destiny, over which the emblem of nationalism is hoisted. The following is a rather long quote in which Brenna explains the dynamic of the invention and idealization of one's own identity and the exclusion of the identity of others:

> *These frontiers end up being a space of tension: identity illusions shared with those inside, conflicting categories of differentiation from those outside. It speaks of the space where, rather than taking on the differences, we underline them, we measure them out and use them; we need to categorize the unknown in order to ensure that the unknown does not bring us unrest or threatens us; we need categories; we cannot live without them.[12]*

We may conclude from this quote, that the defence of national identity operates from a dynamic that in social psychology appears as the dynamic between the *in-group* and the *out-group*.[13] This dynamic operates with mechanisms of negative attribution values placed on the non-nationals. A discourse emerges, which is imposed, consumed, and is taken on socially as a true experience which becomes a part of the common meaning, such as investigations from the perspective of the critical analysis of discourse so advocate.[14] Lastly, a government resolves to prevent the entrance of bearers of so-called ethical, cultural, or social counter values, which represent a "danger" to national identity. Nevertheless, what are the effects of this discourse, formulated as a border policy, when the foreigners or the migrants are already inside the nations? How is it possible to build a society with people whose position, traditions or religious beliefs are constantly being devaluated? Obviously, society needs to build different types of discourses within their frontiers in order to avoid the divisions that are built on the outside to permeate them and make them ungovernable, due to xenophobia or intolerance.

One of these discourses is that of assimilation, which aims to colonize the migrant so that he or she is not different and is able to fully reproduce the characteristics of the dominating social group. Another discourse is that of multiculturalism, which opposes assimilation and presupposes that social cohesion can be achieved through the preservation of the identity of each group.

12 Brenna 2011, 12.
13 Verkuyten 2014.
14 Van Dijk 2004.

The type of tolerance of this second discourse rises over an essentialization of cultures as if these could be perpetuated or reduced to a single one, and it lacks, as well, a proposal able to dynamize the interaction between the various groups comprised within social multiculturalism. In this same manner, it reflects the so-called mosaic of cultural diversity that characterizes many destination societies, but defends the autonomous identity of the groups in such a way that it deepens social segmentations. We can therefore understand that the fear of the loss of national identity has generated assimilationist and multiculturalist discourses, with inappropriate proposals. First of all because they have a bearing on the negative perception of the migrant outside and inside the frontiers of the nation states. And, secondly, because the critical search for intercultural affinities and interactions that are able to foster social cohesion or human conviviality are not taken into account.

Fortunately, even though the echoes of fear due to the presence of migrants in destination societies grab the main focus of the communications media, there are groups that are in solidarity with the migrants both in the transit countries as well as in the destination societies. These groups organize rescue missions in the seas or deserts; they hold protests in order to lobby governments to humanize their frontiers and to receive those who are persecuted and who are refugees; they participate as volunteers in hospitality centres and open the doors of their homes to the recent arrivals. According to Kymlicka this second attitude towards migrants can be understood within the tendencies that comprise the "new progressive's dilemma: the fear that there is a trade-off between being pro-immigrant and being pro-welfare state".[15] It is a dilemma heavily politicized by the political parties that use fear in society with electoral intentions. Lastly, we also have the political and ideological interests that have the power of channeling or hegemonizing social fear that translates into migratory policies.[16]

In conclusion, and making reference to the question of how to explain the existence of frontier control mechanisms that endanger the lives and increases the suffering of migrants, I would answer, supported by various authors, that there is a fear based on a negative image of the other, that provokes the formulation of strict border policies. The fear of losing security, identity and comfort, also provoke identity shaping policies that lack a vision and a *pathos* to foster intercultural relations. Both within and outside the frontiers these policies have a bearing on exclusion and even on the death of the non-national. They also have a bearing on the loss of a sense of responsibility, for example, for the 25,000 human beings that have died in the waters of the Mediterranean in the new millennium, because as the Pope said in Lampedusa, "they don't concern us".

---

15 Kymlicka 2015, 1.
16 Boswell, Geddes & Scholten 2011.

3.3   *A culture of Welcome* - The Magisterium of Pope Francis in matters concerning migration

In this second part I will analyze the considerations and proposals made by Pope Francis to face the current challenges of human mobility and in this way clarify the main contributions in order to achieve what he has called "a culture of welcome". I will start with a reflection on Francis' prophetic reading on migration, and then on his proposal for change.

3.3.1   Prophetic reading regarding a culture that discards the meaning of community and places limits on human life

Together with the interdisciplinary analysis presented in the previous section regarding the fear that legitimizes restrictive border policies, the Pope holds true that the craving for well-being and the determination to conserve it leads to the exclusion of the other. A repressive border policy is a reflection of this aim as we note in his prophetic denunciation of a social injustice with connotations for the whole world:

> *The culture of comfort, which makes us think only of ourselves, makes us insensitive to the cries of other people, makes us live in soap bubbles which, however lovely, are insubstantial; they offer a fleeting and empty illusion which results in indifference to others; indeed, it even leads to the globalization of indifference.*[17]

The "globalization of indifference" that Pope Bergoglio denounces is not limited to the walls of exclusion, because in fact it extends throughout the routes of death, already mentioned in the first part of this paper, with the intention of restraining the entry and intermixing with him or her that "bothers me in my life and my wellbeing".[18] The Pope denounces, therefore, a logic of exclusion based on materialism and a pattern of consumerism that places the needs and the lives of migrants at the lowest level of their value scale. Because they are on the other side of the border, because of their non-national classification, the life of the other is less valuable and can even be dispensed with.

Certainly, this rationality has been pointed out by the liberation theologians based on Franz J. Hinkelammert's denouncement of an "ethics" of the sacrificial economic policies. In his words: "This ethic is demanding and entails sacrifice. It rises over the loser and leaves him lost. It is the ethic of the elected by success; the success that elects the elected and condemns the losers".[19]

---

17   Francis 2013.
18   Francis 2013.
19   Hinkelammert, 2001, 170; 1977; 1989; Richard 1983.

In this sense, Jon Sobrino affirms that "in the face of postmodernity there is a need to express the passion and the struggle of God against the idols in order to overcome indifference—even the tolerance with what this indifference may have of falsity—as though history were a mere wandering of whatever is human, without the powerful forces in place to oppose them".[20] The struggle against the death of the victims and the unmasking of the idols of death, have given way to a rethinking of the image of God, of the hope placed in God and the way we speak of God. This rethinking of the radical "no" of God to human sacrifice, exposed exemplarily by Monsignor Óscar Arnulfo Romero, has been coined as "the theology of the God of Life".[21]

The Pope is very close to the theology of the God of life, when he states that God is life, Jesus Christ is the font or source of life and the Holy Spirit sustains life, while contrasting this image to the image of ideologies and logic that limit human life. In *Evangelii Gaudium* he insists that the idols, the idolatry of money, or the "deified market", provoke an anthropological crisis that is manifested in "the denial of the primacy of the human person".[22] He therefore emphasizes later that "following God's way leads to life, whereas following idols leads to death".[23]

This brief reflection regarding one of the backdrops of his words at Lampedusa, allows us to understand why Pope Francis warns that the world cannot continue without understanding that the *modus vivendi* of societies must break off from the ideologies that do away with the sense of community and uphold patterns of exclusion and even the death of the other. In his words: "New ideologies, characterized by rampant individualism, egocentrism and materialistic consumerism, weaken social bonds, fueling that 'throw away' mentality which leads to contempt for, and the abandonment of, the weakest and those considered 'useless'".[24]

3.3.2   Proposals for a Better World

A short time after his visit to Lampedusa (8 July 2013), Pope Francis broadcasted his "Message for the World Day of Migrants and Refugees" for the year 2014, in which he complemented his prophetic homily with proposals for change. Is it possible to distinguish between the various contexts to which he directs his social teachings? In fact, yes; the Pope focuses on the different fields in which change can begin in order to avoid the death of migrants and the prevalent social indifference in the face of this human drama, and to embrace Christ revealed in the migrant.[25] Let us consider this further.

---

20   Sobrino 1995, 83.
21   Romero 1980.
22   Francis 2013b, no. 55.
23   Francis 2013c.
24   Francis 2013d, no. 1.
25   Francis 2013e.

3.3.3   International Cooperation

At the international level, the Pope revisits the main lines from the social teachings of the Catholic Church regarding migration, and accordingly exposes that migration needs a new international policy based on cooperation and attitudes of solidarity. Countries cannot, on their own, continue the search for solutions to the dilemmas they face in dealing with migration, because the problems they are attempting to solve are only one of the manifestations of a process that investigators propose as a transnational issue.

International cooperation is necessary in order to avoid seeing emigration as the only alternative for a life with dignity, justice, work and security. Pope Francis' proposal is supported by affirmations made in the Social Doctrine of the Church, regarding the right to not need to emigrate.[26]

In his Message for the Day of the Emigrant and the Refugee for the year 2016, Pope Francis makes another proposal at the international level: that countries pay attention to migration according to a new value scale that prioritizes the problems according to their importance. This means that the first thing that needs attention is the emergency of human beings involved in the migratory process. Secondly, the need to address the problems that emigration entails for other societies and peoples. The concern for the problems of migrants and particularly regarding refugees does not imply that attention is being denied regarding its effects in other societies, as is evidenced by the social repercussions of the so-called crisis of refugees in Europe. The Pope is suggesting, rather, a logic to implement policies that take the most vulnerable into consideration first, and then attend to the other problems, following the criteria of the common good.

3.3.4   Recovery of truth

Secondly, the Pope reminds us of the responsibility of the communications media, in spreading an image of the migrant free of prejudice; that they understand the problems that they cause, and to remember that these people comprise a fraction with regard to the majority that deserve the portrayal of a fair image. This responsibility entails, among other aspects, to correctly report the contributions that migrants make to their societies in their countries of origin and destination, in various fields.[27] For example, in recent years there has been a generalization of an extremely negative image on the subject of the religions that migrants introduce to the destination societies. However, empirical data report that Muslim and Christian migrants participate constructively in public spaces, when they invest their social capital to foster social cohesion both inside and outside their communities. In other words, the Pope encourages the media to report the truth and not fall prey to generalizations or assumptions regarding

---

26   John XXIII 1963, no. 25; Luciani 2005, 280.
27   Castillo Guerra 2015c.

the negative impact of migration, their cultures or religions on the destination societies.[28] It should also, be borne in mind that the propagation of correct information reduces the risk of falling into the trap of *political correctness*, which hides the social tensions and problems in the relationship between migrants and the rest of society. By the same token, correct information does not fall prey to biased positions that support a monocultural or multicultural discourse with regard to the insurmountable incompatibility between migrants and the destination society.

Information therefore, plays a crucial role in counteracting the fear of losing security, wellbeing and identity which has a bearing on many people and incites the "culture of rejection" in the destination societies. An adequate image of the migrant, free of hostility and fear is a fundamental step in overcoming the so-called culture of rejection and leads to the construction of a "culture of encounter". Paraphrasing the words of the Pope when he spoke before the Congress of the United States of America, quoted above, it can be said that the role of the communications media is to disseminate truth so that society can recover its notion of belonging to only one humanity, and from that truism, is able to come together as one.[29]

3.3.5   Ecclesial Mission: welcome without discrimination

The third proposal of Pope Francis implies concern for migrants as a constitutive element of an ecclesial mission that takes into account that "each person belongs to humanity and shares with all the peoples, the hope of a better world".[30] However, the construction of a better world presupposes a missionary task that highlights that each and every one is entitled to a life with dignity. This is a task that begins with a transformation of the understanding of migrants, where the human being is discovered within them, where there is acceptance of the fact that they have been created in the image and likeness of God and "flesh of Christ".[31] The Pope uses arguments taken from the theology of creation, as well as from Christology to propose fundamental criteria for the ecclesial mission within the context of migration, that is, to value the human genre as a family with only one origin and dignity that shares creation.

In his Message for the World Day for Migrants 2015, the Argentinian Pope clarifies the breadth of the understanding of the migrant as the "flesh of Christ", for the ecclesial mission. By way of that identification he calls on us to discover Jesus in the migrant, while at the same time he reminds that this has its roots in the following of the evangelizing message of Jesus. It is Jesus who invites us to care for those who are suffering and to discover him within them, just as is

---

28   Pontificia Comisión para los Medios de Comunicación Social 1971, no. 17.
29   Francis 2015.
30   Francis 2013e.
31   Francis 2013f.

mentioned in the Gospel of Matthew 25, 35-36.[32] The discovery of Jesus, as we read the Papal message, has to correspond with a mission of the Church as a mother who receives migrants without discrimination, *without frontiers,* because this is the way of testifying the sending off of the Church into the world, to proclaim God's love and compassion.

3.4   Church to the world, to proclaim God's love and compassion

The mission of a Church that is faithful to the sending by Jesus, has a universal reach that is made specific through the service of the Church to migrants, when she reacts to its urgencies, and when she overcomes the barriers between religions and cultures and when she does not allow herself to be intimidated by human diversity. We observe that the Pope interprets the ecclesial mission as a message translated and witnessed through the specific embracing of the other, and without exclusion of any distinct trait or orientation. However, we ask, what is the scope of this acceptance mission in the face of the religious plurality of migrants? Is the reception and acceptance being instrumentalized for conversion to Catholicism?

During his visit to a shelter for refugees in Rome, the Pope had already expressed the interreligious extent of the ecclesial mission in a sense that can clarify our questions: "Many of you are Muslim or members of another religion. You come from various countries, from different situations. We mustn't be afraid of differences! Brotherhood enables us to discover that they are riches, gifts for everyone! Let us live in brotherhood!".[33]

In the words of the Pope we find elements of the mission of welcoming. The first is the acceptance of the cultural or religious diversity of the persons involved, and the second element is valuating this as enriching. The reception of persons with different cultural or religious orientations has fraternity as an underpinning and predisposes persons to a religious and intercultural dialogue which can contribute to overcoming extreme positions, when they understand, appreciate their differences and share the common elements. It also encompasses the incentive of the values that support a "peaceful coexistence between persons and cultures", such as solidarity, by letting go of attitudes against migrants and by embracing a "culture of encounter".[34] Therefore, the ecclesial mission of reception or welcome acquires an interreligious perspective, first of all, through the religious diversity of its recipients and of those who collaborate in this mission. Second, when the reception of migrants becomes an encounter with diversity that has no pretention of religiously colonizing the other but rather that favours his or her fidelity to the ethical imperatives of his or her own

---

32 Francis 2014.
33 Francis 2013g.
34 Francis 2014.

religion. In other words, an inverted proselytism, that invites a constant conversion to each person's own religion through that food for thought that emerges in the encounter with religious otherness.

This missionary work leads the Church towards those contexts linked by human mobility in the countries of origin, and the countries of transit and destination. And, by inserting herself into them she educates to provide an understanding of the causes of migration, to denounce the dangers and injustices that emerge in the day-to-day experiences of the emigrant and immigrant, and to offer support to groups and institutions in solidarity with migrants and, in particular, with refugees. Lastly, from that context, the Church is able to contribute criteria for judgment in order to face the dilemmas that migration poses to destination societies.

3.5   Conclusion: A Church Without Boundaries: her mission and identity

In this chapter I have highlighted the points made by the Pope regarding the effects of the attitudes and border policies that provoke the suffering, exclusion or death of migrants. With the aid of interdisciplinary studies, I have reflected on the social concerns that these policies engender. Now, in closing, I propose to answer a question posited in the introduction regarding the repercussions of a mission oriented towards an ecclesial identity on the topic of migration.

In my analysis, I note that the Pope affirms that in her path towards migrants and refugees, the Church walks together with them, and in that way she recovers her identity as a pilgrim Church, a Church on route, "without boundaries", because to approach others is an approach without distinctions.

Francis offers other theological insights in favour of the identity of a Church without boundaries. Migration is not a mere ethical issue, rather, it is a faith issue. In his arguments, the Pope holds true that the origin of a Church that understands herself as being without boundaries, relies on Jesus and his Spirit. In Jesus, through the calling to receive and adore him through those who need the most. And in the Spirit, manifested at Pentecost, that invigorates the Church to overcome fear, to understand the message of the Reign of God, each in his or her own language and, to give testimony to the world, of the love of God.

In fact, from its origin, as illustrated by the Council of Jerusalem (*Acts* 15, *Galatians* 2) the Church feels the calling and feels invigorated to go into the world; to answer that vocation, in the midst of limitations and errors, she is present in various countries, where she is incarnated in the cultural diversity of peoples. It has to do with what Jon Sobrino explains as partial incarnations, particularly from the margins of the world. These are precisely the incarnations that enable the Church to be truly catholic, that is, Universal.[35]

---

35   Sobrino 1978, 17.

Finally, the identity of a Church "without boundaries" conveys the image of a Church that serves the mission of a single people of God and precisely by carrying out this service, she exceeds the frontiers that divides it.

References

Baggio, M. & L.C. Susin (2012), 'O clamor das migrações eo magisterio da Igreja', *REMHU* 29 (39), p. 211-228.

Battistella, B. (2003), 'The Human Rights of Migrants: A Pastoral Change', in: G. Campese & P. Ciallella (eds.), Migration, *Religious Experience, and Globalization,* New York: Center for Migration Studies, p. 76-102.

Blume, M. (2003), 'Migration and the Social Doctrine of the Church', in: G. Campese & P. Ciallella (eds.), *Migration, Religious Experience, and Globalization*, New York: Center for Migration Studies, p. 62-75.

Boswell, C., A. Geddes & P. Scholten (2011), 'The Role of Narratives in Migration Policy-Making: A Research Framework', *The British Journal of Politics & International Relations* 13(1), p. 1-11.

Brenna, B. (2011), 'La mitología fronteriza: Turner y la modernidad', *Estudios Fronterizos*, 12(24), p. 9-34.

Campese, G. (2008), *Hacia una teología desde la realidad de las migraciones: Método y desafíos,* Guadalajara: Sistema Universitario Jesuita.

Castillo Guerra, J.E. (2010), 'Diaconía de la cultura y la relación: contribuciones de migrantes para una transformación intercultural de las sociedades de acogida', in: R. Fornet-Betancourt (Ed.), *Alltagsleben: Ort des Austausch oder der neuen Kolonialisierung zwischen Nord und Süd,* Aachen: Verlagshaus Mainz, p. 331-356.

Castillo Guerra, J.E. (2004), 'Naar een theologie van de migratie: context perspectieven en thematiek', *Tijdschrift voor Theologie,* 44(3), p. 241-258.

Castillo Guerra, J.E. (2010), 'Diaconía de la cultura y la relación: contribuciones de migrantes para una transformación intercultural de las sociedades de acogida', in: R. Fornet-Betancourt (ed.), *Alltagsleben: Ort des Austausch oder der neuen Kolonialisierung zwischen Nord und Süd*, Aachen: Verlagshaus Mainz, p. 331-356.

Castillo Guerra, J.E. (2011), 'Diaconie en katholieke migranten', in: H. Crijns *et al.* (eds.), *Diaconie in beweging: Handboek Diaconiewetenschap*, p. 294-313, Kampen: Kok.

Castillo Guerra, J.E. (2013), 'Teología de la migración: movilidad humana y transformaciones teológicas', *Theologica Xaveriana* 63(176), p. 367-401.

Castillo Guerra, J.E. (2015a), 'Contributions of the Social Teaching of the Roman Catholic Church on Migration: From a 'Culture of Rejection' to a 'Culture of Encounter'', *Exchange* 44(4), p. 403-427.

Castillo Guerra, J.E. (2015b), 'From the Faith and Life of a Migrant to a Theology of Migration and Intercultural Convivencia', in: J. Gruber & S.

Rettenbacher (eds.), *Migration as a Sign of the Times: Towards a Theology of Migration,* Leiden/Boston: Brill-Rodopi, p. 107-129.

Castillo Guerra, J.E. (2015c), 'Beyond conflict: understanding the deprivitazation of religion from the social capital of religious migrant's organizations', in: C. Sterkens & P. Vermeer (eds.), *Religion, migration and conflict,* Wien: Nijmegen Studies in Development and Cultural Change, Lit. Verlag, p. 127-168.

Congregation for Bishops (1969), *Instruction De Pastorali Migratorum Cura,* Rome: 22 August.

Dijk, T.A. van (2004), 'Discourse, Knowledge and Ideology', in: M. Pütz, J. Neff & T.A. van Dijk (eds.), *Communicating ideologies. Multidisciplinary perspectives on language, discourse and social practice,* Frankfurt a. M.: Peter Lang, p. 5–38.

El País (2013), 'El Papa clama en Lapedusa contra la globalización de la indiferencia', 7 July : <www.internacional.elpais.com/internacional/2013/07/08/actualidad/1373270412_332935.html> [April 2017].

Fargues, P. & S. Bonfanti (2014), *When the best option is a leaky boat: why migrants risk their lives crossing the Mediterranean and what Europe is doing about it,* Firenze: Migration Policy Centre.

Ferrer-Gallardo, X. & H. van Houtum (2014), 'The deadly EU border control', *ACME: An International E-Journal for Critical Geographies,* 13(2), p. 295-304.

Francis (2013a), Homily of Holy Father Francis, 'Arena' sports camp. Lampedusa: Salina Quarter, 8 July: <w2.vatican.va/content/francesco/en/homilies/2013/documents/papa-francesco_20130708_omelia-lampedusa.html> [July 2014].

Francis (2013b), *Apostolic Exhortation: Evangelii Gaudium,* Vatican: 24 November.

Francis (2013c), *Homily, Holy Mass for "Evangelium Vitae" Day,* Saint Peter's Square, Vatican: 16 June.

Francis (2013e), *Message* for the *World Day of Migrants and Refugees 2014: 'Migrants and Refugees: Towards a Better World'.* Vatican: 15 August.

Francis (2013g), *Visit to the 'Astalli Centre', The Jesuit Refugee Service in Rome,* Vatican: 10 September.

Francis (2014), *Message* for the *World Day of Migrants and Refugees 2015: 'Church without frontiers, Mother to all',* Vatican: 3 September.

Francisco (2013f), *Discurso a los participantes en la Plenaria de Consejo Pontificio de los Emigrantes e Itinerantes,* Vatican: 24 May.

Francis (2015), *Visit to the joint session of the United States Congress,* Washington, D.C., 24 September.

Gutiérrez, G. (1989), *El Dios de la vida.* Lima: Instituto Bartolomé de las Casas, CEP.

Hinkelammert, F.J. (1977), *Las armas ideológicas de la muerte: las raíces económicas de la idolatría,* San José de Costa Rica: DEI.

Hinkelammert, F.J. (1989), *Der Glaube Abrahams und der Ödipus des Westens: Opfermythen im christlichen Abendland,* Münster: Ed. Liberacion.

Hinkelammert, F.J. (2001), *El nihilismo al desnudo en tiempo de la globalización.* Santiago de Chile: Lom.

Houtum, H. van & R. Pijpers (2007), 'Angst en protectie in het grens- en immigratiebeleid van de Europese Unie. Over 'tsunami', 'cherry picking' en 'gated communities'', in: E. Brugmans, P. Minderhoud & J. van Vugt (eds.), *Mythen en misverstanden over migratie,* Nijmegen: Valkhof Pers, p. 115-143.

John XXIII (1963), *Encyclical: Pacem in Terris,* Vatican.

Kessler, T. (ed.) (2014), *Migration als Ort der Theologie,* Regensburg: Verlag Friedrich Pustet.

Kim, S.C. (2012), 'Origin and Destination: A Theology of the Migrant's Trail', in: D. Kaulemu (ed.), *Faith Perspectives on Migration and Human Trafficking,* Mount Pleasant, Harare: The African Forum for Catholic Social Teaching, p. 98-103.

Kymlicka, W. (2015), 'Solidarity in diverse societies: beyond neoliberal multiculturalism and welfare chauvinism', *Comparative Migration Studies,* 3(1), p. 1-19.

Leo XIII (1891), Encyclical *Rerum Novarum, Rights and Duties of Capital and Labor,* Vatican: 15 May, no. 47.

Luciani, A. (2005), *Catecismo social cristiano: historia, principios y orientaciones operativas,* Bogotá: Ed. San Pablo.

Menjívar, C. (2014), 'Immigration Law Beyond Borders: Externalizing and Internalizing Border Controls in an Era of Securitization', *Annual Review of Law and Social Science,* 10, p. 353-369

OIM (2013), *Es hora de actuar y de salvar las vidas de los migrantes atrapados en situaciones de crisis. Comunicado de la OIM,* Ginebra: 17 December.

Pius XII (1950), *Apostolic Constitution: Exsul familia nazarethana,* Vatican.

Pontifical Council for the Pastoral Care of Migrants and Itinerant People (2004), *Instruction*: *Erga Migrantes Caritas Christi,* Vatican: 3 May.

Pontificia Comisión para los medio de comuni (1971), *Instrucción Pastoral Communio et Progressio, Sobre los Medios de Comunicación Social,* Vatican: 18 May.

Pontificio Consejo para la Pastoral de los Emigrantes e Itinerantes y Pontificio Consejo 'Cor Unum' (2013), *Acoger a Cristo en los refugiados y en los desplazados forzosos, Orientaciones Pastorales*, Vatican.

Richard, P. (ed.) (1995), *The idols of death and the God of life: a theology.* Maryknoll, N.Y.: Orbis.

Romero, O.A. (1980), *La dimensión política de la fe desde la opción por los pobres. Una experiencia eclesial en El Salvador, Centroamérica,* Discurso *al recibir el doctorado honoris causa por la Universidad de Lovaina, 2 febrero 1980:* <servicioskoinonia.org/relat/135.htm> *[January 2016].*

Schroeder, R. (2015), 'Prophetic dialogue and interculturality', in: C. Ross & S. Bevans (eds.), *Mission on the road to Emmaus,* London: SCM Press, p. 215-226.

Sobrino, J. (1978), *Iglesia de los pobres. Esbozo de eclesiología sistemática,* CRT 37, San Salvador: UCA.

Sobrino, J. (1995), 'La pascua de Jesús y la revelación de Dios desde la perspectiva de las víctimas', *RLT* 12 (34), p. 79- 91.

Strik, M.H.A. (2015), 'Frontex en de grenzen van zijn mandaat', *Justitiële Verkenningen,* 42(3), p. 45-58.

Tassello, G.G. (2010), 'Church social teaching on migration. Issues and challenges', *REMHU: Revista Interdisciplinar da Mobilidade Humana,* 18(35), p. 229-246.

Tulud Cruz, G. (2010), *An Intercultural Theology of Migration,* Leiden: Brill.

Verkuyten, M. (2014), *Identity and Cultural Diversity: What Social Psychology Can Teach Us,* Abingdon, Oxon, UK: Routledge.

Zapata-Barrero, R. (2012), 'Teoría Política de la Frontera y la movilidad humana', *Revista Española de Ciencia Política,* 29(7), p. 39-66.

Chapter 4   Immigration and Talmudic Law

4.1   Introduction

The topic - Immigration and Talmudic Law - directs me to look at Talmudic law for the answer to questions of immigration policy. These questions are not new to any established culture or group of people, and certainly not new to the Jews who have substantial millennial experience in immigration, as well as being strangers and aliens in many strange countries. Let me pose that the subject matter of immigration may rest on two principles.

The first principle is that of granting rights of immigration - that is, someone with the power to permit or deny immigrants entry. The second principle is the responsibility and latent, if not active, power of the immigrant to get along in his or her new country and refuse the temptation of bending the will of a country to suit his own cultural or economic interests. Before I touch upon these two principles in more detail, I will review the general principles of Talmudic law.

First, all Jewish law and thus what we may refer to as Talmudic law is based upon the Bible or the Five Books of Moses, commonly referred to as the Old Testament. This is the source of all Jewish biblical law, and if it is explicit on a topic, it is the final and only word.

But ambiguity has a righteous place in Jewish law, as often the question is far more important than the answer. Sharp edges in discussions of Jewish law, particularly among friends, is required; this requirement for sharp discussion is put clearly in focus when one understands that the Hebrew word for pepper is the same root as the Hebrew word for discussion. Aggressive discussion is a watchword of Talmudic interpretation.

Following the Old Testament, which I may refer to as the Torah or Bible, there were commentaries on the day-to-day implementation of the Bible's principles of law. These commentaries were in the form of case disputations and answers to questions brought before the rabbinic authorities over the ages. This process set the tone and structure that is referred to in Jewish history as the making of the Oral Law and for deciding a myriad of questions facing the Jewish people. This process of questioning helped form the Jewish people into a structure which thankfully has lasted for centuries and enabled Jews to contribute and survive in small communities as well as in larger non-Jewish communities.

NOTES

As he is scrupulous...like Raḥava – דְּהָיֵיק...כְּרָחֲבָא: Various interpretations were suggested in explanation of Raḥava's unique precision. Some *geonim* explain that Raḥava was uncertain whether he heard the statement in the name of Rabbi Yehuda, the *tanna*, or Rav Yehuda, the *amora*, and he therefore repeated the statement in a manner that included them both. Others reject this (Rabbeinu Ḥananel, Rashi) and say that he repeated what he learned from his teacher verbatim.

He transforms the attributes of the Holy One, Blessed be He, into mercy – שֶׁעוֹשֶׂה מִדּוֹתָיו שֶׁל הַקָּדוֹשׁ בָּרוּךְ הוּא רַחֲמִים. אֵינָן אֶלָּא גְּזֵרוֹת: The Rambam explains that compassion is not the reason for this mitzva, as if that was the case, God would have prohibited slaughtering animals for food. Although in midrash, this mitzva is interpreted as a manifestation of compassion, it should be understood as guidance for man to act with compassion toward creatures, not as an indication of God's compassion on those creatures (Ramban on the Torah).

LANGUAGE

Colonnade [stav] – סְטָיו: From the Greek στοά, *stoa*, meaning a roofed row of columns, *stav* refers to a row of columns that is attached to a building. The Gemara refers to a double *stav*, two rows of columns.

Colonnade

HALAKHA

The havdala of: And You have made known to us, etc. – הַבְדָּלָה דְּוַתּוֹדִיעֵנוּ: According to Rav Yosef's conclusion, the addition to the evening prayer on Festivals that occur at the conclusion of Shabbat: And You have made known to us, is the accepted formula for havdala on that occasion (Rambam Sefer Ahava, Hilkhot Tefilla 2:12; Shulḥan Arukh, Oraḥ Ḥayyim 491:2).

One who recites: Just as Your mercy is extended to a bird's nest... – הָאוֹמֵר עַל קַן צִפּוֹר וכו׳: Those who hear one who recites in this prayer: Just as Your mercy is extended to a bird's nest or a similar formula, should silence him, as per our mishna (Rambam Sefer Ahava, Hilkhot Tefilla 9:6).

One who recites: We give thanks, we give thanks – הָאוֹמֵר מוֹדִים מוֹדִים: Those who hear one who recites: We give thanks, should silence him, as per our mishna (Rambam Sefer Ahava, Hilkhot Tefilla 9:4; Shulḥan Arukh, Oraḥ Ḥayyim 121:2).

One is required to bless God for the bad, etc. – חַיָּיב אָדָם לְבָרֵךְ עַל הָרָעָה וכו׳: One is required to bless God for the bad that befalls him with devotion and enthusiasm just as he does when good befalls him (Rambam Sefer Ahava, Hilkhot Berakhot 10:3; Shulḥan Arukh, Oraḥ Ḥayyim 222:3).

רַבִּי יוֹחָנָן אָמַר: מוֹדִים; וְרַבִּי חִיָּיא
בַּר אַבָּא אָמַר: גְּרָאִין.

אָמַר רַבִּי זֵירָא: נְקוֹט דְּרַבִּי חִיָּיא
בַּר אַבָּא בִּיְדָךְ, דְּדָיֵיק קָן וְגָמַר
שְׁמַעְתָּא מִפּוּמָא דְּמָרָהּ שַׁפִּיר
כְּרָחֲבָא דְּפוּמְבְּדִיתָא.

דְּאָמַר רָחֲבָא אָמַר רַב יְהוּדָה:
הַר הַבַּיִת סְטָיו כָּפוּל הָיָה, וְהָיְה
סְטָיו לְפְנִים מִסְטָיו.

אָמַר רַב יוֹסֵף: אֲנָא לָא הָאי
יָדַעְנָא וְלָא הָאי יָדַעְנָא, אֶלָּא
מִדְּרַב וּשְׁמוּאֵל יָדַעְנָא דְּתַקִּינוּ
לָן מַרְגְּנִיתָא בְּבָבֶל:

וְתוֹדִיעֵנוּ ה' אֱלֹהֵינוּ אֶת מִשְׁפְּטֵי
צִדְקֶךָ, וַתְּלַמְּדֵנוּ לַעֲשׂוֹת חֻקֵּי
רְצוֹנֶךָ, וַתַּנְחִילֵנוּ זְמַנֵּי שָׂשׂוֹן
וְחַגֵּי נְדָבָה וַתּוֹרִישֵׁנוּ קְדוּשַׁת
שַׁבָּת וּכְבוֹד מוֹעֵד וַחֲגִיגַת הָרֶגֶל.
בֵּין קְדוּשַׁת שַׁבָּת לִקְדוּשַׁת יוֹם
טוֹב הִבְדַּלְתָּ וְאֶת יוֹם הַשְּׁבִיעִי
מִשֵּׁשֶׁת יְמֵי הַמַּעֲשֶׂה קִדַּשְׁתָּ,
הִבְדַּלְתָּ וְקִדַּשְׁתָּ אֶת עַמְּךָ יִשְׂרָאֵל
בִּקְדוּשָּׁתֶךָ, וַתִּתֶּן לָנוּ וכו':

מַתְנִי׳ הָאוֹמֵר "עַל קַן צִפּוֹר
יַגִּיעוּ רַחֲמֶיךָ", וְ"עַל טוֹב יִזָּכֵר
שְׁמֶךָ", "מוֹדִים מוֹדִים" –
מְשַׁתְּקִין אוֹתוֹ.

גמ׳ בִּשְׁלָמָא "מוֹדִים מוֹדִים"
מְשַׁתְּקִין אוֹתוֹ – מִשּׁוּם דְּמֵיחֲזֵי
כִּשְׁתֵּי רְשׁוּיוֹת, וְ"עַל טוֹב יִזָּכֵר
שְׁמֶךָ" – נַמֵי מַשְׁמַע עַל הַטּוֹבָה
וְלֹא עַל הָרָעָה, וּתְנַן: חַיָּיב אָדָם
לְבָרֵךְ עַל הָרָעָה כְּשֵׁם שֶׁמְּבָרֵךְ עַל
הַטּוֹבָה. אֶלָּא "עַל קַן צִפּוֹר יַגִּיעוּ
רַחֲמֶיךָ" מַאי טַעְמָא?

פְּלִיגִי בָּהּ תְּרֵי אֲמוֹרָאֵי בְּמַעְרְבָא,
רַבִּי יוֹסֵי בַּר אָבִין וְרַבִּי יוֹסֵי בַּר
זְבִידָא: חַד אָמַר: מִפְּנֵי שֶׁמַּטִּיל
קִנְאָה בְּמַעֲשֵׂה בְרֵאשִׁית, וְחַד
אָמַר: מִפְּנֵי שֶׁעוֹשֶׂה מִדּוֹתָיו שֶׁל
הַקָּדוֹשׁ בָּרוּךְ הוּא רַחֲמִים, וְאֵינָן
אֶלָּא גְּזֵרוֹת.

Rabbi Yoḥanan said that there is no dispute here, and the Rabbis **agree** with Rabbi Eliezer. **And Rabbi Ḥiyya bar Abba** said that it was established that Rabbi Eliezer's opinion **appears** to be correct.

With regard to this difference of opinion **Rabbi Zeira said: Take this statement of Rabbi Ḥiyya bar Abba in your hand, as he is scrupulous and he learned the *halakha* well from the mouth of its originator, like the Sage Raḥava**[N] **from the city Pumbedita.** Raḥava was famous for the precision with which he would transmit material that he learned from his teacher.

The Gemara cites an example: **Raḥava said that Rabbi Yehuda said: The Temple Mount was a double** *stav*,[1] **and there was a** *stav* **within a** *stav*. Here Raḥava used his Rabbi's language in describing the structure of the Temple and the rows of columns it contained, a row within a row; but he did not employ the common term *itzteba*, portico, but rather *stav*, as he heard it from his Rabbi.

Rav Yosef said the conclusive *halakha* on this topic: **I don't know this and I don't know that, but I do know from the statements of Rav and Shmuel they have instituted a pearl for us in Babylonia.** They established a version that combines the first blessing of the Festival with the formula of *havdala*, parallel to the opinion of the Rabbis who include *havdala* in the first blessing that follows the first three blessings. They instituted to recite:

You have made known to us,[H] **Lord our God, Your righteous laws, and taught us to perform Your will's decrees.**
You have given us as our heritage seasons of joy and Festivals of voluntary offerings.
You have given us as our heritage the holiness of Shabbat, the glory of the festival and the festive offerings of the Pilgrim Festivals.
You have distinguished between the holiness of Shabbat and the holiness of the Festival,
and have made the seventh day holy over the six days of work.
You have distinguished and sanctified Your people Israel with Your holiness,
And You have given us, etc.

MISHNA Concluding the laws of prayer in this tractate, the mishna raises several prayer-related matters. This mishna speaks of certain innovations in the prayer formula that warrant the silencing of a communal prayer leader who attempts to introduce them in his prayers, as their content tends toward heresy. **One who recites** in his supplication: **Just as Your mercy is extended to a bird's nest,**[H] as You have commanded us to send away the mother before taking her chicks or eggs (Deuteronomy 22:6–7), so too extend Your mercy to us; **and one who recites: May Your name be mentioned with the good** or one who recites: **We give thanks, we give thanks**[H] twice, they silence him.

GEMARA Our mishna cited three instances where the communal prayer leader is silenced. The Gemara clarifies: **Granted,** they silence one who repeats: **We give thanks, we give thanks, as it appears like he is** acknowledging and praying to two authorities. And granted that **they also silence one who says: May Your name be mentioned with the good,** as clearly he is thanking God only **for the good and not for the bad, and we learned** in a mishna: **One is required to bless God for the bad**[H] just as he blesses Him for the good. **However, in the case of one who recites: Just as Your mercy is extended to a bird's nest, why do they silence him?**

Two *amora'im* **in Eretz Yisrael disputed this question; Rabbi Yosei bar Avin and Rabbi Yosei bar Zevida; one said** that this was because **he engenders jealousy among God's creations,** as it appears as though he is protesting the fact that the Lord favored one creature over all others. **And one said** that this was **because he transforms the attributes of the Holy One, Blessed be He, into expressions of mercy,**[N] when they are nothing but decrees of the King that must be fulfilled without inquiring into the reasons behind them.

The Jews recognized that government and respect for rule of law, whether Jewish or non-Jewish, was essential to prevent chaos. This concept of respect for order is extremely important and is aptly summed up in a quote from *Pirkei Avot* (Ethics of Our Fathers 3:2):

> *Pray for the integrity of the government, for were it not for the fear of its authority a man would swallow his neighbor alive.*

Hillel, a well-known Hebrew scholar, summed it up more homiletically when he said:

> *If I am not for myself, who is for me? And if I am only for myself, what am I? If not now, when?* (Ethics of Our Fathers 1:14)

> *Whoever destroys a soul, it is considered as if he destroyed an entire world; and whoever saves a life it is considered as if he saved an entire world.* (Sanhedrin 4:9)

> *What is hateful to you, do not to your neighbor: that is the whole Torah, the rest is the commentary, go and learn it.* (Shab. 31A)

Thus, over thousands of years, scholars and rabbis interpreting principles of the Bible into everyday life developed an oral discourse much like one may find in a case book in a law school outlining problems and giving answers. If a co-worker broke down his neighbor's fence, what was the outcome? If one was encroaching on another's rights, who prevails? Does it matter if the parties are both residents or if one is an alien or foreigner?

Decisions on such questions over literally thousands of years affected a great deal of the basis for Western common law. In Talmudic terms, the general body of this oral law is sometimes referred to as the Mishnah. The Mishnah was finally recorded in writing somewhere around 200 A.D. Generally, the Mishnah was a series of statements of the law without necessarily the process by which decisions leading to that law were made. In other words, the Mishnah is a collection of legal statutes without discussion and without footnotes. A few hundred years later, rabbinic scholars began capturing both the statements of legal principles, called the Mishnah, and the peppery discussion which formed the decision-making process. This process gave birth to the Talmud.

There were two groups of rabbis and scholars putting together two separate Talmuds over many years. One was in Israel, and became known as the Jerusalem Talmud, the other was outside of Israel, which became known as the Babylonian Talmud. The discussion (see previous page for an example) is the implementation and collection of rabbinic opinion over a long period of time, setting forth pros and cons and only citing rabbis by name if they had achieved a sufficient reputation during their lives. Otherwise, the opinion is stated generically 'as the Talmud says' or sometimes 'as the Rabbis said'.

The Talmud, which is the combination of the Mishnah and the implementing discussions, is what we today refer to as the basis of Talmudic law. It obviously has nuances and additions by various Rabbinic authorities over the years. There are 63 volumes of the Talmud with subject matters as diverse as the Sabbath, contracts, conveyances, injuries, et cetera. There is, however, no volume entitled Immigration Policy. For this we must be prepared to ask the right questions in order to get the right answers.

4.2   Immigration status

Now I would like to go back to the first two questions mentioned earlier the conflict and juxtaposition between the two parties in immigration decision: the person who confers the immigration status and the person who receives the immigration status. What does Jewish law say about this potential conflict?

First, as I mentioned to you, the source of all Jewish law is the Bible. But what does the Bible say about immigration law? We know from the story of Joseph that Jewish immigration to Egypt came with a bargain: protection and a place to live in exchange for a contribution to society. Eventually Joseph's contribution was costly as it led to conflict and expulsion. Nonetheless, we are taught by this history to be kind to strangers because in the words of Exodus and Deuteronomy, 'We were strangers in a strange land'. So, Talmudic law starts with the principle, indeed the obligation, for us to be kind to strangers. This means when someone comes to seek permission to enter your country's borders, Talmudic law would require an initial presumption of allowance of that person to enter the country.

But as we shall soon see, there are limits. What if the stranger takes away the job of a resident who now goes on the dole to support his family? What if the stranger is trying to impose his own cultural values and to change the essence of the City to which he immigrated? How are these conflicts resolved in Talmudic law? The answer will give us insight into the question of what Talmudic law requires in the broad case of immigration principles. So now I turn to some examples which I hope will lead us to some answers.

4.3   Examples

The Ten Commandments speak of the obligation to love God, but only to honor one's mother and father. It is obvious that one can honor someone without loving them, and love is a commandment reserved for God. But in the Book of Deuteronomy (10:19, King James Version), we are told:

> *Love ye therefore the stranger: for ye were strangers in the*
> *land of Egypt.*

The obligation to love a stranger is unique from among all ancient civilizations. This concept of loving strangers appears elsewhere and throughout the Bible. For example, in Exodus (22:21) we are told:

> *Thou shalt neither vex a stranger, nor oppress him: for ye*
> *were strangers in the land of Egypt.*

Don't pressure the stranger: you know the feelings of being a stranger, seeing as you were strangers in the land of Egypt. Further, in Deuteronomy (23:15):

> *Thou shalt not deliver unto his master the servant which is*
> *escaped from his master unto thee. He shall dwell with thee,*
> *even among you, in that place which he shall choose in one*
> *of thy gates, where it liketh him best: thou shalt not oppress*
> *him.*

This then sets out the general obligation in non-contextual circumstances to allow open borders and not only protect the foreigner or alien, but love him.

Clearly, this positive and welcome approach to a stranger or immigrant is no doubt one of the foremost missions of the Exodus and the experience in exile which the Jewish people faced over the many years they were held in bondage. Indeed, the promise to the Jewish people to have their own land made early through Abraham came with the understanding that the Jews would be enslaved themselves for 400 years and thus the promise of salvation for the Jewish people was intertwined with the recognition that Jews would one day earn their freedom, but only by recognizing their eternal obligations to others. In Genesis and the story of Jacob and the spies, the brothers themselves are treated kindly -even though they were foreigners to Joseph in the story and the principle of kindness to strangers prevailed.

In the story of Adam and Eve, God said 'Be fruitful and multiply and fill the earth'. The Bible encouraged Adam and Eve and their progeny to spread from each other and not stay in one place. Later the Bible told us that the whole earth had one language and spoke the same words, and a united humanity attempted to build a tower, the Tower of Babel, to reach to the heavens and prevent themselves from being dispersed throughout the world. This effort failed. The people were directed to dwell in tribes, in their respective quarters, so that they were not intermingled.

From this we learn the Talmudic principle that each tribe of Israel was obligated to establish countries and borders for the development of a wide variety of communities. These communities in turn could, over the course of history, be in conflict with each other, and the question now arises: what are the rules for resolving these conflicts when people cross borders?

These national characteristics and the distinct bounded lands that gave rise to them are part of the providential plan in the Bible and place in stark relief questions for supporting those borders and opposing keeping those borders closed. Thus, we come upon the question of how do we solve in a community – small or large – the issues of security, cultural coherence, economics and expectations as well as immigration whether legal or illegal?

While the dispersed people are obligated by the bounds of common humanity to respect each other, the Bible offers no privileges without responsibilities, and the mutual respect of those bearing shared responsibilities have a common goal. The holiday of Passover, which commemorates the exodus of the Jewish people from Egypt where they were enslaved, is a biblical holiday. The obligation to eat only unleavened bread during the holiday is set forth in Exodus (13:8), and fathers are commanded to tell their sons:

> *It is done because of that which the Lord did unto me when*
> *I came forth out of Egypt.*

This concept of identification of modern Jews who celebrate Passover with the Jews who are released from Egypt is carried forward in the Haggadah, the prayer book used during the Passover service, as a recognition of an individual redemption. The specific language of the Haggadah is instructive on this subject. The pertinent part states:

> *In each generation, each individual Jew is obliged to regard*
> *himself or herself as if he or she had personally gone out of*
> *Egypt. (...) And it was not our ancestors alone who the Holy*
> *one did redeem, but he also redeemed us with him.*

Each Passover, biblical and Talmudic law obligates each Jew who participates in the Passover service to identify as one of the Jews who themselves were released from Egypt. Thus, Jews are annually thankful by this holiday observance for being freed. This again is a specific recollection that Jewish history, as well as modern Jewish observances, has an annual reminder that the current Jewish generation only exists because that ancient Jewish civilization was freed from Egypt. This obligation to recognize that communication and personal identification with that exodus forms a powerful recognition of the obligation referred to earlier to be kind to strangers and have empathy for immigrants.

In the Book of Deuteronomy (33:25), Moses, addressing the Jewish people, told Asher: 'Iron and brass shall be thy bars'. Asher's tribe dwelled in the far northern territory on the seacoast and Moses was telling Asher to fortify his borders against enemies and that only mighty warriors should dwell in the border cities in order to 'lock up' or protect the land.

Rashi, the famous French commentator who wrote annotations for the Bible and the Talmud, underscores the necessity of protecting borders from *enemy* immigrants. So now we know that the obligation to love a stranger is biblically modified by the obligation to protect yourself.

In the Talmud volume entitled Bava Batra at page 21B, we see a discussion that makes it clear that residents of a town can prevent an outsider from setting up a business competing with residents in that town. However, a different result obtains if the new person who wishes to open up the new business is willing to contribute and pay local taxes. If that occurs, then according to Talmudic law, the residents cannot prevent the competition from a new business. What we learn from this is the principle that immigration denial is not absolute and that an immigrant who is willing to contribute to the welfare of the city to which he wishes to move, must then be accorded the rights of other citizens.

Over the years this balancing concept has permitted Jewish communities to enact rules with the power to regulate local conditions to prevent immigrants from coming in and taking employment *when* the competition would prevent the residents of the city from earning a living.

Thus, if immigration will prevent the residents of the city to which immigration is sought from earning a basic livelihood, immigrants can be barred from residing in a town but not from contributing to the town. Thus, an immigrant could spend money in the town but not start a business which would not only compete but take away the main earning power of those living in the city. This led to principles of Talmudic law which rendered it appropriate for city leaders to deport anyone who entered without permission; and even people who came with permission can be required to contribute to various tax obligations for the upkeep of the city in order to do business, even if they do not reside there.

And, while the Talmud generally provides that an outsider cannot be rejected if she is willing to pay taxes, *and* there is no ethical backing to ban an outsider from entering the city, the city authorities could, as I have mentioned, entertain enforceable regulations which would prevent the destruction or substantial impairment of the residents' ability to make a living.

4.4   Conclusion

If strangers come to a community because they are fleeing danger, Talmudic law generally provides that such immigrants who are fleeing danger have the right to settle in any community until the crisis passes, and they may remain if it is impossible to return to their homeland. This Talmudic principle emphasizes the overarching principle of Talmudic law, which is the obligation to save a life.

So, going back to the first two principles I mentioned – the power to grant immigration and the obligation of the immigrant to fit in to his new country, we can sum up by recognizing that the presumption of Talmudic law is to help immigration and the power to deny entry is not absolute. Indeed, as we have seen, the power to grant or deny immigration must be exercised by the concept of loving strangers, which mirrors the history of the Jewish people who were strangers in a strange land.

However, equally important is the role of the immigrant. He may not come to a country to take advantage of that country without making contributions, and even with a recognition of an immigrant's obligation to make contributions to the place he wishes to immigrate, his conduct and responsibilities may not be such as to destroy the character of the community or the right of its residents to support themselves.

In the end, we will find that Talmudic law regards immigration policy as circumstantial and transactional. Citizens with roots in a particular place have an obligation to help others but not so that they have to risk destroying the very society which they have built for themselves.

Part 2

Application of Religious Freedom

Chapter 5   Can one still call it ignorance or improper bias?

Nexus test modified, but courts still fail to address international law under the International Religious Freedom Act

Craig B. Mousin

5.1   Introduction

The United States Congress passed the International Religious Freedom Act on October 27, 1998[1] (IRFA) to address what it considered a global scourge of religious persecution. According to Congress, over half "of the world's population lives under regimes that severely restrict or prohibit the freedom of their citizens to study, believe, observe, and freely practice the religious faith of their choice".[2] But Congress also found fault in the unfairness of the United States adjudication of asylum and refugee claims. Congress specifically criticized U.S. government agencies and individuals involved in refugee screening and adjudicating claims, including immigration judges (IJ), Asylum Officers, consular officials, and border enforcement officers for their failure to properly recognize and respond to the many ways persons of faith faced persecution for their religious beliefs and practices.[3] Finding that it was either "improper biases or (...) lack of proper training", many victims of religious persecution had not been treated fairly.[4]

To address this concern, in a particularly rare development in United States immigration law, Congress did not look to United States domestic law or to the Constitution's First Amendment as the primary protector of the religious claims of refugees, but instead named international law the relevant source of

---

1   22 U.S.C. §§ 6401–6481 (2000) (enacted 27 October 1998).
2   22 U.S.C. § 6401(b)(5). 22 U.S.C. § 6401(a)(4)–(6).
3   The House Report on IRFA stated: "The primary impetus behind the immigration provisions of H.R. 2431 is the concern that victims of religious persecution may not be treated fairly by the organizations and individuals responsible for screening applicants for asylum or refugee's status and adjudicating their claims. Such unfair treatment could arise from improper biases or from lack of proper training".
     H.R. REP. NO. 105-480, pt. 3, at 16 (1998), reprinted in 1998 U.S.C.C.A.N. 602, 628. Although Congress made significant changes in H.R. 2431 in enacting IRFA, IRFA retained the mandate for training and eliminating bias and misunderstanding in the final bill.
4   *Id.*

protection.[5] Congress called for reform and mandated new training to ensure the elimination of potential biases to protect religious "practices which would meet the definition of persecution under international refugee law".[6] In addition to legal training, adjudicators needed to understand the "nature of religious persecution abroad, including country-specific conditions, instruction on the internationally recognized right to freedom of religion, instruction on methods of religious persecution practices in foreign countries, and applicable distinctions within a county in the treatment of various religious practices and believers".[7] Confirming the new changes to asylum law, Congress added that "the promotion of international religious freedom requires new and evolving policies (...)".[8]

Initially, the Immigration and Naturalization Service acknowledged this major transformation of asylum law. In particular, the Asylum Officers Basic Training Manual affirmed: "In IRFA, Congress invoked the understanding of religion found in international instruments, such as the Universal Declaration of Human Rights, and the International Covenant on Civil and Political Rights, and found that freedom of religious belief and practice is a universal human right and fundamental freedom".[9] By naming international religious freedom as codified under international law, Congress instructed Asylum Officers and immigration judges to look to both a persecutor's intent and the effect of a law or practice in judging whether violations of religious liberty occurred.[10] By requiring the consideration of effect to asylum law adjudications, IRFA modified existing asylum law regarding nexus. This conclusion presented a radical change in United States asylum law.

---

5   22 U.S.C. § 6401 (a)(2)–(3) provide:
     (2) Freedom of religious belief and practice is a universal human right and fundamental
     freedom articulated in numerous international instruments, including the Universal
     Declaration of Human Rights, the International Covenant on Civil and Political Rights, the
     Helsinki Accords, the Declaration on the Elimination of All Forms of Intolerance and
     Discrimination Based on Religion or Belief, the United Nations Charter, and the European
     Convention for the Protection of Human Rights and Fundamental Freedoms.
     (3) Article 18 of the Universal Declaration of Human Rights recognizes that "Everyone has
     the right to freedom of thought, conscience, and religion. This right includes freedom to
     change his religion or belief, and freedom, either alone or in community with others and in
     public or private, to manifest his religion or belief in teaching, practice, worship, and
     observance".
     Article 18(1) of the International Covenant on Civil and Political Rights recognizes that
     "Everyone shall have the right to freedom of thought, conscience, and religion. This right
     shall include freedom to have or to adopt a religion or belief of his choice, and freedom,
     either individually or in community with others and in public or private, to manifest his
     religion or belief in worship, observance, practice, and teaching".
6   22 U.S.C. § 6473 (2002).
7   22 U.S.C. § 6473(b) (2002).
8   22 U.S.C. § 6401(b)(2) (2002).
9   Immigration & Naturalization Serv., INS Asylum Officer Basic Training Manual, Immi-
     gration Officer Academy (Nov. 20, 2001), 12.
10   See infra note 56.

Although the Refugee Act of 1980[11] brought the United States into confor-
mance with the United Nations Protocol of 1967,[12] subsequent attempts to look
to international law for protection have been rebuffed by the Board of
Immigration Appeals (BIA or Board) and the courts.[13] IRFA, at least for
purposes of asylum and refugee adjudication, recognized the need to include the
protection offered by international law for religious claimants. It stressed the
need to remedy past failures by conducting specific training "on the internationally recognized right to freedom of religion, the nature, activities, and
beliefs of different religions, and the various aspects and manifestations of
violations of religious freedom".[14] Such language corroborates that adjudication
of religious claims of persecution under domestic refugee law prior to IRFA had
failed. Therefore, through the language of IRFA, Congress ordered the federal
agencies, consulates, and judges to follow international law to address this
critical problem of protecting religious liberty.

Despite the initial fanfare and opportunities IRFA offered, however, a search
of the electronic data bases of immigration cases decided since 1998 reveals not
one published decision citing the legal protections offered by IRFA.[15] Congress
enacted a radical change by changing the nexus standard, but the courts, as well
as attorneys representing asylum applicants, have spurned this remedy, leading
to a continuing failure to protect applicants seeking safe haven from religious
persecution.

Indeed, courts continue to downplay the need to examine international law
in asylum cases. In *Romeike v. Holder*, for example, the applicants urged the
court to recognize that Germany violated their right to home school their
children under the International Covenant on Civil and Political Righters art.
18(4) and the Universal Declaration of Human Rights, (UDHR) but the court
said "that, by itself does not require the granting of American asylum
applications".[16] In a concurring opinion, Circuit Judge Rogers flatly stated, "Our

---

11 Refugee Act of 1980, Pub. L. No. 96-212, 94 Stat. 102 (codified as amended in scattered
    sections of 8 U.S.C.).
12 I.N.S. v. Cardoza-Fonseca, 480 U.S. 421, 436 (1987).
13 Bradvica v. I.N.S., 128 F.3d 1009 (7th Cir. 1987), citing In Re Medina, 19 I & N Dec. 734
    (1988), (BIA lacks jurisdiction to hear international claims unless specifically delegated by
    the Attorney General or by Congress). Congress authorized such consideration in IRFA. The
    Act also established the U.S. Commission on International Religious Freedom (USCIRF) to
    monitor the status of freedom of thought, conscience and religion or belief abroad, as defined
    in the universal Declaration of Human Rights and related international instruments, and to
    give independent policy recommendations to the Executive and Legislative branches of
    government. United States Commission on International Religious Freedom,
    <www.uscirf.gov/about-uscirf>.
14 22 U.S.C. § 4028(a)(1); see *id.* § 4028(a)(2); *id.* § 6473(a)–(c).
15 IRFA also tasked the USCIRF to prepare Annual Reports on religious liberty conditions.
    Case law does reveal that parties have cited the Annual Reports and courts have addressed
    the use of the Reports, but no published cases have raised IRFA's international protections
    as part of the asylum or withholding adjudications.
16 718 F.3d 528, 534 (6th Cir. 2013), Rehearing and Rehearing En Banc Den., July 12, 2014,
    cert. den. 134 S.Ct. 1491 (2014).

role, however, is not that of an international court adjudicating Germany's obligation to other countries in respect of its own citizens. Instead we sit as a court of the United States, enforcing statutes that implement some of the international obligations of the United States to other countries in respect of asylum applications".[17] Conceding that some international obligations were initially implemented within the 1980 asylum law, Judge Rogers finds no independent investigation under international principles notwithstanding IRFA's 1998 enactment. As *Romeike* reveals, despite nineteen years of litigation, no court through a published decision has seen fit to respond to Congress' frustration with prior adjudication of religious persecution claims and analyze an applicant's request under international protections. This paper focuses on the consequences of judicial failure to understand the "international" in IRFA and invites courts and attorneys representing asylum applicants to apply IRFA in adjudicating religious persecution cases.

In a 2003 article, I celebrated IRFA's promise for expanded concepts of religious liberty in asylum adjudication and suggested several areas where IRFA provided new tools for courts to evaluate claims of religious persecution.[18] IRFA called for broader comprehension of religious liberty than prior domestic law offered.[19] IRFA required greater sensitivity to the legal and factual issues involved in credibility determinations.[20] IRFA expanded the understanding of religious persecution beyond domestic United States law.[21] IRFA recognized a government's affirmative duty to protect against violations of freedom of belief or religion.[22] No published cases citing these provisions exist, however, leaving the record bare in resolving religious persecution cases under IRFA and perpetuating what Congress perceived as the failure of federal adjudicators to fully understand religious persecution in asylum determinations.

Par. 5.2 of this chapter will discuss how IRFA changes the nexus issue in religious asylum cases. Because international law protects individuals from both intentional persecution as well as persecution resulting from the effect of a law or practice, IRFA should mitigate some of the difficulty religious applicants face under the Supreme Court definition of nexus in *INS v. Elias-Zacarias*.[23] Par. 5.3 will look at one case under IRFA, but its particular procedural history has minimized its impact instead of providing a map for relief. Par. 5.4 suggests as a thought experiment of IRFA's potential, re-litigating one pre-IRFA case to consider what might have happened if IRFA had been applied to the litigation. Par. 5.5 examines the interrelationship between United States First Amendment

---

17 *Id*. at 535.
18 Mousin, Craig B. (2004), 'Standing with the persecuted: adjudicating asylum applications account of religion after the enactment of the international religious freedom act of 1998', *Brigham Young University Law Review*, p. 541.
19 *Id*. at p. 561-568.
20 *Id*. at p. 568-573.
21 *Id*. at p. 573-587.
22 *Id*. at p. 587-590.
23 502 U.S. 478 (1992).

law with IRFA. Finally, Par. 5.6 argues that even if IRFA did not change the law of nexus, IRFA still mandates enhanced training for adjudicators and government attorney to eliminate improper asylum adjudications. International law emphasizes the many manifestations of how religion is practiced, how religion impacts identity, and how persecutors violate religious liberty as compared to the narrow interpretations followed prior to the enactment of IRFA. At the very least, applicants should receive what Congress intended in a fair appraisal of their cases to ensure they retain the universal human right of religious liberty under the "internationally recognized right to freedom of religion, and religious belief and practice".[24]

5.2 The Nexus Problem

The failure to use the tools IRFA provides has had particularly negative consequences in the context of nexus. To prevail in an asylum case the applicant must show he or she possesses one or more of the enumerated grounds, for example, religion, and that the persecutor intended the harm based on the named grounds.[25] When the Supreme Court established the necessity of proving this connection between the enumerated ground and the persecutor's intent, it increased the difficulty in obtaining asylum when neutral laws of general applicability interfere with faith or practice.[26] As I discussed more extensively in my earlier paper,[27] prior to IRFA, the confluence of two United States Supreme Court cases involving First Amendment law and immigration law in

---

24 22 U.S.C. § 6402 (16).

25 The Refugee Act of 1980 defines a refugee, in part, as: "any person who is outside any country of such person's nationality or, in the case of a person having no nationality, is outside any country in which such person last habitually resided, and who is unable or unwilling to return to, and is unable or unwilling to avail himself or herself of the protection of, that country because of persecution or a well-founded fear of persecution on account of race, religion, nationality, membership in a particular social group, or political opinion", 8 U.S.C. § 1101(a)(42). The Refugee Act further included the remedy of non-refoulement. Under Section 241(b)(3) an applicant may not be removed to their native country if his or her "life would be threatened in that country because of the alien's race, religion, nationality, membership in a particular social group, or political opinion". The United States Supreme Court has held that this restriction on removal must meet the higher standard that persecution will be more likely than not, but IRFA's modification of nexus analysis for on account of religion should be the same as addressed in this chapter. I.N.S. v. Stevic, 467 U.S. 407 (1984).

26 To be clear, courts have granted asylum to some applicants seeking asylum or withholding based on religious persecution. Even under the First Amendment to the Constitution intentional restrictions on life or liberty based on persecution on account of religion would make one eligible for asylum. Immigration Judges, the BIA have granted asylum and the Courts of Appeal have remanded cases when they find the nexus, or a direct connection, between the applicant's religious faith and the persecutor's intent to persecute. *See, e.g.*, In re L.K., 23 I. & N. Dec. 677, 2004 WL 2211892 (B.I.A. 2004); Shi v. U.S. Attny. Gen., 707 F.3d 1231(11th Cir. 2013).

27 Mousin, Standing, *supra* note 18, at 547, p. 551-555.

the early 1990s played a significant role in limiting protection of refugees seeking safe haven from religious persecution: *Employment Division, Department of Human Resources of Oregon v. Smith*[28] and *INS v. Elias-Zacarias*.[29] In *Smith*, Justice Scalia stated that First Amendment law held that neutral, generally applicable laws that did not intentionally discriminate against religion did not violate the Constitution. Prior to *Smith*, most claimants alleging violations of the Constitution's Free Exercise clause had the opportunity to request exemptions from neutral laws of general applicability when they were able to demonstrate that their infringed rights were not limited by a compelling state interest in the law and, should such interest exist, no less restrictive means existed to achieve the same ends without violating their beliefs or practices. After *Smith*, the neutrality of a law sustained its validity against a First Amendment claim. The Court subsequently confirmed that any government legislation or action that intentionally discriminated would violate the Free Exercise clause.[30] Since *Smith*, the Court and the Congress have jockeyed back and forth with congressional attempts to restore the earlier balancing test with some success while federal courts still struggle with whether a balancing test for exemptions can be found under federal law.[31]

For asylum purposes, however, the Court's decision in *Elias-Zacarias* further constricted asylum as a remedy. Raised under the aegis of a political opinion case, Justice Scalia, without benefit of precedent or citation to any authority, discovered a new test defining "on account of" under the Refugee Act of 1980.[32] According to Justice Scalia, the ordinary meaning of the phrase "persecution on account of (...) political opinion" is persecution on account of the *victim's* political opinion, not the persecutor's".[33] International law had not recognized nor currently recognizes Justice Scalia's "ordinary meaning" of on account of with such a restricted limitation.[34] In an *Elias-Zacarias* amicus brief, the United Nations High Commissioner for Refugees set forth that international law never required such a restrictive test for nexus limited to the intent of the

---

28   494 U.S. 872 (1990).
29   502 U.S. 478 (1992).
30   Church of the Lukumi Babalu Aye, Inc. v. Hialeah, 508 U.S. 520 (1993).
31   Lupu, Ira C. (2015), 'Hobby Lobby and the dubious enterprise of religious exemptions', *Harvard Journal of Law & Gender*, 38, p. 35; Laycock, Douglas (2009), 'The religious exemption debate', *Rutgers Journal of Law & Religion*, 11, p. 139. *See e.g.*, Gonzales v. O Centro Espirita Beneficente Uniao Do Vegetal, 126 S. Ct. 1211 (2006) (finding exemption for use of restricted drug when used in religious ceremony). *See also* Laycock, Douglas & Steven T. Collis (2016), 'Generally applicable law and the free exercise of religion', *Nebraska Law Review*, 95, p. 1; Lund, Christopher C. (2017), 'Religion is special enough', *Virginia Law Review*, 103, p. 481; Gedicks, Frederick Mark (2017), '"Substantial" burdens: how courts may (and why they must) judge burdens on religion under RFRA', *George Washington Law Review*, 85, p. 94.
32   Elias-Zacarias, *supra* note 29, at p. 482.
33   *Id.* (emphasis in original).
34   Musalo, Karen (1994), 'Irreconcilable differences? Divorcing refugee protections from human rights norms', *Michigan Journal of International Law*, 15, 1179, p. 1191-1192.

persecutor persecuting on account of the applicant's political opinion; rather: "It is enough that the persecution is a consequence of political opinion. Proof of the persecutor's motive is not required to establish this link".[35] Consequently, IRFA's invocation of international religious freedom law sought to correct the failure of the immigration courts and asylum officers to properly adjudicate religious asylum cases. Through IRFA, Congress reinstated the "effects" test as part of the nexus calculation.

In *Elias-Zacarias*, an indigenous young man from Guatemala feared recruitment from guerrillas fighting against the government. He claimed that his refusal to accept their demands to join their forces constituted a political opinion that they would punish him or kill him for rejecting their struggle. He argued that they knew his political opinion by his actions to flee.[36] The Court held that the Refugee Act required adjudicators to examine Mr. Elias-Zacarias' political opinion, not that of the persecutor.[37] Based on a very sparse record, the Court could not determine whether the applicant informed the guerrillas of his specific reason for refusing to join them, leading the Court to conclude that the applicant failed to show that he resisted recruitment due to his political opposition to the guerrillas. The Court, therefore, found that "[e]ven a person who supports a guerrilla movement might resist recruitment for a variety of reasons—fear of combat, a desire to remain with one's family and friends, a desire to earn a better living in civilian life, to mention only a few".[38] In this key ruling, the Court held that Mr. Elias-Zacarias had the burden of proving the persecutor "will persecute him because of that political opinion, rather than because of his refusal to fight with them".[39] Recognizing the high burden this placed on asylum applicants, the Court concluded that applicants did not have to show direct proof of a persecutor's motive, but nonetheless, the applicant needed to provide some evidence of motive, "direct or circumstantial".[40]

The new nexus test of *Elias-Zacarias* had an immediate negative impact on protecting religious liberty. In 1990, prior to *Elias-Zacarias*, two Jehovah's Witnesses from El Salvador claimed that their faith prevented them from participating in the military notwithstanding El Salvador's mandatory military service for all males between the ages of 18 and 30.[41] El Salvador permitted no exceptions to the conscription policy.[42] Moreover, young men who refused the conscription notice were either jailed, murdered or subjected to extrajudicial

---

35 Brief Amicus Curiae of the Office of the United Nations High Commissioner For Refugees in Support of Respondent, 1991 WL 11003984 (U.S.) (Appellate Brief).
36 502 U.S. at 478.
37 *Id.* at 481.
38 *Id.* at 482.
39 *Id* at 483.
40 *Id.*
41 Canas-Segovia v. I.N.S., 902 F.2d 717 (9th Cir. 1990) *vacated and remanded*, I.N.S. v. Canas-Segovia, 112 S. Ct. 1152 (1992), *on remand*, 970 F.2d 599 (9th Cir. 1992).
42 *Id.* at 720.

torture.[43] The brothers sought asylum based on their faith and on account of political opinion. The immigration judge denied their cases based upon their failure to show that the Salvadoran government had intentionally singled out Jehovah's Witnesses for persecution because of their religious beliefs.[44] After the BIA affirmed the denial,[45] the Ninth Circuit Court of Appeals reversed and remanded the case noting first that the Board erred by requiring proof of intent or motive to persecute: "Under the Salvadoran conscription policy, if the Canases refuse to do military service, they will go to prison. Any reasonable person in this position would conclude that the punishment would be on account of his religious beliefs".[46] In addition, their refusal quite possibly would subject them to torture and death on account of their religious beliefs.[47] Indeed, that conclusion revealed a clear probability of persecution, thus satisfying the non-refoulement standard permitting withholding of deportation as well as asylum.[48]

After granting review, the Supreme Court vacated the judgment and remanded the case for consideration after *Elias-Zacarias*.[49] Subsequently, the Ninth Circuit in concise language held, "In light of *Elias-Zacarias's* adoption of a motive requirement, Canas-Segovia can no longer prove religious persecution. In our decision, we took pains to explain that although evidence of a persecutor's intent was relevant, it was not required (…). Because the key 'on account of' language applies equally to religious and political persecution, *Elias-Zacarias* dictates that Canas-Segovia must show some evidence of his persecutor's intent, which he is unable to do".[50] *Elias-Zacarias* simply involved a political opinion case and did not explicitly address if the intent standard applied to all the enumerated grounds. The Ninth Circuit did not cite any authority for the conclusion that it applies equally to religious and political persecution. Instead, the court stated:

> *We reject the argument on rehearing that religion should be treated differently. Political opinion is admittedly a narrow term, encompassing beliefs but not activities. Religion, on the other hand, is much broader, describing both beliefs and practices. Canas-Segovia argues that (1) it is undisputed that his sincere religious conviction **require** him to refuse to serve in the military, (2) his refusal to serve is a religious practice, and (3) he is being persecuted because of his*

---

43 *Id.* at 720-21.
44 *Id.* at 721.
45 *Id.*
46 *Id.* at 727.
47 *Id.* at 729.
48 *Id.*
49 112 S.Ct. 1152.
50 970 F.2d 599, 601 (9th Cir. 1992). *Canas-Segovia II* addressed the asylum claim of only Mr. Jose Canas-Segovia. Prior to this second case, his brother, who was included in the first decision, had obtained lawful status through a different immigration procedure.

> religious practice, i.e. his refusal to serve. But this alone
> cannot satisfy the requirement of demonstrating his per-
> secutor's motive or intent.[51]

Noting that there might be many reasons for refusal to serve, for example, fear of combat or fear of reprisal from opposing forces, the court was not permitted to find that the motive was on account of religion unless the applicant tied "the persecution to a protected cause".[52] Fortunately for Mr. Canas-Segovia, the Court upheld its earlier finding that he was eligible for asylum and withholding based on an imputed political opinion.[53]

Critical for all applicants, but especially those fleeing religious persecution, as Professor Karen Musalo recognized, *Elias-Zacarias* eliminated an effects-based test which looked at the consequences of persecution and replaced it with an intent-based test where the applicant had to demonstrate that he or she possessed at least one of the enumerated grounds and the persecution intended or actually persecuted them on account of that ground.[54] Immediately, this changed the prospects for asylum applicants.

IRFA, enacted subsequent to *Elias-Zacarias*, provides new avenues of relief because international law protects religious freedom from violations of both a law's intent and its effects. IRFA names numerous international protections as critical to a new understanding of protection through international religious liberty. Article 18 of the UDHR protects the "freedom to change [one's] religion or belief, and freedom, either alone or in community with others and in public or private, to manifest [one's] religion or belief in teaching, practice, worship, and observance".[55] Practice can be harmed by a neutral law such as the Salvadoran conscription law. In addition, Article 2 of the Declaration on the Elimination of All Forms of Intolerance and of Discrimination Based on Religion or Belief acknowledges that neutral laws can improperly obstruct freedom of religion or belief, providing, in part, "the expression 'intolerance and discrimination based on religion and belief' means any distinction, exclusion, restriction or preference based on religion or belief and *having as its purpose or as its effect* nullification or impairment of the recognition, enjoyment or exercise of human rights and fundamental freedoms on an equal basis".[56] For Article 2 to fully protect religious liberty, the *Elias-Zacarias* nexus definition must be expanded to include a review of how any laws or actions by purported persecutors impacted the religious freedom of the applicant. Under the Refugee Act of 1980, at least since 1992, neutral laws of general applicability may harm

---

51   *Id.* (emphasis in original).
52   *Id.*
53   *Id.* at 602.
54   Musalo, Irreconcilable, *supra* note 34, at p. 1181.
55   *Universal Declaration of Human Rights*, G.A. Res. 217A (III), U.N. GAOR, 3d Sess., at 71, U.N. Doc. A/810 (1948); *see also* 22 U.S.C. § 6401(a)(3) (2000).
56   G.A. Res. 55, U.N. GAOR, 36th Sess., Supp. No. 51, U.N. Doc. A/36/684 (1981) (emphasis added).

religious liberty, but still preclude grants of asylum because of the failure to show intent to harm religion. Thus, IRFA's absence in published decisions is all the more surprising because the effect of a neutral law might, nonetheless, violate an applicant's religious liberty permitting a grant of asylum otherwise denied under the *Elias-Zacarias* nexus test.

In 2005, Congress further restricted the nexus test. It passed the REAL ID Act requiring that an enumerated ground must be at least "one central reason" for the persecution.[57] Subsequently, the Third Circuit held that

> *Section 208's use of the phrase "**one** central reason" rather than "**the** central reason", which (...) was a deliberate change in the drafting of this provision, demonstrates that the mixed-motives analysis should not depend on a hierarchy of motivations in which one is dominant and the rest are subordinate.*
> ***See** Amicus Br. 8–10; In re J—B—N— & S—M—, 24 I. & N. Dec. at 212–13. This plain language indicates that a persecutor may have more than one central motivation for his or her actions; whether one of those central reasons is more or less important than another is irrelevant.*[58]

As no cases have cited IRFA to date, courts have not yet addressed the REAL ID Act's intersection with IRFA. Congress did not explicitly repeal any aspect of IRFA in enacting the REAL ID Act. Moreover, in its first precedent decision on the REAL ID Act, the BIA stated in *In re J-B-N- & S-M-,*

> *Having considered the conference report and the language of the REAL ID Act, we find that our standard in mixed motive cases has not been radically altered by the REAL ID amendments. The prior case law requiring the applicant to present direct or circumstantial evidence of a motive that is protected under the Act still stands.*[59]

REAL ID made no radical changes to the burden test in mixed motive cases. Often proof of the effect of a law persecuting religious liberty might be shown through circumstantial evidence which retains its relevance after enactment of the REAL ID Act. Congress' great concern about the unfairness of asylum and refugee adjudications, moreover, provides strong support that IRFA still must be followed to protect this fundamental right, necessitating that adjudicators examine both the intent and effect of a persecutor's actions upon a belief or practices as a central reason for the persecution.

---

57   8 U.S.C. § 1158(b)(1)(B)(i) (2005).
58   Ndayshimiye v. Attorney General of the U.S., 557 F.3d 124, 129 (3rd Cir. 2009) (emphasis in the original).
59   24 I & N Dec. 208, 212-213 (2007), footnote omitted.

5.3 The Lost Opportunity: Mr. Li and the Neutral Law of General Applicability

One case suggested the power IRFA could have had in protecting religious asylum applicants, but IRFA's subsequent impact was doomed by its initial success. In *Li v. Gonzalez,*[60] a Chinese Christian who organized a Protestant home church in opposition to the government-approved and regulated Protestant Church was arrested, beaten, and interrogated with electric shocks until he signed a confession. After release, he fled to the United States and sought asylum and withholding of deportation. After the Immigration Judge granted withholding, the Immigration and Naturalization Service appealed his case. The Board sustained the appeal, holding that he was not "punished on account of his religion. Rather, he was arrested for a crime in China. We find that the Government of China has a legitimate right to enforce the laws which it creates".[61] The Fifth Circuit upheld the Board, concluding:

> *The BIA held that Li did not establish that he would be persecuted if he was returned to China because Li did not prove that his punishment was on account of his religion. The BIA held that Li was punished for violating the law regarding unregistered churches and not because of his religion. The BIA noted that "China does not prohibit registered religions and its law is a legitimate sovereign right 'not institutional persecution'".*[62]

The court did express concern for the difficulty of its holding:

> *The issue in this case is perplexing not only because it involves affairs of a foreign state that are contrary to our fundamental ideals but also because the line between religious belief and religious activity here is indeed a fine one and it is colored by sensitive political and religious concerns. However, while we may abhor China's practice of restricting its citizens from gathering in a private home to read the gospel and sing hymns, and abusing offenders, like*

---

60   420 F.3d 500 (5th Cir. 2005), (Dismissed, Opinion Vacated by Li v. Gonzalez 429 F.3d 1153 (5th Cir. 2005).

61   Matter of Li, unpublished decision at 2 (BIA July 17, 2003), quoted in Jonathan Robert Nelson (2006), 'Shaking the Pillars: An Asylum Applicant Shakes Lose Some Unusual Relief', *Interpreter Releases,* 83, 1, p. 1. Mr. Nelson's account provides a fuller description of the procedural steps and impact of IRFA leading to Mr. Li's receipt of withholding of deportation. *See also* Churgin, Michael J. (2016), 'Is religion different: is there a thumb on the scale in refugee convention appellate court adjudication in the United States? Some preliminary thoughts', *Texas International Law Journal,* 51, 213, p. 222-224.

62   Li at 509.

*Li, who commit such acts, that is a moral judgment not a
legal one.*[63]

Jonathan Nelson reports that although Mr. Li's lawyers filed for a rehearing *en banc*, public uproar against this decision changed the course of this case. Nelson noted: "the *coup de grace* in the campaign to overturn the decision (…) came in the form of an unprecedented letter to the Attorney General from the United States Commission on International Religious Freedom".[64] USCIRF's Chair, Michael Cromartie, expressed concern about the *Li* decision and its precedential impact that would "undermine the international leadership of the United States in protecting asylum seekers and advancing the right to freedom of religion or belief".[65] In addition to supplementing the record regarding China's human rights violations, Chair Cromartie emphasized the Commission's concern about "the increasing trend by China and other authoritarian governments to criminalize religious activity on the sole basis that the activity is not approved or the relevant religious organization registered by the government".[66] Chair Cromartie concluded, "as precedent, *Li v. Gonzales* will effectively provide a refuge from international law for those countries that criminalize 'unregistered' religious activity. It will refuse refuge, however, to those who flee persecution from such countries".[67]

Within weeks of the USCIRF letter, the Department of Justice moved to withdraw its appeal. Two days later, the BIA vacated its prior decision and granted Mr. Li withholding of deportation. Subsequently, the Fifth Circuit vacated its decision for mootness.[68] By vacating its decision, the Fifth Circuit contributed to the IRFA void once again – no published decision cites IRFA for its introduction of international law into asylum adjudications – further eviscerating international law from IRFA's asylum protections. The Department of Justice, by moving to vacate the decision cited the Cromartie letter,[69] implicitly acknowledged his argument that the effects of neutral laws should be considered as sufficient to show persecution on account of religion under IRFA. Although Chair Cromartie's letter specifically addressed China, he noted that other countries also persecute religion through criminalization of practice. In lauding the vacated *Li* decision, the USCIRF reported that it was clear that China's policies criminalizing unauthorized religious activity "are clearly in

---

63 *Id.* at 511.
64 Nelson, Relief, *supra* note 60, at 3.
65 *Id.;* Michael Cromartie, United States Commission on International Religious Freedom, *China/Asylum Issues: USCIRF Deeply Troubled by 5th Circuit Decision in Li v. Gonzales* (October 3, 2005), available at <www.uscirf.gov/news-room/press-releases/chinaasylum-issues-uscirf-deeply-troubled-5th-circuit-decision-in-li-v>.
66 *Id.*
67 *Id.*
68 Li v. Gonzales, 429 F.3d 1153 (5th Cir. 2005).
69 Nelson, Relief, *supra* note 60, at 3.

violation of international law with regard to freedom of religion or belief".[70] The effect of the law violated Mr. Li's liberty. The *Li* case underscores how Congress intended international religious liberty law to modify *Elias-Zacarias'* limited understanding of nexus.

The vacated *Li* case also reveals one other issue with the failure to recognize international protection for religion. The Fifth Circuit cited boilerplate language in affirming the Board regarding the definition of persecution: "The term 'persecution' is not defined in the immigration statute, *Chang v. INS,* 119 F.3d 1055, 1060 (3rd Cir.1997), therefore, the court must accept any interpretation by the BIA that is not arbitrary, capricious, or manifestly contrary to the statute".[71] Some courts have criticized the Board of Immigration Appeals for not adequately defining persecution. In *Sahi v. Gonzalez,* Judge Richard Posner complained that "We haven't a clue as to what it [BIA] thinks religious persecution is".[72] Jonathan Nelson observed that although IRFA does not specifically define persecution, it sets forth "[p]articularly severe violations of religious freedom"[73] and "[v]iolations of religious freedom".[74] As such, IRFA gives

---

70   China/Asylum Issues: Fifth Circuit vacates troubling asylum decision on religious freedom in China, November 4, 2005: <www.uscirf.gov/news-room/press-releases/ chinaasylum-issues-fifth-circuit-vacates-troubling-asylum-decision>.

71   Li at 508. Although many courts frequently cite similar boilerplate language that Congress did not define persecution in the Refugee Act, the boilerplate designation does not accurately reveal what Congress has done since its enactment in 1980. For example, Congress modified the definition of refugee when it added language to protect individuals and families fleeing coercive population controls: "For purposes of determinations under this chapter, a person who has been forced to abort a pregnancy or to undergo involuntary sterilization, or who has been persecuted for failure or refusal to undergo such a procedure or for other resistance to a coercive population control program, shall be deemed to have been persecuted on account of political opinion, and a person who has a well-founded fear that he or she will be forced to undergo such a procedure or subject to persecution for such failure, refusal, or resistance shall be deemed to have a well-founded fear of persecution on account of political opinion". 8 U.S.C. § 1101(a)(42). Although not a complete definition of persecution, the statutory language does describe specific conduct pursuant to population control that constitutes persecution providing a relevant example of Congress defining some actions that constitute persecution. Moreover, as discussed in footnotes at 73 and 74, *infra,* IRFA directed adjudicators to examine particularly severe violations and violations of religious freedom in analyzing persecution.

72   416 F.3d 587, 589 (7th Cir. 2005).

73   Nelson, Relief, *supra* note 60. *See also* Mousin, Standing, *supra,* note 18, at p. 573-581. 22 U.S.C. § 6402(11) provides: 'The term "particularly severe violations of religious freedom" means systematic, ongoing, egregious violations of religious freedom, including violations such as:
(A) torture or cruel, inhuman, or degrading treatment or punishment;
(B) prolonged detention without charges;
(C) causing the disappearance of persons by the abduction or clandestine detention of those persons; or
(D) other flagrant denial of the right to life, liberty, or the security of persons'.

74   22 U.S.C. § 6402(13) provides: 'The term "violations of religious freedom" means violations of the internationally recognized right to freedom of religion and religious belief and practice,

guidance to the courts of the wide variety of activities that governments engage in or tolerate to violate religious liberty. By simply adopting boilerplate language and not following IRFA, the courts continue to minimize protection of persecution of persons of faith from the multiple ways religion can be restricted through persecution. The combination of ignoring the effect of a law or practice without understanding the full manifestation of ways religious liberty can be constrained, limits asylum protection. Not only does IRFA provide more than a clue, many of the international covenants and declarations cited by Congress delineate the types of activities that constitute severe violations of religious liberty – the type of violations previously ignored by the courts that inspired Congress to enact IRFA's asylum reforms. International protection would guide courts who otherwise defer to an agency that is overworked and has been criticized by Congress for not comprehending the full scope of religious persecution, and therefore, not protecting religious freedom. Mr. Li's eventual receipt of withholding of deportation and the *Li* case's unique procedural result as a vacated appellate court case, however, contributed to the failure of IRFA to protect persons of faith.

5.4 A Thought Experiment of Re-litigating the *Canas-Segovia* Cases Under IRFA

The *Canas-Segovia* cases provide an excellent example of how IRFA should be applied to religious asylum cases. Consider the thought experiment of asking what would have happened if the Canas-Segovia brothers' cases came before the Ninth Circuit after IRFA. It was the first case to address religious persecution after *Elias-Zacarias*. The Ninth Circuit concluded that *Elias-Zacarias* required it to find that the persecutor intended to persecute the brothers because of their religious beliefs. Because the Salvadoran conscription laws were found to be neutral laws of general applicability, the Court determined that it could not grant relief based on religious persecution. With the passage of IRFA, persecution can now be found based on the effects of a law, not just the intent. IRFA protects religious practice as well as belief while simultaneously critiquing governments that not only engage in persecution, but also tolerate it.

---

as set forth in the international instruments referred to in section 6401(a)(2) of this title and as described in section 6401(a)(3) of this title, including violations such as:

(A) arbitrary prohibitions on, restrictions of, or punishment for: (i) assembling for peaceful religious activities such as worship, preaching, and prayer, including arbitrary registration requirements; (ii) speaking freely about one's religious beliefs; (iii) changing one's religious beliefs and affiliation; (iv) possession and distribution of religious literature, including Bibles; or (v) raising one's children in the religious teachings and practices of one's choice; (B) any of the following acts if committed on account of an individual's religious belief or practice: detention, interrogation, imposition of an onerous financial penalty, forced labor, forced mass resettlement, imprisonment, forced religious conversion, beating, torture, mutilation, rape, enslavement, murder, and execution'.

The record contained no dispute that both brothers, who were practicing Jehovah's Witnesses since their early childhood, possessed a genuine faith. *Canas-Segovia I* had found that "the tenets of their faith prohibit them from participating in military service of any kind".[75] The Salvadoran government recognized no exemptions for young males to avoid military service. If they refused to serve, they faced imprisonment from six months to 15 years.[76] More important, at the time, the record was undisputed that many Salvadorans who avoided conscription were not sent to jail, but faced extrajudicial torture and murder by the authorities.[77] The effect of the law and the government's extrajudicial punishments meant the brothers faced either lengthy imprisonment, torture, or death as soon as they informed the authorities that their faith prevented them from serving in the military. The Ninth Circuit acknowledged that United States constitutional law might be relevant to the analysis, and cited *Wisconsin v. Yoder*[78] for the proposition that a religious exemption could be granted under a neutral law of general applicability.[79] According to the Court, "the mere facial neutrality of the Salvadoran conscription policy does not preclude it from amounting to persecution".[80]

Given those facts, although the conscription law was neutral on its face, the effects of the law to bona fide believers such as the Canas-Segovia brothers led to either imprisonment, torture or death. *Canas-Segovia II* dismissed the religious persecution claim for failure to show a nexus to religion. IRFA provided a new test for nexus permitting the effect of a law to be considered as well as the intent and expanded how manifestations of belief or practice could be protected. First, Article 2 of the Declaration on the Elimination of All Forms of Intolerance and of Discrimination Based on Religion or Belief protects persons suffering from the effect of a law, stating, in part, "the expression 'intolerance and discrimination based on religion and belief' means any distinction, exclusion, restriction or preference based on religion or belief and *having as its purpose or as its effect* nullification or impairment of the recognition, enjoyment or exercise of human rights and fundamental freedoms on an equal basis".[81]

The effect of El Salvador's conscription law left the Canas-Segovia brothers with no choice but to abdicate their beliefs, leave their nation, or serve up to 15 years in prison, face torture or death. El Salvador offered them no options—

---

75 Canas-Segovia, *supra* note 41.
76 *Id.* at 721.
77 *Id.* at 720-21.
78 406 U.S. 205, 220 (1972). The Court also cited Thomas v. Review Bd., 450 U.S. 707 (1981) and Sherbert v. Verner, 374 U.S. 398 (1963) for granting exemptions from neutral laws. Canas-Segovia I was decided on April 24, 1990. Employment, 494 U.S., was decided on April 17, 1990.
79 Canas-Segovia I at 723.
80 *Id.* at 724.
81 G.A. Res. 55, U.N. GAOR, 36th Sess., Supp. No. 51, U.N. Doc. A/36/684 (1981) (emphasis added).

either practice their faith and die or abdicate their faith through conscription. Compare the choice the Canas-Segovia brothers had to Mr. Li's choice—practice and go to prison or abdicate his practice. To paraphrase Chair Cromartie's letter, El Salvador left no "refuge" but only persecution for the brothers.[82] The brothers could not simultaneously practice their pacifist faith and serve in El Salvador's military. Mr. Li could not practice his faith within a registered house church. In both cases, practicing their faith put them in line for at a minimum, criminal violations, and at most beatings, torture or death. Chair Cromartie's letter noting that "criminalizing religious activity on the sole basis of that activity" underscores that international protections protect the effects of a law as well as its intent.[83]

Second, by linking asylum claims to international religious freedom, IRFA points to additional international resources for understanding the many manifestations of religious persecution such as the 2004 UNHCR Guidelines which state: "religious belief, identity, or way of life can be seen as so fundamental to human identity that one should not be compelled to hide, change or renounce this in order to avoid persecution".[84] For the Canas-Segovia brothers to thrive and survive in El Salvador they would have had to deny their belief, identity, and way of life. Paragraph 25 states "in conscientious objector cases, a law purporting to be of general application may, depending on the circumstances, nonetheless be persecutory where, for instance, it impacts differently on particular groups…where the punishment itself is excessive or disproportionately severe, or where the military service cannot reasonably be expected to be performed by the individual because of his or her genuine beliefs or religious convictions".[85] All of these factors address the nexus issue. Other religious youth in El Salvador faced extrajudicial torture or murder for refusing to serve. Paragraph 14 of the Guidelines adds:

> In this context, the well-founded fear "need not necessarily be based on the applicant's own personal experience". What, for example, happened to the claimant's friends and relatives, other members of the same religious group, that is to say to other similarly situated individuals, "may well show that his [or her] fear that sooner or later he [or she] also will become a victim of persecution is well-founded".[86]

---

82   See Cromartie, supra note 64.
83   Id.
84   UNHCR, Guidelines on International Protection: Religion-Based Refugee Claims under Article 1A(2) of the 1951 Convention and the 1967 Protocol relating to the Status of Refugees: <www.refworld.org/cgi-bin/texis/vtx/rwmain?docid=4090f9794> [28 April 2004].
85   Id.
86   Id.

El Salvador provided a significant example in the life and death of the Salvadoran Archbishop. In 1980, Archbishop Oscar Romero preached a sermon urging the young men of El Salvador to refuse to serve in the military, to put their guns down and not kill. One day later, Archbishop Romero was assassinated while presiding over a Catholic Mass.[87] The Canas-Segovia brothers were neither clergy nor leadership, but the public interpreted Archbishop Romero's assassination as a message to those who might refuse to serve such as the Canas-Segovia brothers. IRFA would have enabled the brothers' advocates to present Romero's assassination as evidence of the effect of El Salvador's murderous treatment of conscientious objectors.

Moreover, IRFA's international protections place an affirmative duty on the state to protect religious minorities.[88] In the case of the Canas-Segovia brothers, the government of El Salvador failed that duty in a number of ways. First, it enacted a law that provided no exemption for persons whose very religious identity was tied to not participating in military service. It offered no protection for them despite this duty. Moreover, in light of the extrajudicial torture and murder, El Salvador failed its affirmative duty to protect the brothers even if they were willing to face the consequences of legal penalties, thus leaving them no option but to seek asylum. By pointing to international protection against the effects of a law, Congress, through IRFA, sought to remedy the unfair treatment previously experienced by persons of faith claiming asylum on account of religion.

The *Canas-Segovia II* precedent further limits religious liberty. Because of the narrow nexus limitations, many bona fide persons of faith seek to fit their cases within social group or imputed political opinion categories, further marginalizing religion in asylum adjudication. Often parties use political opinion or particular social group in what appears to be obvious situations where a full-blown religion argument would be more effective. For example, the meaning of particular social group has been intensely litigated over the last fifteen years, with different courts of appeals establishing distinctive tests and the BIA regularly modifying its tests as cases are remanded, leading to "jurisprudential confusion".[89] Thus, attorneys ignore a faith-ful life or membership in a recognized church or denomination as a primary enumerated ground of protection, and instead, base their argument on a purported social group that requires additional complex tests to meet one's burden.[90]

87 *See, e.g.*, Ana Carrigan (1984), *Salvador witness: the life and calling of Jean Donovan*, NY: Orbis Books, p. 157–158. On 23 March 1980, Archbishop Romero urged all members of the military to lay down their arms and "remember instead the voice of God: 'Thou Shalt Not Kill!' God's law must prevail".

88 *See* Mousin, Standing, *supra* note 18, at p. 589–590.

89 Ardala, Sabrineh & Thomas Boermann (2016), 'Dynamics between gangs and the church: An overlooked dimension of Central American asylum claims', *Immigr. Briefings*, 16-07, 1, p. 2.

90 *Id.* at 2 ("Yet, within the larger story of gang warfare in Central America, one aspect is too often overlooked: the targeting of individuals on the basis of religion". Note omitted).

International law has developed a broader conception of what religion is and demands careful inquiry into how a law or persecutory acts interfere with a belief or practice.

Similarly, given the narrow scope of the nexus standard, courts have denied asylum to persons of faith who have refused to join criminal or guerilla gangs in Central America by holding the guerillas would harm them due to their refusal to join rather than based on their religious beliefs to avoid murder, rape, or assault of other persons. In *Tecun-Florian,* a young Guatemalan who held sincere religious beliefs preventing him from killing anyone refused to join a criminal gang.[91] The gang watched him go to church and then kidnapped and tortured him for ten days until he was freed through the efforts of a human rights group. He fled to the United States and sought asylum. The court acknowledged that Mr. Tecun-Florian refused to join the guerrillas because they violated his religious beliefs, but under the *Elias-Zacarias* nexus test, "the BIA could reasonably determine that the guerillas tortured Mr. Tecun-Florian solely in retribution for refusing to join their group—and not because of his religious or political beliefs".[92] In dissent, Judge Ferguson wrote, "he was deeply devoted to the Catholic faith, attending its services twice a week, and actively partici-pating in other activities. His faith taught him that killing for any purpose is wrong. It was for this reason that he resisted joining the guerrilla's cause despite their many efforts to conscript him".[93] His belief taught him to resist which led to torture and detention — it was part of his identity. The effect of his belief led to the retribution.

Similarly, in *Bueso-Avila v. Holder*, a young Honduran Christian actively proselytized other youth to join his church, the largest evangelical church in Honduras.[94] A criminal gang tried to recruit him, including at least once when he was leaving the church. He frequently carried his Bible with him. His faith defined his identity, yet the court rejected his claim on nexus. International law recognizes that belief and practice have consequences, sometimes fatal consequences that Congress intended to be mitigated through the remedy of asylum. The failure to follow IRFA has forced persons of faith to seek relief under the confused jurisprudence of social group, at a time when Congress sought to provide more protection for religious liberty.

5.5 Romeike Family and Home Schooling

Another case of interest that reflects the failure of the litigants and the courts to follow Congress' direction to look at international protections involved German natives who sought asylum in the United States because they faced financial

---

91   207 F.3d 1107 (9th Cir. 2000).
92   *Id.* at 1109.
93   *Id.* at 1114, (Ferguson, J., dissenting).
94   663 F.3d 934 (7th Cir. 2011).

penalties and potential loss of custody of their children when they chose to home school their children in violation of German law requiring attendance at public school.[95] As with *Canas-Segovia II*, the court may have had a fuller discussion of the impact of international law on religious liberty if it followed IRFA's direction to include analysis of the effect of a law or practice.

In *Romeike,* the immigration judge granted asylum on account a particular social group of homeschooling families. The BIA reversed. The Romeikes appealed the denial to the Sixth Circuit Court of Appeals which upheld the Board and denied their request for asylum.[96]

In a strange twist on the issue I have raised about expanded protection for religion under IRFA, the court opened its opinion by stating, "[h]ad the Romeikes lived in America at the time, they would have had a lot of legal authority to work with in countering the prosecution", citing three United States Supreme Court cases including *Wisconsin v. Yoder*, the same case that *Canas-Segovia I* had applied to find protection for the applicants.[97] *Yoder* provides strong constitutional protection for parents' faith in determining the appropriate education for their children when they decide not to send their children to public schools. Apparently, both the litigants and the court ignored the Convention's Travaux Préparatoires which note that although one of the five enumerated grounds of protection, religion "is the only article in the convention where treatment is 'at least as favorable' as that accorded to nationals of the contracting states".[98] Instead, the court stated, "Congress might have written the immigration laws to grant a safe haven to people living elsewhere in the world who face government strictures that the United States Constitution prohibits. But it did not".[99] Even without IRFA, the Travaux Préparatoires suggest that the court should have looked at the parental rights protections under the Constitution as the minimum standard for asylum applicants. Although protections of the Convention and the Protocol were fully integrated into the Refugee Act of 1980, IRFA and its inclusion of international law further strengthens the Travaux Preparatoires' relevancy. The court's discussion of the First Amendment protections under *Yoder* becomes relevant and not simply discarded as dicta.

Here, too, the court's failure to rely on IRFA doomed the Romeike's chances for asylum. First, although mentioning that the Romeikes sought to home school based on their faith, the court primarily examined the Board's decision that the Romeikes failed to establish themselves as homeschoolers who were within a particular social group in Germany. The court noted, "there is a difference between the persecution of a discrete group and the prosecution of those who violate a generally applicable law".[100] The court found that Germany neither

---

95   Romeike, *supra* note 16, at 528.
96   *Id.*
97   *Id.* at 530.
98   The Refugee Convention (1951), Travaux Préparatoires analysed 42–43 (Paul Weis ed., 1995).
99   Romeike, *supra* note 16, at 530.
100 *Id.*

selectively applied the compulsory school attendance law to the Romeikes or that they were more severely punished than other parents who broke the law.[101] But IRFA demands more, requiring the court to determine if religious persecution could be found under violations of international religious freedom which includes, "arbitrary prohibitions, restriction of, or punishment for (...) raising one's children in the religious teachings and practices of one's choice".[102] At the very least the international treaties require a more sensitive analysis of how a law impacts a person of faith. The UNHCR Guidelines, for example, state:

> *Each claim requires examination on its merits on the basis of the individual's situation. Relevant areas of inquiry include the individual profile and personal experiences of the claimant, his or her religious belief, identity and/or way of life, how important this is for the claimant, what effect the restrictions have on the individual, the nature of his or her role and activities within the religion, whether these activities have been or could be brought to the attention of the persecutor and whether they could result in treatment rising to the level of persecution.[103]*

Although the Romeikes raised international protections, the court failed to cite IRFA in dismissing those claims.

Instead the court acknowledged that although international treaties signed by Germany might give the Romeikes the right to decide the education of their children, "that by itself does not require the granting of an American asylum application".[104] IRFA does not require the granting of asylum, but as the USCIRF letter in the *Li* cases stated, it would have provided a more expansive analysis of a violation of a generally applicable law.[105]

The court, apparently unaware of the reasons Congress reacted so strongly to the improper adjudications of religious claimants was because over half the world's population lives under regimes that persecute on account of religion,[106] quoted then-Judge Alito from a pre-IRFA case: "If persecution were defined that expansively, a significant percentage of the world's population would

---

101 *Id.*

102 See supra note 24.

103 UN High Commissioner for Refugees (UNHCR), *Guidelines on International Protection No. 6: Religion-Based Refugee Claims under Article 1A(2) of the 1951 Convention and/or the 1967 Protocol relating to the Status of Refugees*, 28 April 2004, HCR/GIP/04/06: <www.refworld.org/docid/4090f9794.html> [8 September 2017]

104 *Id.* at 534.

105 Erin Welch writes in a student note that the court ignored significant evidence of selective punishment against religious homeschoolers in Germany. Welch, Erin (2015), 'Disguised persecution in Germany: the Romeike asylum case', *University of Cincinnati Law Review*, 83, 1029, p. 1043-1051.

106 22 U.S.C. §§ 6401–6481 (2000) (enacted 27 October 1998).

qualify for asylum in this country – and it seems most unlikely that Congress intended such result".[107]

Contrary to the Romeikes' court's reliance on Judge Alito's assumption, Congress specially cited the great numbers, especially in terms of religious persecution, as cause for chastising the government adjudication of religious claims and seeking expansive protection.[108] The concern of courts that great numbers of asylum applicants would flood the system ignores the particular requirement for asylum that in addition to examining whether the intent or effect of a law was directed at an applicant, the applicant must still prove harm or fear of harm that meets the definition of persecution. That is, the Romeikes would still have had to show that their fears of a government school violated their religious freedom to the extent, for example, that Mr. Yoder experienced in seeking to exercise his religious freedom to raise children within his faith. A speculative fear about too many applicants should not override congressional findings of improper bias or unfairness against bona fide applicants. Seemingly oblivious of IRFA, however, the court citing *Elias-Zacarias,* concluded,

> *The question is not whether Germany's policy violates the American Constitution, whether it violates the parameters of an international treaty or whether Germany's law is a good idea. It is whether the Romeikes have established the prerequisites of an asylum claim – a well-founded fear of persecution on account of a protected ground.*[109]

If the court does not provide the opportunity to explore homeschooling as a religious liberty issue, it ignores the many manifestations of religious persecution. Congress intended through IRFA to expand the protection beyond the bare minimum set by *Elias-Zacarias.* The USCIRF letter in the *Li* case pointed to the parameters of international law on religious liberty to question the effect of a nation's law when it criminalizes religious conduct. It further called for those individuals adjudicating cases to show more sensitivity to the individual's faith and impact of such laws on faith. Through IRFA, courts must fully plumb all the manifestations of religious liberty rather than dismissing claims for failure to meet the *Elias-Zacarias* nexus test — something clearly not accomplished in the *Romeike* case.[110]

---

107 *Id.* at 535, citing Fatin v. INS, 12 F.3d 1233, 1240 (3rd Cir. 1993).

108 *Id.*

109 Romeike, *supra* note 16, at 535.

110 Fred Gedicks describes an issue in United States First Amendment jurisprudence. He argues that courts have not fulfilled their obligation to address the severity of the burden when persons of faith seek accommodations under the First Amendment. *See generally* Gedicks, Substantial, *supra* note 31. In asylum cases, adjudicators must decide when the intent or effect of the purported persecutor's actions constitute persecution and not a necessary inconvenience of living in a pluralist nation. Mr. Yoder and his community feared their faith community would not survive if children were not raised in its faith without the competing demands of a public-school education. IRFA's requirement that adjudicators understand the

5.6 Even if the courts refuse to modify the Nexus Test for religious asylum claims, IRFA still calls for greater sensitivity to religious claims of persecution.

Even if the courts decide that IRFA did not change the nexus requirement for religious asylum claims, the bias or ignorance that Congress chastised adjudicators for still appears in court cases to the detriment of religious liberty. Congress demanded additional training on international religious liberty law for adjudicators precisely because either improper bias or lack of training led to federal unfairness. Indeed, eight years after its enactment, USCIRF Chair Michael Cromartie testified before Congress that the training had mixed results.[111] He expressed concern that DOJ and DHS attorneys had taken positions contrary to IRFA's intent, stating: "the Commission has recommended that both the Board and the Office of Immigration Litigation should be subject to mandatory training under IRFA".[112] Now, ten years since that testimony, the BIA and the Office of Immigration Litigation continue to reveal that government officials still do not understand that the extensive manifestations of religious persecution, including when laws tolerate religious persecution or forced conversions, constitute serious violations of religious liberty. Similarly, living in secret to avoid persecution should not eviscerate a legitimate claim. International religious liberty cannot coincide with governments that tolerate persecution, but courts continue to misconstrue all of these issues absent more effective training.[113]

5.6.1 Failure to Understand the Context of a Nation's Law and Culture

By not understanding the many manifestations of faith, courts fall prey to IRFA's conclusions about unfair treatment of religious asylum claimants. In

full range of potential violations of religious freedom necessitates a broader understanding of religious persecution.

111 Testimony by United States Commission on International Religious Freedom (USCIRF Chair Michael Cromartie, Hearing on the U.S. Refugee and Asylum Programs, May 10, 2006, <www.uscirf.gov/advising-government/congressional-testimony/testimony-united-states-commission-international>.

112 *Id.*

113 It appears that even the limited training that occurs will soon be reduced or eliminated. *See* Sherman-Stokes, Sarah (2017), 'Immigration Judges Were Always Overworked. Now they'll be untrained, too', *The Washington Post*, July 11: <www.washingtonpost.com/opinions/immigration-judges-were-always-overworked-now-theyll-be-untrained-too/2017/07/11/e71bb1fa-4c93-11e7-a186-60c031eab644_story.html ?tid=sm_tw&utm_term=.cb49e698dba7>. "Justice Department confirmed that it has eliminated what little continuing judicial education and professional development once existed for immigration judges".

Faour v. Gonzalez,[114] Faour, a Christian shopkeeper in Syria, was accosted by a female customer. When he resisted her advances, she left the store. Shortly thereafter, her brothers returned and demanded that he marry their sister or they would kill him. Mr. Faour refused. He claimed that he refused to convert to Islam which was required if he were to marry their sister. He then left his home and moved around the country, hiding from his tormentors before he was able to travel outside of Syria. He sought asylum based on persecution on account of religion. After explaining that her brothers demanded that he marry their sister, the immigration judge asked: "What does the religion have to do with anything?".[115] Mr. Faour replied: "Because if I ever wanted to marry the woman, I would have been a Muslim, I would have converted to Islam, and I don't want to convert to Islam". The immigration judge responded: "Okay. That's all right, you don't have to convert".[116] Mr. Faour later testified that if returned to Syria, the brothers would kill him because he did not marry their sister. In her opinion denying asylum, the immigration judge held: "Although a feeble attempt has been made to allege religion as the statutory ground, the evidence is devoid or the record is devoid of any evidence".[117] She also found: "the respondent has not carried his burden and the testimony is not credible".[118]

The Board, in affirming the decision, noted that even if "respondent's testimony were found to be true (...) the respondent has not met his burden of establishing that he was a victim of past persecution".[119] Mr. Faour testified that he faced the tragic choice of a forced conversion or death. IRFA mandated immigration judges to attend training to understand the complexity of religious liberty issues in different nations. Syrian law offers the possibility of exemption from criminal penalties for honor killings.[120] At the time of the brothers' threat, Syrian law exempted murderers of either the woman or the man involved in the conduct that led the brothers to threaten Mr. Faour.[121] Mr. Faour would have had reasonable grounds to believe the brothers could act with impunity if they murdered him, or at least face a very limited incarceration. The Syrian government not only tolerated religious persecution, its laws enabled it.

---

114 125 Fed. Appx. 863 (9th Cir. 2005). The Ninth Circuit opinion had a limited review of the record. These facts were taken from the government's brief to the Ninth Circuit unless otherwise noted.

115 2004 WL 3155108 (C.A.9) (Brief for Respondent), 6.

116 *Id* at 7.

117 *Id* at 9.

118 *Id.*at 8.

119 *Id* at 10.

120 Syrian Penal Code, art. 548. *See also* Abu Odeh, Lam (2010), 'Honor killings and the construction of gender in Arab societies', *American Journal of Comparative Law*, 58, 911, p. 929-930.

121 On July 1, 2009, Syria amended Article 548 which waived punishment for honor killings, but caps the punishment at a sentence of two years. *See* Syria: No Exceptions for 'Honor Killings', (2009, July 28), *Human Rights Watch*. Retrieved from <www.hrw.org/news /2009/07/28/syria-no-exceptions-honor-killings>.

Despite the immigration judge's retort that Mr. Faour did not have to convert, his fear of a forced conversion also was reasonable within the Syrian legal system. Article 3 of the Syrian Constitution states that "Islamic jurisprudence is a main source of legislation".[122] Muslim women cannot marry Christian men. If Mr. Faour was to remain in Syria and escape death, he had no choice but to convert. Notably, IRFA lists forced conversions as violations of religious liberty.[123] If the training that IRFA mandated was effective, it would be almost impossible for the IJ to hold the record was devoid of evidence of religious persecution of Mr. Faour given the laws and culture of Syria. At the very least the IJ should not have terminated testimony about the forced conversion simply by concluding that Mr. Faour did not have to convert – perhaps a right held within the United States, but not within Syria.

5.6.2   Worship in Secrecy

Mr. Faour's case also highlights another element that IRFA's enactment should have at least shed some light in understanding the religious liberty implications of his case. One difficulty some religious claimants face in proving their cases involves the impossible choice of worshipping in the open and facing persecution or worshipping in secret, but then facing the possibility that their case would be denied because the persecutor did not know they possessed this enumerated ground. Be public and be persecuted or be private, survive, but perhaps lose their asylum case. Unlike political opinion which can sometimes be expressed in private through anonymous social media sources or distribution of unsigned publications, religion often requires community worship or worship at sacred spaces that may be public, but limited to a specific location. In Mr. Faour's case, he fled his home and lived in Syria for three years, hiding and moving about to keep from discovery.[124] In the meantime, his parents continued to worship in their hometown. The IJ and the BIA interpreted his three years in Syria as proof of his safety, totally disregarding that he could not worship publicly, nor remain at home and worship with his family. The Ninth Circuit found no reason to disagree with the BIA. In contrast, Judge Posner in a Seventh Circuit case rebuked an immigration judge's decision denying a Jehovah's Witness religious persecution claim:

> *But the fatal flaw in the immigration judge's opinion lies (...) in the assumption – a clear error of law – that one is not entitled to claim asylum on the basis of religious persecution if (...) one can escape the notice of the persecutors by concealing one's religion. Christians living in the Roman Empire before Constantine made Christianity*

---

122 Constitution of the Syrian Arab Republic Feb.26, 2012, art. 3.
123 *See supra* note 74.
124 2004 WL 3493875 (C.A.9) (Petitioner's Opening Brief), 6.

> *the empire's official religion faced little risk of being thrown
> to the lions if they practiced their religion in secret; it
> doesn't follow that Rome did not persecute Christians, or
> that a Christian who failed to conceal his faith would be
> acting "unreasonably". (...) One aim of persecuting a
> religion is to drive its adherents underground in the hope
> that their beliefs will not infect the remaining population.[125]*

IRFA defines forcing persons of faith from publicly expressing their faith as a violation of religious liberty. In *Faour*, the Board found, however, that his three years living in Syria without harm undermined his case.[126] The Board committed the same fatal flaw found by Judge Posner in *Muhur*. Given that the Board examined the record as if Mr. Faour's testimony was true which included his not returning home and hiding in several different locations during those three years, his safety amounted to emulating the pre-Constantine Christians, not the absence of objective evidence of his faith.

The government's argument demonstrates the specific problem that IRFA sought to alleviate and why Chair Cromartie called for more training for judges and attorneys with the Office of Immigration Litigation. The government brief stated:

> *Faour has clearly stated that his fears of persecution arise
> from his refusal to convert to Islam and to marry the woman,
> but not that he was sought out because of his religion. Thus,
> for the same reasons that were found to be inadequate in
> Elias-Zacarias (...), Faour has failed to present any
> evidence that the men's intent was to persecute him on
> account of his religion, that is, because he was Christian.[127]*

Examine that argument closely: Mr. Faour refused to convert from his faith to one demanded by his purported persecutors who could make such a demand with impunity from prosecution by Syria. Yet the government attorney claims such a conversion had nothing to do with Mr. Faour's religion. Mr. Faour's purported persecutors threatened to kill him if he did not marry, but if he married, he would have been required him to convert to Islam. Yet the government brief claims it had nothing to do with his religion. Ignoring IRFA's many manifestations of ways persecutors persecute on account of religion, the government brief argues that simply because the persecutors did not say they

---

125 Muhur v. Ashcroft, 355 F.3d 958, 960 (7th Cir. 2004). *See also* Kazemzadeh v. U.S. Attny. Gen., 577 F.3d 1341, 1358, (Marcus, Circuit Judge, specially concurring): the right to practice one's faith and to do so in public stands at the heart of free exercise. *See also* Mousin, Standing, *supra* note 18, 580: historical understanding of the early Christians hiding in the catacombs of Rome demonstrated that the fear of persecution was reasonable and subject to remedy.
126 2004 WL 3155108 (C.A.9) (Appellate Brief), 9.
127 *Id.* at 18.

wanted to harm him because he was a Christian, there was no nexus to a specific religion. The Ninth Circuit agreed, however, denying Mr. Faour's claim holding that

> *Substantial evidence supports the BIA's determination that Faour's alleged persecutors did not and would not, act on account of his Christian faith. Faour himself stated that "[the brother] will kill [him] (...) because [he] didn't marry their sister". As a result, the record does not compel the conclusion that Faour demonstrated a nexus between the claimed persecution and a protected ground.[128]*

Here again the limitations based on the nexus test of *Elias-Zacarias* combined with Congress' concern of either ignorance or bias against religious claims limits remedies of persons of faith who face either murder or forced conversion. IRFA holds murder as a serious violation of religious liberty and forced conversion as a serious violation of religious liberty. Both together constitute persecution on account of religion, hardly a record devoid of religion. The combination of impunity for murder, sanctioned by custom and Syrian law, with the cultural requirement of forced conversion provides a perfect example of the dismissive ways government officials have treated religious asylum claims that Congress tried to remedy through IRFA.

Admittedly, Mr. Faour's case contained a relatively meager record and credibility issues existed, but the government brief reveals the lack of sensitivity to national laws, cultures and practice that silence religious belief and practice. To ignore the full context of a person's faith at a time of forced global migration undermines all asylum cases. The lack of sensitivity to a nation's laws and customs denigrates the United States commitment to the fullness of this universal freedom.

5.7 Conclusion

Congress chastised the government for failing to live up to our national promises of religious freedom. Congress infrequently accuses federal adjudicators of bias or ignorance based on improper training. In 1998, however, Congress enacted IRFA to overcome the unfairness it found in the government determination of religious claims for asylum. Recognizing that such institutional unfairness undercut a universal right of religious liberty, it instructed that religious asylum claims should be analyzed under international religious liberty principles. Those principles were broader and more protective than domestic United States law had been interpreted previously. International religious liberty law examines both the intent and effect of a law. Moreover, Congress specifically listed

---

128 Faour, *supra* note 114, at 864.

particularly severe violations of religious liberty and violations of religious liberty underscoring the complex and diverse variety of ways governments and their agents persecute persons of faith. Despite this concern, no published cases cite IRFA for its international law principles. Despite this congressional intent, persons of faith, living lives endangered by their belief or practice, remain unprotected by United States asylum laws. Can one still call this refusal to follow IRFA simply bias or improper training? Greater protection on account of religion would occur, moreover, by the recognition that IRFA also modified the nexus test for religious claims by requiring courts and adjudicators to explore the persecutory effect of a law or practice on one's religion. IRFA remains the law. For the United States to truly stand with the persecuted and to recognize the fundamental universal right of religious liberty with the full protection of international law, advocates and adjudicators must bring IRFA into all asylum and refugee determinations.

References

Supreme Court (United States of America)
Church of the Lukumi Babalu Aye, Inc. v. Hialeah
                508 U.S. 520   1993
Employment Division, Dpt of Human Resources of Oregon v. Smith
                494 U.S. 872   1990
Gonzales v. O Centro Espirita Beneficente Uniao Do Vegetal
                546 U.S. 418   2006, (126 S.Ct. 1211)
I.N.S. v. Cardoza-Fonseca   480 U.S. 421, 436   1987
I.N.S. v. Elias-Zacarias   502 U.S. 478   1992
I.N.S. v. Stevic   467 U.S. 407   1984
Sherbert v. Verner   374 U.S. 398   1963
Thomas v. Review Bd.   450 U.S. 707   1981
Wisconsin v. Yoder   406 U.S. 205, 220 1972

Federal Court of Appeals (United States of America)
Bradvica v. I.N.S.   7th Cir. 1987   128 F.3d 1009
                citing *In Re Medina*, 19 I & N Dec. 734 (1988)
Canas-Segovia v. I.N.S.   9th Cir. 1990   902 F.2d 717
                vacated and remanded
Faour v. Gonzalez   9th Cir. 2005   125 Fed. Appx. 863
Fatin v. INS   3rd Cir. 1993   12 F.3d 1233, 1240
I.N.S. v. Canas-Segovia   9th Cir. 1992   970 F.2d 599
                on remand, 112 S. Ct. 1152 (1992)
Kazemzadeh v. U.S. Atty.G. 11th Cir. 2009   577 F.3d 1341, 1358,
                Marcus, Circuit Judge, *specially concurring*
Li v. Gonzales   5th Cir. 2005   429 F.3d 1153

Muhur v. Ashcroft	7th Cir. 2004	355 F.3d 958, 960
Ndayshimiye v. U.S. Atty.G.	3rd Cir. 2009	557 F.3d 124, 129
Romeike v. Holder	6th Cir. 2013	718 F.3d 528, 534
		Rehearing and Rehearing En Banc Den., July 12, 2014, cert. den. 134 S.Ct. 1491 (2014)
Sahi v. Gonzalez	7th Cir. 2005	416 F.3d 587, 589
Shi v. U.S. Attny. Gen.	11th Cir. 2013	707 F.3d 1231
Tecun-Florian v. I.N.S.	9th Cir. 2000	207 F.3d 1107

Board of Immigration Appeals (United States of America)
L.K.   23 I. & N. Dec.   677, 2004 WL 2211892 (B.I.A. 2004).

Statutes
Refugee Act of 1980, Pub. L. No. 96-212, 94 Stat. 102 (codified as amended in scattered sections of 8 U.S.C.)
8 U.S.C. § 1101(a)(42).
8 U.S.C. § 1158(b)(1)(B)(i) (2005)
22 U.S.C. § 4028(a)(1)
22 U.S.C. § 4028(a)(2)
22 U.S.C. § 6401(a)(2)–(3)
22 U.S.C. § 6401(a)(4)–(6)
22 U.S.C. § 6401(b)(2) (2002)
22 U.S.C. § 6401(b)(5)
22 U.S.C. §§ 6401–6481 (2000) (enacted 27 October 1998)
22 U.S.C. § 6402 (16)
22 U.S.C. § 6473 (2002)
22 U.S.C. § 6473(a)–(c)

Literature

Ardala, Sabrineh & Thomas Boermann (2016), 'Dynamics between gangs and the church: An overlooked dimension of Central American asylum claims', *Immigration Briefings* 16-07, p.1-2.

Carrigan, Ana (1984), *Salvador witness: the life and calling of Jean Donovan*, NY: Orbis Books, p. 157–158.

Churgin, Michael J. (2016), 'Is religion different: is there a thumb on the scale in refugee convention appellate court adjudication in the United States? Some preliminary thoughts', *Texas International Law Journal*, 51, 213, p. 222-224.

Gedicks, Frederick Mark (2017), '"Substantial" burdens: how courts may (and why they must) judge burdens on religion under RFRA', *George Washington Law Review*, 85, p. 94.

Laycock, Douglas (2009), 'The religious exemption debate', *Rutgers Journal of Law & Religion*. 11, p. 139.

Laycock, Douglas & Steven T. Collis (2016), 'Generally applicable law and the free exercise of religion', *Nebraska Law Review* 95, p. 1-36.

Lund, Christopher C. (2017), 'Religion is special enough', *Virginia Law Review*, 103, p. 481.

Lupu, Ira C. (2015), 'Hobby Lobby and the dubious enterprise of religious exemptions', *Harvard Journal of Law & Gender*, 38, p. 35.

Mousin, Craig B. (2004), 'Standing with the persecuted: adjudicating asylum applications account of religion after the enactment of the international religious freedom act of 1998', *Brigham Young University Law Review*, 541.

Musalo, Karen (1994), 'Irreconcilable differences? Divorcing refugee protections from human rights norms', *Michigan Journal of International Law*, 15, 1179, p. 1191-1192.

Nelson, Jonathan Robert (2006), 'Shaking the pillars: an asylum applicant shakes loose some unusual relief', *Interpreter Releases* 83, 1, p. 1.

Odeh, Lam Abu (2010), 'Honor killings and the construction of gender in Arab societies', *American Journal of Comparative Law*, 58, 911, p. 929-930.

Sherman-Stokes, Sarah (2017), 'Immigration Judges Were Always Over-worked. Now they'll be untrained, too', *The Washington Post,* 11 July: <www.washingtonpost.com/opinions/immigration-judges-were-always-overworked-now-theyll-be-untrained-too/2017/07/11/e71bb1fa-4c93-11e7-a186-60c031eab644_story.html?tid=sm_tw&utm_term=.cb49e698dba7.

HRW (2009), 'Syria: No Exceptions for 'Honor Killings'', *Human Rights Watch,* July 28, <www.hrw.org/news/2009/07/28/syria-no-exceptions-honor-killings>.

Welch, Erin (2015), 'Disguised persecution in Germany: the Romeike asylum case', *University of Cincinnati Law Review*, 83, 1029, p. 1043-1051.

Constitutions and foreign law
Constitution of the Syrian Arab Republic (26 February 2012), art. 3.

Syrian Penal Code, art. 548.

U.S. Congressional and Administrative Material
China/Asylum Issues: Fifth Circuit vacates troubling asylum decision on religious freedom in China, 4 November 2005: <www.uscirf.gov/news-room/press-releases/chinaasylum-issues-fifth-circuit-vacates-troubling-asylum-decision>.

H.R. REP. No. 105-480, pt. 3, at 16 (1998), reprinted in 1998 U.S.C.C.A.N. 602, 628.

Immigration & Naturalization Serv., I.N.S. Asylum Officer Basic Training Manual, Immigration Officer Academy (20 November 2001), 12.

Michael Cromartie, United States Commission on International Religious Freedom, *China/Asylum Issues: USCIRF Deeply Troubled by 5th Circuit Decision in Li v. Gonzales* (October 3, 2005): <www.uscirf.gov/news-

room/press-releases/chinaasylum-issues-uscirf-deeply-troubled-5th-circuit-decision-in-li-v>.

The Refugee Convention (1951): The Travaux Préparatoires analysed 42–43, Paul Weis ed.

Testimony by United States Commission on International Religious Freedom (USCIRF) Chair Michael Cromartie, Hearing on the U.S. Refugee and Asylum Programs, 10 May 2006: <www.uscirf.gov/advising-government/congressional-testimony/testimony-united-states-commission-international>.

United Nations Material

Brief Amicus Curiae of the Office of the United Nations High Commissioner For Refugees in Support of Respondent, 1991 WL 11003984 (U.S.) (Appellate Brief).

G.A. Res. 55, U.N. GAOR, 36th Sess., Supp. No. 51, U.N. Doc. A/36/684 (1981).

UNHCR, Guidelines on International Protection: Religion-Based Refugee Claims under Article 1A(2) of the 1951 Convention and/or the 1967 Protocol relating to the Status of Refugees 14 (Apr. 28, 2004): <www.refworld.org/cgi-bin/texis/vtx/rwmain?docid=4090f9794>.

Universal Declaration of Human Rights, G.A. Res. 217A (III), U.N. GAOR, 3d Sess., at 71, U.N. Doc. A/810 (1948); *see also* 22 U.S.C. § 6401(a)(3) (2000).

Chapter 6   A challenge for Muslim migrants

Entering the EU as well as into a sharī ͑ah-compliant relationship. The Italian case

Federica Sona

6.1   Introduction

Pious Muslims have a religious obligation to marry. When adopting the point of view of European Muslim communities, entering into a *sharī͑ah*-compliant[1] relationship is perceived as a pivotal part of the exercise of religious freedom as granted by domestic and international legal provisions on European soil.

This chapter focuses on the right to contract a valid marriage with civil (and religious) effects and, then, to claim related family reunification rights with respect to alien Muslims, in particular, Muslim migrant prospective spouses (ir)regularly settled in Italy. The foreign nationals' statutory right to individual religious freedom is therefore analysed, whilst investigating whether this is *de facto* affected by the actual or assumed religious belonging of the non-EEA partner, as well as by the fiancé(e)'s migrant status.

Examining the impact of state and Islamic laws on the agency of prospective migrant Muslim spouses-to-be, a dichotomy becomes increasingly evident. On the one hand, Muslim migrant partners may be (unintended) victims of discriminatory provisions based on the fiancé(e)'s religious affiliation, as enacted by the national legal systems of European and Muslim majority countries. On the other hand, Muslim purported spouses, as well as official bodies, may gradually learn to elaborate on antidotes to the discriminatory effects of some state provisions.

Building upon empirical data,[2] this chapter thus aims to discuss whether the Italian legal system can meet the needs of Muslim migrants, with regard to the

---

1   *Sharī͑ah* is the Arabic word indicating Islamic divine law, in: real terms, this word designates a path (to a watering place). From the wording of the *Qur'ān* (V: 48; XLII: 13 and 42; XLV:18) it can be inferred that the word *sharī͑ah* (as well as the terms and verbs which derive from the same root) identifies the way that shall be followed by Muslims, in this chapter, the expression *sharī͑ah*-compliant is used to indicate Islamic and/or Muslim nuptial unions. For a clarification of the meaning of the adjective Islamic and Muslims see *infra* section 3 and footnote No. 16.

2   The discussed empirical data was collected from 2004 to 2017. With respect to the employed research methodology, qualitative data were collected through a combination of oral (predominantly semi-structured research interviews and focus groups) and written

statutorily granted right to form a family. Analysing the nuptial prerequisites to be satisfied by prospective spouses (national and alien), the proposed analysis pinpoints the impairment of Muslim migrant fiancé(e)s' right to marry, including the (impelled) shadowy exercise of the Islamic right-&-duty to enter into a nuptial union.

In the attempt to consider to what extent the examined European Member State has withdrawn from religious provisions (with respect to nuptial requirements)[3] or, alternatively, Muslim partners have withdrawn from official state rules, strategically refined remedies - as elaborated either by Italian official bodies, or by Muslim parties (prospective spouses or Muslim majority countries) - are investigated. As a result, habitually unnoticed *sharīʿah*-compliant or civil nuptial patterns, as well as Muslim family reunification techniques, are brought to light in the next sections.

6.2   Freedom of religion and *Islām*

Freedom of religion is a key principle in the Italian legal system, a prerogative of every human being that is guaranteed under the 1947 Constitution of the Italian Republic.[4] As a matter of fact, article 19 proclaims that anyone is entitled

---

(predominantly document examination and self-designed questionnaires) surveys, and field observations. Socio-legal deductive-inductive methods were relied upon and methodological triangulation techniques were combined. The interviewees were selected combining area sampling, stratified random sampling, accidental sampling and snowball techniques. On social research methods, see *inter alia* Weber (1949), Denzin (1989), Gray and Guppy (1994); Ringer (1997), Bryman (2001), Weinberg (2002), Bulmer (2003), Huff (2003), Banakar and Travers (2005), Walliman (2006). With respect to qualitative research, including empirical investigations, interviews, narrative, and evaluation, see respectively Denzin and Lincoln (1994; 1998), Flick (1998). Hollway and Jefferson (2000), Yanow and Schwartz-Shea (2006), Patton (2002). As far as the more specific legal field and Muslim peculiarities are concerned, see McConville and Chui (2007), and Jeldtoft and Nielsen (2012). Details concerning the interviewed diplomatic personnel (foreign country and Italian cities) are not reported in order to protect the participants and this is due to the highly sensitive nature of the released information. With respect to the diplomatic premises, the embassies/consulates of the countries of origin of Muslims settled on Italian soil were contacted and invited to take part in my research project. The percentages of relevant countries varied over the years; they included Afghanistan, Albania, Algeria, Bangladesh, Bosnia-Herzegovina, Burkina Faso, Egypt, India, Iran, Iraq, Kosovo, Lebanon, Libya, Mali, Morocco, Nigeria, Pakistan, SA, Senegal, Somalia, Sri Lanka, Sudan, Syria, Tunisia, Turkey, UAE, and Yemen.

3   Although the Italian legal system has withdrawn from including religious requirements in the Civil Code, (unintended) religious-based discrimination might be enacted, as the discussion reveals. Additionally, part of the legal vocabulary used to describe civil nuptial requirements is borrowed from Canon law; see *infra* footnote No. 20.

4   Italian Constitution, 'Costituzione della Repubblica Italiana', 22.12.1947, in *Gazzetta Ufficiale* 27.12.1947 No. 298.

to freely profess his or her religious belief in any form, individually or with others.[5] Additionally, article 3, states:

> *All citizens have equal social dignity and are equal before the law, without distinction of sex, race, language, religion, political opinion, personal and social conditions. It is the duty of the Republic to remove those obstacles of an economic or social nature which constrain the freedom and equality of citizens, thereby impeding the full development of the human person and the effective participation of all workers in the political, economic and social organisation of the country.*

Accordingly, individual religious freedom cannot be constrained to the point where it impedes the full development of the human person.[6]

When adopting the Islamic point of view, an essential aspect for the full development of the human person is marriage. Indeed, according to *sharīʿah*, marriage is not simply an expression of individual agency, a manifestation of personal autonomy, but it is a 'right-&-duty' of the practising Muslim. The *Qurʾān* - chapter (*sūrah*) XXIV, verse (*āyah*) 32 - exhorts Muslims to marry:

> *And marry the unmarried among you and the righteous among your male slaves and female slaves. If they should be poor, Allāh will enrich them from His bounty, and Allāh is all-Encompassing and Knowing.*

The imperative form of the verb 'to marry' adopted in the verse reported above is further corroborated by the *sūrah* XXX, *āyah* 21, as it clarifies that

> *And of His signs is that He created for you from yourselves mates that you may find tranquillity in them; and He placed between you affection and mercy. Indeed in that are signs for a people who give thought.*[7]

The creation of mates - literally of spouses (*azwāǧan*) - is thus perceived as one of the signs of God. Also, the *Sunnah*[8] warmly recommends Muslim believers

---

5   The social dimension of freedom of religion is indeed explicitly recognised by the Italian Constitution, specifically by articles 8, 19, 20 117. For a study of the constitutional provisions granting religious freedom, see Barsotti *et al.* (2015: 114-122).

6   As stressed by the Italian judiciary, see *infra* section 7.

7   I am here reporting the English translation of the text as provided by *The Qurʾan: Saheeh International,* published respectively by Dar Qiraat (2010), Umm Muhammed Al-Muntada al-Islami (2004), and Abul Qasim Publishing House (1997), as this is widely available in worship prayer centres and therefore well-known by European Muslims. The same publication is relied upon for the *āyāt* reported below in section 5.

8   The Arabic word *sunnah* means 'practice'. The *Sunnah* is usually referred to the Prophet Muḥammad's living habits reported through *aḥādīth* (sing. *ḥadīth*), which give an account

to contract marriage: for instance, a *ḥadīth* recites: 'I fast, eat, pray and sleep and marry women, and who does not follow my *Sunnah* does not belong to me'.[9] A family based on a nuptial union is regarded as the basis of human society,[10] and Muslims commonly recite the saying that 'marriage is the half of the religion (*dīn*)'.[11]

Accordingly, when dealing with the religious freedom of (pious) Muslim partners, not only the 'right' to marry but also the 'duty' to marry is to be carefully taken into consideration. An Islamic or Muslim marriage is at the same time a religious, social and a civil duty when some requirements are satisfied: a Muslim man can afford to pay the dower (*mahr* or *ṣadāq*), he can support a family and he is afraid to commit sins as an unmarried person.[12]

Theoretically, this *sharī'ah*-compliant right-&-duty is not challenged on Italian soil. From a legal perspective, the right to marry and form a family is protected and granted by both Italian and European black letter laws. Article 29(1) of the Italian Constitution recognises the rights of the family as a natural society founded on marriage, indeed it states that

> *The Republic recognises the rights of the family as a natural society founded on marriage. Marriage is based on the moral and legal equality of the spouses within the limits laid down by law to guarantee the unity of the family.*

The same approach reverberates throughout the contemporaneous wording of the Convention for the Protection of Human Rights and Fundamental Freedoms and its Protocols.[13] Article 12 ECHR indeed stresses the right of men and women of marriageable age to marry and to found a family. Similarly, article 9

---

of the Prophet's life as a role model behaviour. The *Sunnah* represents the second Islamic source, following the *Qur'ān*.

9   As reported as *al-Saḥīḥ al-Bukhārī*, 7: 2 by Arabi (2001a: 150) and 67: 1 by 'Ali (1936: 602; 1944: 269).

10 See *inter alia* 'Ali (1936: 268); al-Faruqi (1982: 160).

11 This sentence is widely reported by scholars, but regrettably they tend to cite different sources for the same expression. For instance, Arabi (2001a: 150) regards it as a proverb. The very same expression is an *ḥadīth* reported in the *al-Mishkāt al-Masābīḥ* by 'Ali (1936: 603), and referred by al-Bayhaqī in the opinion of Maqsood (2003: 1). Some authors generally mention *al-Bukhārī* or *al-Ġazhālī* - see e.g. Wiktorowicz and Farouki (2000: 690), and Blank (2001: 332, note No. 35) respectively; or some scholars simply do not report the source of the *ḥadīth* - see e.g. Lapidus (1976: 95) and Hoodfar (1997: 52). Islamic scholars and fieldwork informants almost unanimously reported this expression to me. With respect to empirical evidence, see *infra* footnote No. 2.

12 See Santillana (1919: 157).

13 Convention for the Protection of Human Rights and Fundamental Freedoms and its Protocols (Rome, 04.11.1950), as amended by Protocols Nos. 11 and 14, in *Council of Europe Treaty Series*, No. 5, 01.06.2010. This is generally addressed as the European Convention on Human Rights (ECHR) and entered into force on 01.06.2010 in its last amended form.

of the Charter of Fundamental Rights of the European Union recognises the right to marry and to found a family as granted by domestic laws.[14]

This chapter thus intends to explore the ways in which migrant Muslim partners can exercise their own statutory right to individual religious freedom in the form of a (*sharīʿah*-compliant) nuptial union in Italy.

6.3 Marrying and forming a family in Italy

On Italian soil, Muslim migrant intended spouses can marry in compliance with Italian laws or *sharīʿah*. Muslim migrant fiancé(e)s can indeed contract a civil-only nuptial union as regulated by Italian laws, or they can marry in compliance with *sharīʿah*. Specifically, Muslim partners can enter into a 'religious-Islamic' or a 'customary-Muslim' marriage. The former is the nuptial union perfected in compliance with religious provisions, namely the *Qurʾān*, the *Sunnah* and other acknowledged sources of Islamic laws.[15] The adjective customary-Muslim instead refers to the partners' *sharīʿah*-compliant relationship as recognised by the spouses, their kinship(s), their (local) Muslim community, or the law of the Muslim majority country of origin of one of the parties.[16]

An Islamic or Muslim marriage can then be recognised as valid with civil effect by the Italian legal system when some requirements are satisfied. Three options exist: the wedding is celebrated by an appointed religious minister; the nuptial union is perfected in compliance with the laws of a foreign country; the competent foreign authorities or diplomatic premises of a foreign country recognise as valid and register a Muslim-only or Islamic-only marriage.

In the above listed cases, a *sharīʿah*-compliant marriage is also (potentially) valid with civil effect on Italian soil.[17] In other words, Muslim migrant spouses-to-be can enter into a civil, religious, or religious-*plus*-civil marriage. In this chapter, the discussion concerns a specific model of *sharīʿah*-compliant nuptial unions, specifically civil marriages of Muslim migrant partners.

---

14 Charter of Fundamental Rights of the European Union, (2010/C 83/02), in *Official Journal of the European Union*, 30.03.2010, C 83/391.

15 The other sources of Islamic law (e.g. consensus, analogical reasoning) and methods of scriptural interpretation are arranged following a different hierarchy by Islamic jurisprudence, *Sunni* and *Shīʿi* various denominations, sects and schools of thought. Accordingly, different interpretations are given with respect to the requirements and the validity of a *sharīʿah*-compliant marriage. Since this chapter focuses on the Muslim migrants' statutorily granted right to form a family on Italian soil and does not refer to a specific Muslim community, addressing all the conditions for validity of a Islamic and/Muslim marriage contract(s) is beyond the scope of the present work.

16 For a study of the semantic meaning of the adjectives 'Muslim' and 'Islamic' frequently improperly used as synonyms, see Sona (2014: 116; 2015: 38; 2016a: 22; 2016c: 17-18). On the meaning of the word *sharīʿah*, see *supra* footnote No. 1.

17 Empirical evidence disclosed that, whereas the former two cases are well-known, the last hypothesis seems to be frequently overlooked by scholarship and judiciary alike.

The necessary conditions for entering into a civilly valid marriage are listed in Section I, Chapter III, Title VI of the Italian Civil Code.[18] Accordingly, the vital statistics officer (*ufficiale di stato civile*) can perfect a civil matrimonial union between (Muslim) migrant parties when some legal requirements are satisfied;[19] contrariwise diriment or impedient nuptial impediments arise.[20] Among the legal requirements, some prerequisites differ for Italian and foreign national fiancé(e)s, the nuptial conditions for a civilly valid marriage are thus examined in the following sections, whilst paying specific attention to Islamic principles and Muslim intended spouses.

6.4   Nuptial prerequisite for nationals and aliens alike

On Italian soil, the first nuptial prerequisite similarly affects Italian and foreign nationals. The marriage preliminaries required by the Italian Civil Code (articles 93-96 and 106) clarify that the wedding celebration shall be preceded by publication (*pubblicazioni*) by the vital statistics officer.[21] The publication is an impedient impediment to the celebration of a valid marriage: the spouses and the vital statistics officer who celebrate the marriage without prior publication are in fact punishable by administrative penalty.

The fiancé(e)s, or a person specially appointed by them for that purpose, are compelled to apply for the publication of matrimony to the vital statistics officer of the commune where one of the intended spouses resides. In the case of migrant partners, the procedure might differ: in effect, when a fiancé(e) is resident (not only domiciled) abroad, and the partners wish to marry in foreign diplomatic premises (e.g. embassy or consulate of a Muslim majority country), the vital statistics officer shall request that the foreign diplomatic premises proceed with the publication.[22] The publication is however not necessary if the parties marry abroad, before foreign authorities.[23] As a result, if a migrant

---

18 For an English language translation of the Italian Civil Code see Beltramo et al. (1969-2007); a comment on the Italian legal system can be found in Cappelletti et al. (1967).
19 For an in-depth analysis of civil marriages of foreign Muslim spouses-to-be, see also Sona (2015, 2016a, 2016c, 2017).
20 This lexicon is borrowed from Canon law. The marriage between the parties is invalid in the case of diriment impediment. When the impediment is impedient, instead, the parties may simply be impelled to pay an administrative penalty.
21 Articles 93-101 Italian Civil Code; arts. 50-53, Decree of the President of the Republic No. 396 of 2000. From 01.01.2011, the publication is made online in compliance with Memorandum (*circolare*) of the Ministry of Interior No. 1, 05.01.2011; Memorandum of the Ministry of Interior No. 13, 21.04.2011; Memorandum of the Ministry of Interior No. 26, 28.10.2011.
22 Article 11 of the Decree of the President of the Republic 05.01.1967 No. 200 (1), 'Disposizioni sulle funzioni e sui poteri consolari' (1/circ), *Gazzetta Ufficiale* 19.04.1967 No. 98 SO. See also Legal Decree 03.02.2011 No. 71, 'Ordinamento e funzioni degli Uffici consolari', *Gazzetta Ufficiale* 13.05.2011 No. 110.
23 Article 13(2), Legal Decree No. 71 of 2011.

Muslim couple contracts a marriage outside the country, publications are not needed for the validity of their civil nuptial union. (Muslim) foreign partners marrying in a Muslim majority country are thus not affected by this provision.

Intended spouses can also request a reduction in or omission of the publication period.[24] The tribunal, having heard the public prosecutor, may reduce the period required for publication by a decree non-susceptible to appeal and issued in chambers. The tribunal may also authorise the omission of publication for serious reasons and when the spouses-to-be give assurances (on their own responsibility) that the marriage is not prevented by the impediments specified by articles 85-89 Italian Civil Code.[25] Additionally, the publication may be omitted if there is imminent danger of the fiancé(e)'s death. In these situations, the vital statistics officer can proceed with the celebration of the marriage without the publication and without the tribunal's assent to the marriage, if the parties swear that there are no impediments susceptible to dispensation between them. It is worth mentioning that a marriage celebrated without publication is valid even if the spouses falsely declared the imminent danger of death of one future spouse.[26] The provision of article 100 Italian Civil Code may thus represent an effective remedy for foreign Muslim fiancées who cannot produce a certificate called *nulla osta* to the vital statistics officer, as explained in the next sections 5-6.

With respect to the procedural aspects, the Italian legal system requires the intended spouses to provide their personal details - namely, name, surname, date of birth, citizenship, residence, and matrimonial status - to the vital statistics officer. The mention of the prospective spouse's identity seeks to ascertain that no impediments to the marriage exists according to both Italian and the parties' foreign laws, as clarified by the Ministry of Interior's Instructions (2011a: 113, and 2012a: 119-120). The fiancé(e)s shall also give assurances that their marriage is not prevented by the nuptial impediments specified by articles 85-89 Italian Civil Code – fiancé(e)s' minor age, parties' already married status, prohibited degrees of relations between the spouses-to-be, and partners' interdiction for mental incapacity.[27] As clarified further in the discussion, empirical evidence discloses that these conditions might specifically affect Muslim migrant spouses.[28] The vital statistics officer is also entitled to ask intended spouses to produce additional documents;[29] in particular, non-Italian

---

24 Article 100 Italian Civil Code.
25 On this aspect, see *infra* section 5.
26 Court of Cassation, 24.01.1967 No. 216, *Foro Italiano* 1967, I, 230. This provision can therefore be potentially abused by unscrupulous partners.
27 Article 51(1), Decree of the President of the Republic No. 396 of 2000.
28 For further details on the empirical evidence relied upon in this chapter please see *supra* footnote No. 2.
29 Article 110, Decree of the President of the Republic No. 396 of 2000 repealed article 97 Italian Civil Code; a formal comprehensive list of the necessary documents is not provided by the Italian Civil Code.

prospective spouses are compelled to satisfy further requirements, as scrutinised below in sections 5 and 7.

Once the above-mentioned procedures are concluded before the vital statistics officer, there are two possible scenarios. Either a public record is published and displayed on the commune's main door for at least eight consecutive days;[30] or, the officer deems that he or she cannot proceed with the publication and, accordingly, he or she issues a certificate reporting the reasons for the denial. In this case, the parties can bring a complaint against the denial before the competent tribunal, which shall ascertain whether the prerequisites can be satisfied by the partners and if the intended spouses can contract a valid civil marriage.

6.5   Current *ad hoc* aliens' nuptial prerequisites

In addition to the prerequisites detailed above, alien intended spouses must satisfy two further conditions in order to contract a valid marriage with civil effect in the Italian legal system.[31] Two additional documents are[32] to be submitted to the vital statistics officer: a certificate of no nuptial impediments, and a regular residence permit. The first condition and its impact on the agency of Muslim migrant partners is discussed in the following sections 5-6; whereas the effects and the consequences of the second prerequisite are examined in sections 7-8.

First of all, the foreign purported spouse is impelled to present to the vital statistics officer a document called *nulla osta* from the Latin expression *nihil obstat.* This expression indicates a certificate of no impediments to a nuptial union. The certificate is to be issued by the foreign fiancé(e)'s diplomatic premises and it must prove that no impediments to the marriage exist 'under the laws to which he is subject'.[33]

Two types of *nulla osta* can be submitted by non-Italian fiancé(e)s: either a document attesting that no nuptial impediments exist, or a certificate of legal capacity to marry. The intended foreign spouse shall submit a 'certificate of

---

30   Articles 54-58, Decree of the President of the Republic No. 396 of 2000.

31   A reviewer underlined that '[t]he author treats all Muslims in Italy as one homogenous group and does not mention whether there are differences between, for example, Muslims from Turkey and Morocco in terms of their eligibility to marry on Italian soil'. It should be pinpointed that, when adopting the point of view of the Italian legal system, aliens - independently form their religious affiliation - must satisfy the same nuptial requirement(s). The only difference in the treatment of foreign (Muslim) purported spouses that can be legally enacted by a European Member State is the one reported and explained in the next paragraph.

32   The second condition was eventually repealed; see *infra* section 7.

33   Article 116 Italian Civil Code, and Royal Decree 16.03.1942 No. 262, 'Approvazione del testo del Codice Civile', in *Gazzetta Ufficiale* 04.04.1942 No. 79. This provision does not necessarily refer to the foreign citizen's national laws, due to the principle of *renvoi* (Ballarino, 2008: 136).

legal capacity to marry', when the foreign fiancé(e) is a national of a country bound by the Munich Convention on the Issue of a Certificate of Capacity to Marry,[34] or by the previous Hague Convention relating to the Settlement of the Conflict of the Laws Concerning Marriage.[35] A 'no nuptial impediment declaration' is instead to be submitted by non-European citizens, who are nationals of a country which is not bound by the above-mentioned international treaties.

Introduced as a measure against cross-national polygamous nuptial unions,[36] this Italian provision *de facto* undermines the individual religious freedom statutory right of migrant Muslim parties, specifically their right to enter into a civil marriage in Italy. This discrimination can be described as a 'side effect' of a non-culturally-sensitive norm. Indeed, problems arise not in cases of polygynous nuptial unions - as originally intended by the Italian legislator - but in cases of inter-religious marriages. As a result, polygamous unions, which may in fact be valid in compliance with the laws of some Muslim majority countries, are not tackled by this provision, whereas inter-faith marriages are *de facto* impeded in cases of nationals of Muslim majority countries.

The explanation for this (unintended) reduction in the Muslim alien's right to marry is grounded in the fact that the legal systems of Muslim majority countries have the tendency to comply with *sharī'ah* with respect to nuptial impediments. Accordingly, inter-faith marriages are limited. The *Qur'ān* prescribes that Muslims cannot validly marry idolaters and unbelievers. For instance, the *sūrah* II (*āyah* 221) declares:

> *And do not marry polytheistic women until they believe. And a believing slave woman is better than a polytheist, even though she might please you. And do not marry polytheistic men until they believe. And a believing slave is better than a polytheist, even though he might please you. Those invite to the Fire, but Allāh invites to Paradise and to forgiveness, by His permission. And He makes clear His verses to the people that perhaps they may remember.*

Similarly, the *sūrah* V (*āyah* 5) and the *sūrah* LX (*āyah* 10) reiterate the ban when reciting as follows:

> *This day good foods have been made lawful, and the food of those who were given the Scripture is lawful for you and your food is lawful for them. And chaste women from among the believers and chaste women from among those who were*

---

34 International Commission on Civil Status (ICCS), Munich Convention No. 20 of 05.09.1980.
35 Hague Convention of 12.06.1902.
36 For a discussion on polygamous unions in Italy, see *inter alia* Campiglio (1999, 2008); Colaianni (2009); Galoppini (2000); Mancini (2003, 2008). For a study on Italian *Islām* see also Allievi and Castro (2000), Ferrari (2004, 2008).

> *given the Scripture before you, when you have given them*
> *their due compensation, desiring chastity, not unlawful*
> *sexual intercourse or taking lovers. And whoever denies the*
> *faith - his work has become worthless, and he, in the*
> *Hereafter, will be among the losers.*
> *O you who have believed, when the believing women come*
> *to you as emigrants, examine them. Allāh is most knowing*
> *as to their faith. And if you know them to be believers, then*
> *do not return them to the disbelievers; they are not lawful*
> *for them, nor are they lawful for them. But give them what*
> *they have spent. And there is no blame upon you if you*
> *marry them when you have given them their due*
> *compensation. And hold not to marriage bonds with*
> *disbelieving women, but ask for what you have spent and let*
> *them ask for what they have spent. That is the judgement of*
> *Allāh; He judges between you. And Allāh is Knowing and*
> *Wise.*

Accordingly, a Muslim man can validly marry a Muslim, Jewish, or Christian woman; whilst a Muslim woman can marry a Muslim man only. As disclosed by fieldwork evidence, in some situations, even Jewish or Christian prospective wives can similarly be required or advised to embrace *Islām* in order to enter into a valid marriage with a Muslim man. In compliance with a more restrictive interpretation, indeed, unless the partners live in a *sharī'ah*-compliant environment such as a Muslim majority country, a Muslim man cannot validly marry a 'woman of the Book'.[37]

Controversial situations therefore arise when a Muslim, or a supposedly Muslim fiancé(e), wishes to marry a non-Muslim partner on Italian soil. Satisfying the *nulla osta* preliminary nuptial requirement can be highly challenging for a migrant intended spouse, who is a Muslim majority country national, whose domestic legal system prohibits inter-faith nuptial unions. It is worth mentioning that, in effect, this limit impacts both Muslim and non-Muslim migrant prospective brides and grooms; a national of a Muslim majority country can indeed belong to a minority religious group, or the prospective bride or groom can abandon *Islām* and embrace another religion or become an atheist.

Furthermore, field-collected data indicate that the right of a foreign national to marry can be denied on the ground of his or her religious belonging and this data can also be simply presumed. Empirical evidence indeed revealed that the fiancé(e)'s religious affiliation (when not explicitly stated by the fiancé(e), or reported in the intended spouse's documents establishing his or her identity) was assumed to be relying upon the family name and the given name of the future spouse(s). The diplomatic personnel of Muslim majority countries'

---

37   The *Qur'ān* refers to Jews and Christians with the expression *ahl al-kitāb*, which means 'people of the Book'. A Christian or Jewish bride is thus called *kitābiyyah*.

consulates and embassies I interviewed in Italy clarified that *sharīʿah*-compliant nuptial impediments apply in the competent Muslim majority country's diplomatic premises in EU countries when it is declared, or it can be inferred, that the prospective spouse's parents are Muslim. This assumption is usually made relying upon the fiancé(e)'s personal names - such as patronymic, forename, surname - the (modest) behaviour of the intended spouses, or the parties' dress code.

6.6 The impairment of Muslim migrant fiancé(e)s' right to marry

A number of remedies to the above-mentioned limit to civilly valid marriages grounded in foreign religious impediments have been elaborated by the diplomatic premises of Muslim majority countries, as well as by the Italian judicial and administrative authorities. These two classes of remedies to the impairment of Muslim migrant fiancé(e)s' right to civilly marry are analysed in this section.

With respect to diplomatic premises, the empirical investigation I conducted unveiled three different patterns followed by the embassies and consulates of Muslim majority countries: some diplomatic premises refuse to issue the *nulla osta*; some embassies and consulates of Muslim majority countries release either a negative document, or a conditional certificate of no nuptial impediments.

In the first case scenario, the diplomatic authorisation for an Italian civil marriage is provided only when the act of conversion to *Islām* is submitted by the non-Muslim partner. The requirements and the procedures significantly vary: in some cases, the foreign diplomatic premises may need a *shahādah*[38] released by a named Italian worship centre, or the religious authority of a determined Muslim majority country. The listed centres and authorities differ depending upon the Muslim majority country and the Ambassador or (vice) Consul's interpretation of the foreign domestic legal system. As a result, diverse diplomatic premises can either accept or refuse the 'profession of faith' certified and released by the same Islamic authority.[39] The diplomatic premises of Muslim majority countries on Italian soil, normally, address the 'big mosque in Rome' as the proper place in which to officially embrace *Islām*. This mosque is indeed the seat of the Centro Islamico Culturale d'Italia (CICI), the sole Islamic

---

38 This word comes from the Arabic verb *shahida* which means 'to witness, to testify'; *shahādah* can thus be translated as 'profession of faith', and it is one of the five pillars of *Islām*. This word is also used to identify a person's conversion to *Islām*.

39 It is worth mentioning that the professions of faith of *Sunnī* and *Shīʿī* Islamic denominations slightly differ. The former states 'There is no God but God, and Muḥammad is His messenger'; *Shīʿī* Muslims add that 'and Ali is the *walī* of God'.

organization recognised as a religious legal entity (*ente morale di culto*) in Italy.[40]

To further embroil the requirements to be met by the prospective Muslim spouse, diverse religious authorities can ask aspiring Muslim converts to follow different procedures in order to embrace *Islām*. In some contexts, obtaining a *shahādah* certificate may be relatively easy; whereas in some Islamic or Muslim centres, course attendance - sometimes including a final examination - may be compulsory. The mandatory syllabi usually encompass Islamic theology or history, *Qur'ān* recitation and memorisation, and Arabic language classes.

In the second case scenario, a conditional *nulla osta* is released. Field-collected data indicate that there are two options. Sometimes, a consulate or embassy of a Muslim majority country issues a negative *nulla osta* on the ground of the religious belonging of the non-Muslim prospective spouse. In some cases, diplomatic premises release a conditional certificate of no nuptial impediments; in other words, the requested document is issued, but the certificate is valid only provided the non-Muslim fiancé(e) embraces *Islām* and proves his or her conversion.

In the third case scenario, the *nulla osta* is issued even if the conversion to *Islām* of the intended groom of the Muslim majority country national bride-to-be is not submitted to the diplomatic personnel. An additional condition is to be satisfied for this to happen: the parties have to agree that this inter-faith marriage will never be acknowledged and registered in the migrant bride's Muslim majority country of origin. Therefore, once a wife agrees not to register her marriage with a non-Muslim fiancée in the nuptial record of her Muslim majority country of origin and its foreign diplomatic premises, her certificate of no nuptial impediment is released.

The impact of this course of action on the spouses' life is quite significant, as this choice implies consequences regarding the family member's inheritance rights and the status of the couple's offspring in Muslim majority countries. Additionally, the same person's nuptial status under civil law differs in the legal system of the two states. To put it differently, the migrant Muslim majority country national is 'married' in the settlement country, whilst she remains 'unmarried' in the country of origin. Accordingly, she would be able to legally and religiously enter into an Islamic or Muslim marriage. If this migrant Muslim woman (re)marries, she would then become a polyandrous wife only in the eyes of the (European and possibly Western) legal systems since these acknowledge as valid her marriage to a non-Muslim man. Naturally, the recognition of her multiple married status can happen only if and when her *sharī'ah*-compliant marriage is disclosed to the competent authorities in a European legal system. It should be pinpointed that the controversial situations described above are not

---

40 Decree of the President of the Republic 21.12.1974 No. 712, 'Riconoscimento della personalità giuridica dell'ente "Centro Islamico culturale d'Italia" con sede in Roma Via A. Casella n. 51', *Gazzetta Ufficiale* 10-11.01.1975 No. 10, p. I.

just hypothetical cases or anecdotal narratives, as the fieldwork investigations I conducted revealed.

Apart from the typologies of documents released by the diplomatic premises of Muslim majority countries, the *nulla osta* requested by Italian authorities raises controversial issues. In effect, the fulfilment of this legal requirement may lead to religious prejudice toward the migrant Muslim fiancé(e) wishing to marry in compliance with Italian law.

Administrative and judicial remedies have thus been created to tackle this unintended religious discrimination of alien prospective spouses, who can bring the case before the Italian judiciary. The Italian judge can be asked to state that the *nulla osta* limits the nuptial right of non-nationals and therefore that this requirement can be contrary to the Italian public order.[41] The relevant Italian case law dates back to the mid-eighties and mid-nineties and is consistent. When the capacity to contract marriage to the non-Italian Muslim purported spouse has been made subject to the religious belonging of his or her fiancé(e), the Italian judge orders the vital statistics officer to proceed with the publication without the *nulla osta*, so that the inter-faith civil marriage can be perfected.[42]

Religiously discriminated migrant prospective spouses are however not impelled to resort to the *ad hoc* judicial remedy as described above. Where the *nulla osta* has been denied on the ground of the fiancé(e)'s religious belonging, or the certificate is negative or conditional on the party's conversion, the marriage can nonetheless be celebrated by the vital statistics officer, as clarified by the Italian Ministry of Interior's Instructions.[43] Any conditions inserted by Muslim majority countries' diplomatic premises regarding the purported spouses' religious belonging, in essence, are contrary to the Italian public order, and thus do not prevent the marriage celebration between the parties - as

---

41 Nonetheless, the Constitutional Court clarified that the requirement of a *nulla osta* does not *per se* infringe the inviolable rights of the person as protected by article 2 Italian Constitution. The Court order clarifies that the *nulla osta* is a 'document that in the majority of cases does not limit but rather facilitates the enactment of the freedom of marriage' (Constitutional Court, 16-30.01.2003 No. 14, *Gazzetta Ufficiale* 05.02.2003; *Diritto di Famiglia e delle Persone*, 2003, 331).

42 Cases frequently concern non-Italian Muslim women impeded from marrying non-Muslim men; some case law regards foreign men whose *nulla osta* was denied by the diplomatic premises of their own country of origin on the ground that they were non-Muslims. See *inter alia* Tribunal of Reggio Emilia, 29.09.1986, *Diritto di Famiglia e delle Persone* 1987, 268; Tribunal of Verona, 06.03.1987, *Foro Italiano*, Rep. 1987, Matrimonio, 152; Tribunal of Potenza, 30.11.1989, *Diritto di Famiglia e delle Persone*, XXX, 2001, 558; Tribunal of Camerino, 12.04.1990, *Diritto Internazionale Privato e Processuale*, XXVII, 1991, 800-1; *Rivista di Diritto Internazionale Privato Processuale* 1991, 750; Tribunal of Genova, 04.04.1990, *Giurisprudenza di Merito*, 1992, 1195; Tribunal of Torino, 24.02.1992, *Rivista di Diritto Internazionale Privato Processuale* 1992, 985; Tribunal of Torino, 24.06.1993, *Diritto di Famiglia e delle Persone*, 1993, 1181; Tribunal of Barcellona 09.03.1995, *Diritto di Famiglia e delle Persone*, 1996, 164; *Giurisprudenza di Merito*, 1996, 702; Tribunal of Napoli, 29.04.1996, *Famiglia e Diritto*, 5/1996, 454; Tribunal of Taranto, 13.07.1996, *Famiglia e Diritto*, 5/1996, 444. See also Sona (2014: 125).

43 Ministero dell'Interno (2011a: 109; 2012a: 115-6).

underlined by the Italian Ministry of Interior.[44] Furthermore, the more recent version of the Ministry of Interior's Instructions explicitly states that 'the lack of publication does not nullify the validity of the marriage deed'.[45]

Notwithstanding judicial and ministerial exhortations, field-collected data demonstrate that some Italian communes still assume that they are not authorised to proceed with the nuptial publication when a foreign purported spouse submits a *nulla osta* that is contrary to the Italian public order. Accordingly, this remains a case-by-case solution-seeking situation,[46] in particular for migrant Muslim fiance(é)s.

6.7 Amended aliens' nuptial requirement

As clarified *supra* in section 5, the *nulla osta* is only one of the two nuptial prerequisites that were to be satisfied by foreign partners wishing to marry in Italy.

In addition to the certificate of no nuptial impediments, from 2009 to 2011, non-national fiancé(e)s had to submit to the Italian vital statistics officer, 'a document attesting the regularity of his or her stay in the Italian territory'.[47] This requirement implied that the capacity to enter into a civil marriage was contemporarily subordinated to the religious belonging of the intended spouse(s), as well as to the fiancé(e)'s regular permit to stay in Europe, in cases of non-European national migrant Muslim prospective spouses.[48]

The religious freedom right of foreign nationals irregularly settled on Italian soil was thus specifically challenged by this *de facto* 'blanket prohibition' of civil marriage.[49] Although originally aimed simply to tackle marriages of convenience, the amended version of article 116(1) of the Italian Civil Code was eventually declared the unconstitutional by the Italian Constitutional Court.[50] In July 2011, the *Consulta* asserted that this provision violated both

---

44 See Memorandum (*circolare*) of the Ministry of Interior No. 46, 11.11.2007 and Ministero dell'Interno (2009a: 96; 2011a: 109; 2012a: 115-6; 119).
45 Ministero dell'Interno (2012a: 119).
46 See for instance Tribunal of Milano, 13.03.2007, *Quaderni di Diritto e Politica Ecclesiastica*, 2007, 829, and Tribunal of Piacenza, 05.05.2011, Sez. II, July, 2011, available online at http://www.stranieriinitalia.it/briguglio/ immigrazione-e-asilo/2011/luglio/trib-pc-nullaosta-nozze.pdf (last accessed 01.02.2013).
47 Article 116(1) Italian Civil Code as amended by article 1(15), Law 15.07.2009 No. 94, 'Disposizioni in materia di sicurezza pubblica', in *Gazzetta Ufficiale* 24.07.2009 No. 170 SO No. 128.
48 The Directive of the Ministry of Interior No. 2, 28.01.2010 clarified that European nationals were exempted from that provision.
49 On this aspect, see also Sona (2014: 125-126; 2016a: 42-43). For a legal analysis of the phenomenon see Ferrando (2009), Morozzo della Rocca (2009a/b/c, 2010, 2011), Casoni (2010), Consorti (2010, 2011a/b), Nascimbene (2011), Spina (2011), Zanobetti (2011).
50 As amended by article 1(15) of the Law No. 94 of 2009.

constitutional and international norms.[51] In particular, the Constitutional Court elucidated that:

> *the inviolable rights of article 2 Italian Constitution are owed to any person not since he or she may belong to a particular political community, but to human beings as such.*

The right of migrant partners to exercise their religious freedom in the form of a civilly valid marriage was thus stressed by the Court relying upon statutory provisions. Furthermore, the Court added that the blanket prohibition on the exercise of the right to enter into a civil nuptial union violated constraints deriving from international obligations.[52] The national state's margin of appreciation indeed cannot be broadened to the extent that this implies 'a general, automatic and indiscriminate restriction of a fundamental right', specifically of article 12 of the European Convention on Human Rights.[53]

Although stating that a national state has to control (im)migration flows, and national borders are to be protected and defended, the 'imposed sacrifice' of the matrimonial freedom should not be disproportionate, the Court clarified.[54] Irregularly settled migrant partners, therefore, cannot be prevented from marrying when not submitting a valid permit to stay. The impact of the amended version of article 116(1) Italian civil Code on migrant prospective spouses' individual religious freedom was indeed beyond the protected statutory right.

6.8   Provisional antidotes: Civil and *sharīʿah*-compliant marriages

From 2009 to 2011, Muslim spouses-to-be not owning a valid permit to reside in Europe had to elaborate on effective counteractions in order to enter into a valid marriage. Field-collected data disclosed that two possible provisional

---

51   Constitutional Court, 20-25.07.2011 No. 245, *Gazzetta Ufficiale* 27.07.2011. See also Memorandum (*circolare*) of the Ministry of Interior No. 21 of 26.07.2011.

52   As recognised by article 117(1) Italian Constitution.

53   See para 3.2, Constitutional Court, 20-25.07.2011 No. 245, *Gazzetta Ufficiale* 27.07.2011, where the Italian Constitution Court also quoted *O'Donoghue and Others v the United Kingdom*, Application No. 34848/07, 14.12.2010 - 14.03.2011, [2011] All ER (D) 46 (Jan).

54   See para 3.1, Constitutional Court, 20-25.07.2011 No. 245, *Gazzetta Ufficiale* 27.07.2011. It should be mentioned that the Court also conceded that citizens and foreigners differ. In particular, aliens have a merely 'acquired and temporary' relationship with the Italian state; nonetheless, the "foreign legal status" should not be regarded as 'a justification allowing diversified or pejorative treatments'. The *Consulta* built upon the following: Constitutional Court, 19-26.06.1969 No. 104, *Gazzetta Ufficiale* 02.07.1969 No. 165; Constitutional Court, 10-24.02.1994 No. 62, *Gazzetta Ufficiale* 02.03.1994; Constitutional Court, 05-08.07.2010 No. 249, *Gazzetta Ufficiale* 14.07.2010.

antidotes were soon identified: civil or *sharīʿah*-compliant matrimonial unions, as discussed below.

With respect to civilly valid nuptial unions, migrant non-European national Muslim fiancé(e)s learned that they could still enter into a civil marriage compliant with a legal system other than the Italian one. In the examined interval of about three years, alternative non-Italian nuptial paths were soon identified. Muslim intended spouses could in fact marry in another state (European or Muslim majority country), or in a foreign country's diplomatic premises while being on Italian soil.[55] Provided that the foreign nuptial law did not require a residence permit to contract a valid marriage, the spouses-to-be could enter into a valid nuptial union with civil effect.

This procedure also implied that the irregularly settled migrant married partner could then submit an application to join as a validly married spouse his or her partner on Italian soil. Consequently, the Muslim migrants married in compliance with one of the two above-mentioned procedures were entitled to claim the recognition of their foreign nuptial certificate through private international law principles. Therefore, a Muslim fiancé(e) - who was originally irregularly settled in a European country - was then entitled to benefit from family reunification procedures (specifically to claim a spouse's visa in Italy) on the ground of a civil marriage, which was originally prevented by Italian law, but recognised as valid if perfected abroad.

The fieldwork investigation I completed disclosed that, amid the concurrent possible categories of alternative legal systems,[56] the favourite countermeasure chosen by irregularly settled Muslim partners on Italian soil was represented by a marriage celebrated in a European country. And, amongst European domestic legal systems, a micro-state called San Marino was soon identified as the best option. Thus, from 2009 to 2011, migrant Muslim spouses-to-be rapidly identified and skilfully learned how to take advantage of a loophole in the Italian legislation.

In real terms, in the Republic of San Marino, prospective spouses are requested to satisfy conditions that are nearly analogous to the Italian ones;[57] nonetheless, the alien fiancé(e)'s permit to stay is not listed among the necessary nuptial prerequisites. In addition, the marriage deed is automatically transmitted between the Italian and San Marinian administrative offices, and the marriage act is instantly valid in the other country.[58] As a result, partners married in San

---

55 Naturally, when the marriage was contracted in the embassy or the consulate of a Muslim majority country, this union was not only civilly valid, but also *sharīʿah*-compliant.

56 As stated above, these are a Muslim majority country, the fiancé(e)'s foreign diplomatic premises, or a European state characterised by less demanding nuptial provisions.

57 A notarial act signed by the purported spouses and four Italian national witnesses are also requested.

58 Articles 38(1) and 39(1) of the Law 06.06.1939 No. 1320, 'Esecutorietà della Convenzione di amicizia e buon vicinato stipulata in Roma, fra l'Italia e la Repubblica di San Marino il 31 marzo 1939', in *Gazzetta Ufficiale* 16.09.1939 No. 217. Accordingly, the marriage act is not further examined by the Italian administrative competent offices when recording it.

Marino are almost immediately also regarded as civilly married under the Italian legal system. Skilfully manoeuvring across the provisions of two diverse but connected European legal systems, Muslim foreign intended spouses identified a way to benefit from a legal loophole. Consequently, migrant Muslim intended spouses learned how to legitimise the spouse's reunification claim on the ground of the very same marriage that was forbidden by Italian authorities, but recognised as civilly valid when perfected in San Marino.[59]

As far as *sharī'ah*-compliant marriages were concerned, the prospective Muslim spouses increasingly resorted to unregistered Islamic-only or Muslim-only marriages. The nuptial unions mentioned could be perfected either in Italy or abroad. In these cases, irregularly settled migrant Muslim partners were compelled to exercise their Islamic right-&-duty to marry in the shadow of European domestic legal systems; in other words, since the migrant parties' right to religious freedom had been violated by the provisions of the Italian legal system, Muslim fiancé(e)s began to resort to the Islamic-religious or Muslim-customary legal order to contract the marriage, as discussed above in section 3.

A second antidote to the shadowy exercise of the right-&-duty to marry as imposed by the Italian discriminatory provisions was elaborated by some Muslim majority countries and their diplomatic premises on Italian soil. Privately solemnised *sharī'ah*-compliant marriages were in practice recognised and recorded by foreign Muslim countries.

In this situation, the procedure was knotty but effective, as disclosed by the empirical investigations I carried out. Muslim prospective spouses first entered into a religious or customary marriage in Europe or abroad. This Islamic-only or Muslim-only marriage was then 'raised' to the standard of a nuptial union with civil effect when acknowledged as valid and, therefore, registered by foreign authorities or a Muslim majority country's diplomatic premises. In other words, a Muslim-only or Islamic-only marriage contract was acknowledged as legally valid and therefore registered in the official civil record by the diplomatic premises of a Muslim majority country; consequently, a formerly religious or customary-only nuptial union also acquired (potential) civil effect on European soil.

Amid these legally acknowledged marriages there were Islamic or Muslim nuptial unions which had been previously solemnised in small Islamic worship centres. In real terms, an uncounted number of Islamic or Muslim worship centres celebrate religious-only marriages in Italy.[60] Theoretically, only a *'aqd al-zawāǧ*[61] perfected in the *Grande Moschea di Roma* (as well as in its affiliated worship centres and mosques) is to be recognised as valid and therefore

---

59 For an in-depth analysis of these nuptial procedures and their effects, see Sona (2015; 2016b).

60 In 2007, the Chamber of Representatives reported 774 Islamic worship centres (Camera dei Deputati, 2008: 69). The research conducted by Allievi and Ethnobarometer (2009: 33) counted 661 non-purpose-built mosques and 3 purpose-built mosques in 2009. *Cf.* Coglievina (2013: 357).

61 This is the traditional way to address an Islamic marriage contract in the Arabic language.

officially recorded by the diplomatic premises of Muslim majority countries.[62] This is due to two main reasons. First of all, the big mosque in Rome is the seat of the Centro Islamico Culturale d'Italia (CICI), which is the sole Italian Muslim organisation having the status of a non-profit corporation.[63] Secondly, the CICI board of directors is constituted predominantly of ambassadors of Muslim majority countries accredited by the Holy See and the Italian state.[64]

As far as the privately solemnised *sharīʿah*-compliant nuptial contracts eventually recorded with civil effect, the diplomatic personnel interviewed described this conduct partly as a reaction to the discriminative Italian immigration laws, and partly as the result of a mistake. Although this matter was sometimes taken lightly by some informants, the (un)wanted or (un)expected consequences were however worthy of attention. In particular, when a foreign legal system legitimises nuptial unions, which are otherwise religious-only or customary-only, notable implications arise for European states. In effect, if an alien *sharīʿah*-compliant legal system recognises as civilly valid a Muslim-only or an Islamic-only marriage,[65] this customary or religious-only nuptial union can have civil effect on European soil, and related rights (such as family reunification claims) can be exercised by the parties.

It should be mentioned that, according to field-collected data, Muslim partners relied upon these remedies predominantly when the blanket prohibition to marry for irregularly settled migrants was enforced on Italian soil; however, in some cases these procedures are still followed. Regrettably, this marriage route was often left unnoticed by judicial authorities as well as academic literature.

6.9 Conclusions

Within the broader framework of interaction between (secular) (im)migration laws and religious autonomy, this chapter explored the extent and effectiveness of individual religious freedom as enshrined in domestic and international legal provisions, with respect to (ir)regularly settled migrant Muslim intended spouses on Italian soil. In particular, the potential or actual impairment of

---

62   For instance, the recently built Turin mosque could also release Islamic marriage certificates which can be recognized as valid with civil effect by some Muslim majority countries and/or some diplomatic premises on European soil. Nonetheless, it seems that they prefer to refer Muslim fiancé(e)s to the Rome mosque and/or to foreign diplomatic premises (interviews conducted by the author in February 2017).

63   As clarified above when analysing the recognition of a valid conversion to *Islām*. See above footnote No. 39.

64   This centre is indeed considered the 'official Italian' *Islām*. See *inter alia* Roggero (2002: 136-7); Allievi (2002: 87; 2003: 73-9); Aluffi Beck-Peccoz (2004a: 184; 2004b: 136).

65   For instance, in European legal systems, a foreign *sharīʿah*-compliant marriage is not recognised as valid when it is against the public order and morality.

(pious) Muslim migrant fiancé(e)s' right-&-duty to marry was investigated alongside the challenges faced by migrant Muslims.

When relying upon European statutory declarations, individual religious freedom is a key prerogative largely acknowledged to every person: this principle cannot be constrained eventually impeding the full development of a human being, not even when relying upon the European Member State's margin of appreciation. As a fundamental inviolable right, which is statutorily proclaimed and widely granted, Muslim migrant fiancé(e)s have theoretically recognised the possibility to exercise their religious freedom in the form of a civilly valid or *sharī'ah*-compliant nuptial union. Nonetheless, some matrimonial restrictions might *de facto* be (in)voluntarily imposed on alien Muslim partners therefore limiting the foreign Muslim party's agency. In particular, in the Italian legal system, some nuptial prerequisites - although originally intended to tackle marriages of convenience as well as polygamous nuptial unions - *de facto* limit the capacity of Muslim migrants to marry. Muslim partners might thus be compelled to favour shadowy nuptial routes.

Building upon more than a decade of extensive empirical evidence, the discussion discloses frequently unperceived tactics, which were gradually developed as antidotes to (unintended) discriminatory state provisions. When trying to enforce their right to form - and to reunify - a family on European soil, migrant Muslim prospective spouses might thus rely upon two different strategies. They can elaborate for themselves anti-prejudicial nuptial patterns; or they can refer to official authorities of European as well as Muslim majority countries. By way of illustration, a claim can be brought before the Italian judiciary when one of the foreign fiancé(e)s cannot produce a valid certificate of no nuptial impediments. Additionally, a Muslim majority country's diplomatic premises can recognise, and therefore register with civil effect, religious-only (Islamic) or customary-only (Muslim) marriages even though these were privately perfected in unauthorised Islamic worship centres. (Ir)regularly settled alien spouses-to-be can also enter into a civil marriage compliant with a legal system other than the Italian one. The consequences of these actions are rather significant, in effect, once legally wed, the spouses can submit - and obtain - a valid residence or settlement permit as a married partner.

In the explored and scrutinised scenarios, it is clear that Muslims have learned to manage intricate legal provisions in order to find remedies aimed at forming a family founded on an Islamic or Muslim marriage in Europe. Nonetheless, Muslim fiancé(e)s might be impelled to opt for knotty implementations of their partly impaired religious freedom right. For this reason, whereas entering into a civilly valid *sharī'ah*-compliant relationship in Italy might be even more challenging than entering the EU, (some) migrant Muslim prospective spouses appear to be versed in coping with their (unintendedly) limited Islamic right-&-duty to marry.

References

al-Fārūqī, I.R. (1982), *Tawhid: Its implication for thought and life,* Hemdon (VA): International Institute for Islamic Thought.

Ali, M.M. (1936), *The religion of Islām. A comprehensive discussion of the sources, principles and practices of Islam,* Lahore: The Aḥmadiyya Anjuman Ishā'at Islām.

Ali, M.M. (1944), *A manual of ḥadīth,* Lahore: The Aḥmadiyya Anjuman Ishā'at Islām.

Allievi, S. (2002), *Musulmani d'occidente. Tendenze dell'Islam europeo,* Roma: Carocci.

Allievi, S. (2003), *Islam italiano. Viaggio nella seconda religione del paese,* Torino: Einaudi.

Allievi, S. & Ethnobarometer (2009), *Conflicts over mosques in Europe. Policy issues and trends,* London: Alliance Publishing Trust.

Allievi, S. and F. Castro (2000), 'The Islamic presence in Italy: Social rootedness and legal questions', in: S. Ferrari & A. Bradney (eds.), *Islam and European legal systems,* Dartmouth: Ashgate, p. 155-180.

Aluffi Beck-Peccoz, R. (2004a), 'Islam in the European Union: Italy', in: R. Potz, & W. Wieshaider (eds.), *Islam and the European Union,* Leuven: Peeters, p. 181-198.

Aluffi Beck-Peccoz, R. (2004b), 'The legal treatment of the Muslim minority in Italy', in: R. Aluffi Beck-Peccoz, & G. Zincone (eds.), *The legal treatment of Islamic minorities in Europe,* Leuven: Peeters, p. 133-158.

Arabi, O. (2001a), *Studies in modern Islamic law and jurisprudence,* The Hague: Kluwer Law International.

Arabi, O. (2001b), 'The dawning of the third millennium on shari'a: Egypt's Law No.1 of 2000, or women may divorce at will?', *Arab Law Quarterly,* 16/1, p. 2-21.

Ballarino, T. (2008), *Manuale breve di diritto internazionale private* (3rd ed.), Padova: CEDAM.

Banakar, R. & Travers, M. (eds.) (2005), *Theory and method in socio-legal research,* Oxford and Portland (OR): Hart.

Barsotti, V., P.G. Carozza, M. Cartabia & A. Simoncini (2015), *Italian constitutional justice in global context,* Oxford: OUP.

Beltramo, M., E.G. Longo, J.H. Merryman, & S. Beltramo (eds.) (1969-2007), *The Italian civil code,* Dobbs Ferry (NY): Oceana.

Blank, J. (2001), *Mullahs on the mainframe: Islam and modernity among the Daudi Bohras,* London: University of Chicago Press.

Bryman, A. (2001), *Social research methods,* Oxford and New York: Oxford University Press.

Bulmer, M. (ed.) (2003), *Sociological research methods. An introduction* (2nd ed.), Piscataway (NJ): Macmillan Press.

Camera dei Deputati. (2008), *Relazione sulla politica dell'informazione per la sicurezza. Anno 2007*. Doc. XXXIII No. 4, 29.02, Roma: Tipografia del Senato.

Campiglio, C. (1999), 'La famiglia islamica nel diritto internazionale privato italiano', *Rivista di Diritto Internazionale Privato e Processuale*, XXXV, p. 21-42.

Campiglio, C. (2008), 'Il diritto di famiglia islamico nella prassi italiana', *Rivista di Diritto Internazionale Privato e Processuale*, XLIV, 1, p. 343-376.

Cappelletti, M., J.H. Merryman & J.M. Perillo (1967), *The Italian legal system*, Stanford: Stanford University Press.

Casoni, G. (2010), 'Il nulla osta al matrimonio ed il titolo al soggiorno previsti dall'art. 116 del codice civile: identità documentale e validità temporale, *Lo Stato Civile Italiano*, 2, p. 9-10.

Coglievina, S. (2013), 'Italy', in: J. Nielsen, S. Akgönül, A. Alibašić, & E. Racius (eds.), *Yearbook of Muslims in Europe*, Vol. 5., Leiden: Brill, p. 351-367.

Colaianni, N. (2009), 'I nuovi confini del diritto matrimoniale tra istanze religiose e secolarizzazione: la giurisdizione', *Rivista di Diritto Privato*, 3-4, p. 7-31.

Consorti, P. (2011a), 'Pacchetto sicurezza e fattore religioso', *Stato, Chiese e Pluralismo Confessionale* febbraio, p. 1-20.

Consorti, P. (2011b), 'La nuova disciplina del matrimonio degli stranieri alla luce del pacchetto sicurezza. I suoi riflessi sul matrimonio concordatario', *Stato, Chiese e Pluralismo Confessionale*, febbraio, p. 1-18.

Denzin, N.K. (1989), *The research act: A theoretical introduction to sociological methods*, Englewood Cliffs (NJ): Prentice Hall.

Denzin, N.K. & Y.S. Lincoln (eds.) (1998), *Collecting and interpreting qualitative materials*, Thousand Oaks (Calif) and London: Sage Publications.

Denzin, N.K. & Y.S. Lincoln (eds.) (1994), *The handbook of qualitative research*, London: Sage Publications.

Ferrando, G. (2009), 'Matrimonio e filiazione nella L. n. 94/2009 (c.d. "Pacchetto sicurezza")', *Famiglia, persone e successioni*, p. 957 ff.

Ferrari, S. (2004), 'Islam in Europe: An introduction to legal problems and perspectives', in: R. Aluffi Beck-Peccoz, & G. Zincone (eds.), *The legal treatment of Islamic minorities in Europe*, Leuven: Peeters, p. 1-9.

Ferrari, S. (2008), 'Le questioni normative', in: A. Ferrari (ed.), *Islam in Europa / Islam in Italia tra diritto e società*, Bologna: Il Mulino, p. 77-87.

Flick, U. (1998), *An introduction to qualitative research: Theory, method and applications*, London: Sage Publications.

Galoppini, A.M. (2005), 'Il ripudio e la sua rilevanza nell'ordinamento italiano', *Il Diritto di Famiglia e delle Persone*, 34, 3, 2, p. 969-989.

Gray, G. & N. Guppy (1994), *Successful surveys: Research methods and practice*, Toronto: Harcourt Brace.

Hollway, W. & T. Jefferson T. (2000), *Doing qualitative research differently: Free association, narrative, and the interview method*, London: Sage Publications.

Hoodfar, H. (1997), *Between marriage and the market: Intimate politics and survival in Cairo*, Berkley and Los Angeles: University of California Press.

Huff, T.E. (2003), *Max Weber and the methodology of the social sciences*, New Brunswick (NJ): Transaction Publishers.

Jeldtoft, N. & J. Nielsen J. (eds.) (2012), *Methods and contexts in the study of Muslim minorities: Visible and invisible Muslims*, London: Routledge.

Lapidus, I.M. (1976), 'Adulthood in Islam: Religious maturity in the Islamic tradition, *Daedalus*, 105/2, p. 93-108.

Mancini, L. (2003), 'Società multiculturale, pluralismo normativo e diritto: il caso del matrimonio islamico', in: G. Zanetti (ed.), *Elementi di etica pratica. Argomento normativi e spazi del diritto*, Roma: Carocci, p. 47-58.

Mancini, L. (2006), Il matrimonio islamico in Italia, in: I. Zilio-Grandi (ed.), *Sposare l'altro. Matrimoni e matrimoni misti nell'ordinamento italiano e nel diritto islamico*, Venezia: Marsilio p. 105-118.

Maqsood, R.W. (2003), *Con il mio sposo. Guida islamica al matrimonio*, Imperia: Al Hikma.

McConville, M. & W.H. Chui (eds.) (2007), *Research methods for law*, Edinburgh: Edinburgh University Press.

Ministero dell'Interno (2009a), '*Il Regolamento dello stato civile: guida all'applicazione. Massimario per l'ufficiale di stato civile 2009/4*', authored by R. Mazza, F. De Fanti, F. Vitali, D. Berloco & R. Calvigioni, Roma: Ministero dell'Interno.

Ministero dell'Interno (2011a), *Il Regolamento dello stato civile: guida all'applicazione. Massimario per l'ufficiale di stato civile. Edizione 2011*, authored by R. Mazza, F. De Fanti, F. Vitali, D. Berloco & R. Calvigioni. Roma: Ministero dell'Interno.

Ministero dell'Interno (2012a), *Il Regolamento dello stato civile: guida all'applicazione. Massimario per l'ufficiale di stato civile. Edizione 2012*, authored by R. Mazza, F. De Fanti, F. Vitali, D. Berloco & R. Calvigioni. Roma: Ministero dell'Interno.

Modood, T. & P. Werbner (eds.) (1997), *The politics of multiculturalism in the new Europe: Racism, identity and community*, London and New York: Zed Books.

Morozzo della Rocca, P. (2009a), I limiti alla libertà matrimoniale secondo il nuovo testo dell'art. 116 cod. civ. *Famiglia e Diritto*, X, 945ff.

Morozzo della Rocca, P. (2009b), 'Sul matrimonio in Italia dei cittadini comunitari secondo il nuovo testo dell'art. 116 Cod. Civ.', *Lo Stato civile italiano*, 105/10, p. 734-736.

Morozzo della Rocca, P. (2009c), 'Il matrimonio e gli atti di stato civile', in: P. Morozzo della Rocca (ed.), *Immigrazione e cittadinanza. Profili normativi e orientamenti giurisprudenziali*, Aggiornamento della legge 15 luglio 2009,

n. 94, Disposizioni in materia di sicurezza pubblica, UTET, Milanofiori Assago p. 55 ff.

Morozzo della Rocca, P. (2010), 'Cittadinanza europea, libertà di circolazione e famiglie senza matrimonio,' *Famiglia e Diritto*, 8/9, p. 849-860.

Morozzo della Rocca, P. (2011), 'Immigrazione: la consulta cancella dall'art. 116 c.c., la clausola che ostacolava (anche) matrimoni autentici. Corte Costituzionale 25 luglio 2011, n. 245', *Corriere Giuridico*, 28/11, p. 1532-1542.

Nascimbene, B. (2011), 'La capacità dello straniero: diritti fondamentali e condizione di reciprocità'. *Rivista di Diritto Internazionale Privato e Processuale*, 2/2011, XLVIII, Aprile-Giugno, p. 307-326.

Patton, M.Q. (2002), *Qualitative research and evaluation methods* (3rd ed.), London: Sage.

Pugliese, E. (2002), *L'Italia tra migrazioni internazionali e migrazioni interne*, Bologna: Il Mulino.

Ringer, F.K. (1997), *Max Weber's methodology: The unification of the cultural and social sciences*, Cambridge: Harvard University Press.

Roggero, M.A. (2002), Muslims in Italy, in: Y.Y. Haddad (ed.), *Muslims in the West: From sojourners to citizens*, Oxford and New York: Oxford University Press, p. 131-143.

Sanfilippo, M. & P. Corti (ed.) (2009), *Storia d'Italia. Annali 24. Migrazioni*, Torino: Einaudi.

Santillana, D. (1919), *Il muħtaşar. Sommario del diritto malechita di Khalīl ibn Isḥāq al-Jundī*, Milano, Hoepli.

Sona, F. (2014), 'Defending the family treasure-chest: Navigating Muslim families and secured positivistic islands of European legal systems', in: P. Shah, M.C. Foblets, & M. Rohe (eds.), *Family, Religion, and Law: Cultural Encounters in Europe*, Farnham: Ashgate in Association with Religare, p. 115-141.

Sona, F. (2015), 'Overcoming obstacles through hidden nuptial paths: Foreign Muslim purported spouses marrying in Italy', *The Review of Social Studies*, Gender and Migration, 2/1/Spring, p. 25-53.

Sona, F. (2016a), 'Islām as legal (dis)-empowerment: The dynamic interplay between Italian legal provisions and sharī'ah-compliant norms', in: K. Topidi, & L. Fielder (eds.), *Religion as Empowerment? Global Legal Perspectives*, Abingdon: Routledge, p. 21-52.

Sona, F. (2016b), 'Promessi sposi musulmani e barbatrucchi. Profili di libertà matrimoniale ed accomodamenti tra *islām* e diritto italiano', in: P. Consorti, N. Fiorita, F. Dal Canto, & S. Panizza (eds.), *Corte costituzionale tra diritti e doveri in tempi di crisi economica e di rischi per la sicurezza*, Pisa: Pisa University Press, p. 293-319.

Sona, F. (2016c), 'Griglie di lettura ed analisi dell'*islām* europeo. Diritto interculturale e relazioni sciaraitiche', *Stato, Chiese e Pluralismo Confessionale*, 40, 12/12, p. 1-33.

Sona, F. (2017), 'Riflessioni contemporanee su Europa ed *islām*. Modelli di innesto e di trapianto al crocevia tra stati, religioni e tradizioni', in: I. Zuanazzi (ed.), *Relazioni familiari nel diritto interculturale, Atti del ciclo di incontri Le relazioni familiari nel diritto interculturale. Diritto interculturale tra ordinamenti statali e religioni'*, Libellula University Press, Tricase.

Spina, L. (2011), 'Incostituzionale la norma del "pacchetto sicurezza" che condiziona la capacità matrimoniale dello straniero alla regolarità del suo soggiorno', *Minori Giustizia*, 4, p. 230-234.

Walliman, N.S.R. (2006), *Social research methods.* London: Sage Publications.

Weber, M. (1949), *The methodology of the social sciences,* (Translated and edited by E.A. Shils and H.A. Finch; foreword by E.A. Shils), New York: Free Press.

Weinberg, D. (ed.) (2002), *Qualitative research methods,* Oxford: Blackwell.

Wiktorowicz, Q., & S.T. Farouki. (2000), Islamic NGOs and Muslim politics: A case from Jordan, *Third World Quarterly*, 21/4, p. 685-699.

Yanow, D. & Schwartz-Shea P. (eds.) (2006), *Interpretation and method: Empirical research methods and the interpretive turn,* New York, Armonk and London: M.E. Sharp.

Zanobetti, A. (2011), 'Il diritto di sposarsi dei cittadini stranieri in situazione irregolare: il caso O'Donoghue della CEDU e la sentenza n. 245/2011 della Corte costituzionale italiana', *Diritto, Immigrazione e Cittadinanza*, 3, p. 73-87.

Chapter 7   I could not do otherwise

*Disobeying migration laws under the ECHR on
grounds of religion and conscience*

Dolores Morondo Taramundi

7.1   Introduction

> *I wish, for my own peace of mind, that you would not be
> frightened or disturbed by whatever the sentence they give
> to me (...) My dear mother, I would just like to hug you tight
> and let you know how much I love you and how I would like
> to comfort you for giving you this sorrow: but I could not do
> otherwise. Life is like this, very tough, and sometimes
> children have to give great pain to their moms if they want
> to preserve their honour and dignity as men.[1]*

The Mediterranean Sea is considered one of the deadliest border crossings in
the world. Over the last 3 years, the effort to make it increasingly impenetrable
for people devoid of approved entry clearance has claimed the lives of 13,452.[2]
People fleeing from famine, war, endemic violence or persecution and those
simply searching for a better future have found Europe ever more unwilling to
receive and integrate the less than 15% of international human mobility flows
knocking at our doors.[3]

Against the background of growing xenophobic discourse, political parties
and governments are engaging in what appears more and more clearly as a vain
effort to stop and control migration flows through the use of repressive and
punitive measures, allegedly intended to protect the security of European
citizens and offer them effective rights through the strengthened and modern
management of the Union's external borders.[4]

Yet in the midst of xenophobic prejudice and growing intolerance against
religious and racialized groups, many Europeans have mobilised to support,
help and welcome migrants and refugees while their governments and the

---

1   Gramsci A. (1928), *Letter from prison to his mother*, 10 May.
2   For the period July 2014-June 2017, calculated on data by Missing Migrant Project:
    <missingmigrants.iom.int/mediterranean>.
3   Of the 244 million international migrants in 2015 (UN Migration Report 2015), Europe hosts
    35.1 million people (Eurostat, Migration and migrant population statistics). This does not
    include 19.3 million EU citizens living in another Member State.
4   See, for example: EU Council Conclusions June 2014.

European institutions dawdle. The newspapers all over Europe have reported plenty of cases. An olive farmer in the south of France was given a suspended € 3,000 fine for aiding irregular migrants and housing them in an abandoned railway building.[5] The Spanish government discontinued the access of irregularly resident migrants to universal healthcare provision and hundreds of doctors and nurses refused to abide by the new law.[6] A Danish woman was fined after offering a lift in her car and some refreshment in her house to one of the Syrian families *en route* through the country to claim asylum in Sweden.[7] And the list could continue.

The topic of this chapter is that in supporting, helping or even interacting with persons irregularly present in Europe (that is, without a valid form of residence permit), many Europeans have ignored or violated the law. Some of them knew they were breaking the law, others did not. Most of them did not care. Their reason is that they could not, and cannot, do otherwise: to help bring refugees to the shore of the island of Lesbos, to give a lift to a family to the harbour and get them a ferry ticket to Sweden, to assist them as doctors or nurses, to house them in the winter of the Alps, all those actions were compelled by a sense of human decency, they were the unavoidable corollary of the principle of human dignity.

Contrary to the declared intention of creating a common European immigration policy and led on by the discretionary powers granted to the Member States by European legislation, the application of national laws to these actions has resulted in legal uncertainty and inconsistency, creating a puzzle of cases and sanctions: prison terms, fines, application of humanitarian exemptions from sanction and even absolutions. We cannot focus here on how the different States have treated social interaction with, and even compassionate actions towards, people in irregular situations in Europe.[8] This chapter aims more limitedly at looking at how those actions could be argued in relation to the European Convention on Human Rights (ECHR) in the light of the case law of the European Court of Human Rights in Strasbourg (ECtHR).

Firstly, I shall analyse the increasing criminalisation of irregular migration and of the life around it (para. 7.2). Secondly, I'll examine two routes open for arguing the position of those who have broken the law by assisting or helping so-called irregular migrants. The first route examined (para. 7.3) is for people who belong to faith-based organisations (FBOs) and church communities which undertake the support of marginalised social groups, including irregular migrants, or people who argue that their actions are part of their religion, following the teachings of the Bible or other sacred texts. In the second route

---

5   Adam Nossiter (2017), 'Farmer on Trial Defends Smuggling Migrants: I Am a Frenchman.?', *The New York Times*, 5 January.

6   Giles Tremlett (2012), 'Immigrants in Spain to lose right to public healthcare', *The Guardian*, 31 August.

7   Lizzie Dearden (2016), 'Prominent Danish activist and author prosecuted for 'people trafficking' after giving Syrian refugee family a lift', *The Independent*, 11 March.

8   See: Carrera *et al.* 2016; Provera 2015; FRA 2014.

(para. 7.4), conscience is invoked without any necessary reference to religion. Although, at times, the line that divides these positions blurs and, at times, these actions go further into civil disobedience, I shall assess them separately to see how the claims would fare under the different headings and how human rights protections could be extended.

7.2 The criminalisation of irregular migration and its surroundings

Migration law and policy has become a central item in European political agendas and discourse, both at the level of the European Union (EU) and in every single European State. Growing xenophobic and securitarian discourses have turned the management of migration flows and the reception and integration of migrant groups into a matter of "resistance against invasion", "survival of the European identity", "increased need for control, order and security", or "fight against crime".

Human rights frameworks have been largely neglected in the treatment of this question, when not patently violated. The Council of Europe Commissioner for Human Rights (2013), the United Nations Special Rapporteur on the human rights of migrants (2013), the European Union Fundamental Rights Agency (2011, 2013 and 2014) have all highlighted the risks of trying to manage and deter irregular migration with criminal law measures, and their deleterious impact on fundamental rights, both because those measures often deprive irregular migrants of their basic rights and because they cause irregular migrants to be perceived and treated as criminals, making them more vulnerable to exploitation and abuse.

7.2.1 The criminalisation of irregular migration under EU legislation

The EU has played a decisive role in this trend, adopting legislation which obliges its Member States to punish persons who enter or stay in a territory without the permission to do so, and persons who help irregular migrants to enter and stay in the EU.

Article 79 of the Treaty on the Functioning of the European Union (TFEU) calls on the prevention of "illegal immigration" as one of the aims of the developing common European immigration policy. Its normative framework as regards irregular migration[9] is constituted by the notorious Return Directive[10]

---

9   It is worth noting that not only "irregular migration" but also the EU normative framework and policy for "legal" labour migration raises a number of human rights issues, specifically problems regarding equality (e.g., Friðriksdóttir 2016).

10 Council Directive 2008/115/EC of 16 December 2008 on common standards and procedures in Member States for returning illegally staying third-country national (Return Directive), OJ 2008 L 348.

(which was broadly criticised from the beginning and baptised "the Shame Directive") and the "Facilitation Package", composed of the Facilitation Directive[11] together with its accompanying Council Framework Decision.[12] Some norms can also be found in the Anti-Trafficking Directive.[13] Although it is frequently overlooked, Article 67 TFEU obliges the common immigration policy to respect the rights, freedoms and principles reaffirmed in the Charter of Fundamental Rights of the European Union.

In line with this framework, almost all EU Member States have legislation that criminalise irregular entry and stay as separate offences which might be punished with imprisonment or fines (FRA 2014). The Return Directive has been an object of heightened controversy and has drawn the attention of many scholars, as well as a number of judgments of the Court of Justice of the European Union.[14]

Yet the criminalisation of irregular migrants is not the topic that will be pursued in this chapter. Criminalisation does not stop at migrants themselves but has been progressively expanding to comprise the activity of those who come into contact with actual or even potential irregular migrants. It is, for example, well known that the Carrier Sanctions Directive[15] makes it financially hazardous for shipping companies or airlines to allow on board people who do not have valid visas, which is, arguably, the main reason why refugees and migrants coming to Europe have to resort to smugglers and put their lives at peril instead of taking a plane or a regular ship.

This chapter will focus on the activities which might fall under the Facilitation Directive. Attention has been drawn to the Facilitation Directive because of the so-called solidarity crimes, that is, the criminalisation of acts of help or support to irregular migrants given by those moved by feelings of solidarity or compassion. The range of conduct comprised in solidarity crimes is very extensive: from extreme solidarity acts such as rescuing migrants from the sea or giving them shelter or food in the middle of the winter, to very socially common interaction, such as giving them a lift in the car or inviting them for a coffee in one's own house. Although this might be the most appalling aspect of the Directive and related national legislation, this chapter will also look at other non-charitable activities the criminalisation of which leads to the social

---

11 Council Directive 2002/90/EC of 28 November 2002 defining the facilitation of unauthorised entry, transit and residence (Facilitation Directive), OJ 2002 L 328.

12 Council Framework Decision of 28 November 2002 on the strengthening of the penal framework to prevent the facilitation of unauthorised entry, transit and residence, OJ 2002 L 328.

13 Council Directive 2011/36/EC of 5 April 2011 on preventing and combating trafficking in human beings and protecting its victims, and replacing Council Framework Decision 2002/629/JHA, OJ 2011 L 101.

14 Acosta 2009; Baldaccini 2009; Raffaelli 2016.

15 Council Directive 2001/51/EC, of 28 June 2001, supplementing the provisions of Article 26 of the Convention implementing the Schengen Agreement of 14 June 1985, OJ 2001 L 187, regulates the duty of carriers to return non-admitted third country nationals at their own cost, providing for sanctions against those who transport undocumented migrants into the EU.

exclusion and isolation of irregularly resident migrants. In this section, it will be argued that the indeterminacy of Article 1 of the Facilitation Directive (and related national legislation) criminalises almost every aspect of irregular migrants' lives, the day-to-day social interaction with anyone who treats them *as if they were not criminals*, the most common cases being offering a job or renting a house, but it extends to all sorts of professional provision of goods and services.

The criminalisation of the social interaction with irregular migrants is strictly linked to the spreading of the idea that they are (because they must be treated like) criminals and that regular citizens should (want to) have nothing to do with them. In turn, the forced displacement of irregular migrants towards the realms of illegality (or even criminality), operated by the legislation, increases enormously the vulnerability of irregular migrants to exploitation and abuse, as their illegitimate legal status prevents them from accessing and defending their rights.[16]

7.2.2   Defining punishable assistance

The Facilitation Directive obliges Member States to punish two types of conduct. On the one hand, it establishes the obligation to punish any person who intentionally assists a third-country national to irregularly enter or transit across a Member State (Article 1(1)(a)). On the other hand, it also establishes the obligation to punish anyone who, for financial gain, intentionally assists a third-country national to irregularly reside within the territory of a Member State (Article 1.1(b)).

In relation to the facilitation of irregular entry or transit, Article 1(2) of the Directive allows, but does not compel, the Member States to exempt from punishment the behaviour of those helping others to enter or transit across the territory of a Member State when their intention is to provide "humanitarian assistance to the person concerned". Humanitarian assistance itself is not defined. Yet, the fact that conduct without financial gain is included in the provision and the explicit rejection of an exemption regarding family members[17] have led some authors[18] to argue that "humanitarian assistance" does not mean solidarity assistance but rather conduct, which meets the requirements set by international law for "humanitarian intervention".[19] Furthermore, the Directive makes no reference to international norms or deontological codes that might be in conflict with Article 1(1) of the Directive, such as the UN Convention on the

---

16   A condition named 'Legal isolation' by Provera (2015, 2).
17   An exemption similar to Article 1(2) regarding family members helping irregular entry or transit was dropped during the negotiations in the Council and was not included in the final text of the Directive (Carrera *et al.* 2016, 26).
18   Muñoz 2016.
19   The European Consensus on Humanitarian Aid, for example, stresses the principles of humanity, neutrality, impartiality and independence of humanitarian aid to which all Member States are committed as signatories of the Geneva Conventions of 1949.

law of the sea (UNCLOS) which in Article 98(1) establishes the obligation to provide "assistance to any person found at sea in danger of being lost, and to proceed with all possible speed to rescue".

In relation to the assistance to reside irregularly, the Directive does not give the possibility to Member States to introduce exemptions from punishment. Yet, the definition of the activities punishable under Article 1(1)(b) are delimited by two elements:

- the assistance to irregular residence must be "intentional", and
- must be "for financial gain".

There would remain outside the scope of this provision, therefore, acts which involve the public in general and do not require the identification of the legal status (citizen, regular immigrant, irregular migrant) of the parties (such as selling and buying in shops or supermarkets), since they do not intentionally support irregular residence.

The second element in Article 1(1)(b), financial gain, is more complicated. It seems clear that this element excludes from the scope of application the provision of charity work and gratuitous support or assistance to irregularly residing migrants. But "activities for financial gain" is still a very broad definition and it could comprise any act which helps irregular migrants to remain in the country and involves an economic transaction, e.g. renting an apartment, offering a job, providing legal counselling, etc.

It is noteworthy that the actual endangering or violation of the rights of migrants is not required for the qualification of the conduct under Article 1(1).[20] The Directive seems thus rather clear in directing States to punish people who are not damaging, or intending to damage, the rights of migrants, but are just interacting with them. Some States, on the other hand, have established that the rights of migrants must be affected by the conduct, leaving outside the scope of the national provision those acts of assistance which tend to improve the situation of migrants.[21]

The text of the Directive does not contain much more beyond Article 1.[22] It was the declared aim of the Directive to "provide a definition of the facilitation of illegal immigration" (incipit 4) since a "precise definition of the infringement in question and the cases of exemption" is essential for the approximation of the legal provisions in the Member States (incipit 3). Notwithstanding these intentions, it is precisely the indeterminacy of the kind of conduct aimed at by Article 1 that has raised the alarm regarding both the Directive itself and the domestic legislation adopted to transpose it in the Member States. From the

---

20   The Council Framework Decision requires Member States to ensure custodial sentences with a maximum sentence of not less than eight years if the lives of the migrants are endangered (Article 1.3). The violation of other rights, apart from life, is not contemplated.

21   Spanish Supreme Court, Judgement 1378/2011, 14th December [RJ 2012/453]. Also, for example, the Italian legislation which punishes only those who rent apartments to irregular migrants at prices above the average price for the area.

22   Article 2 extends the obligation to punish also those who instigate, attempt to commit, or are accomplices in the acts contemplated in Article 1(1)(a) or (b).

definition in the Directive it is difficult to know what is the harm that Directive wants to prevent or which is the good protected by the norm. In this respect, the Directive can be usefully compared to the UN Protocol against the Smuggling of Migrants[23] which was adopted two years earlier.

The UN Protocol directs, as the Directive does, State Parties to treat the smuggling of migrants as a criminal offence (Article 6(1)). Yet smuggling of migrants is defined as the "procurement, in order to obtain, directly or indirectly, a financial or other material benefit, of the illegal entry of a person" (Article 3(a)). Also enabling a person to remain illegally in the territory of the State is to be punished, according to Article 6(1)(c) of the UN Protocol, but only when it is done by producing, procuring or providing fraudulent travel or identity documents or by other illegal means. The UN Protocol also contains a clause (Article 19) which establishes that nothing in the Protocol shall affect the rights, responsibilities and obligations of the State or the individuals under international law, including humanitarian and human rights law, with specific mention of the Refugee Convention and its Protocol.

We can therefore note that, on the one hand, the UN Protocol has a much more delimited definition of the punishable conduct. Firstly, because the Protocol is a norm supplementing a Convention aimed at fighting international organised crime. Thus, it defines its own scope of application accordingly in relation to conduct which is transnational and involves an organised criminal group (Article 4). This element, the involvement of an organised criminal group, which is missing in the European norm,[24] is essential for determining the purpose of the legislation. Secondly because it promotes the persecution of activities which are both illegal and intended to produce financial or other material benefit. Differently from the European understanding of facilitation of irregular entry, in the UN Protocol migrant smuggling must be intended for profit; and differently from the European definition of facilitation of irregular residence, which only requires the irregular status of the migrant and the financial gain, the UN Protocol further delimits these actions to those committed through the use of illegal means such as the facilitation of false documentation.

As a result, the aim of the UN Protocol is also more clearly and consistently defined. The Protocol's direction to punish smuggling is clearly placed in the fight against transnational organised criminal groups, because these groups have made a blooming business out of the violation of the States' borders and sovereignty (and their migration legislation). In fact, States are the first victims of migrant smuggling mentioned in the Preamble of the Protocol. However, the UN Protocol adds, smuggling of migrants can also endanger the lives and security of the migrants involved and, therefore, in its provisions the Protocol

---

23 UN Protocol against the Smuggling of Migrants by Land, Sea and Air, Supplementing the United Nations Convention against Transnational Organized Crime, 15 November 2000.

24 It is one of the circumstances for which the States should impose custodial sentences with a maximum sentence of not less than eight years, according to Article 1.3 of the Council Framework Decision.

establishes that migrants shall not be liable to criminal prosecution for having been the object of the conduct persecuted in the norm (which is the transnational, criminal and organised procurement of illegal entry) (Article 5).

Throughout the text, the UN Protocol refers to smuggled migrants as objects of the persecuted conduct and stresses the importance of guaranteeing their rights and well-being in different moments (Articles 2, 4, 6, 16 and 19). From the text of the Directive, and even more so from the EU Plan against migrant smuggling,[25] this clear distinction between smugglers and smuggled migrants is blurred. For the European norm, smuggled migrants are not simply objects of persecuted criminal conduct. They play an active part in that conduct. In relation to smuggled migrants, the action of the EU is not directed primarily at protecting their safety and rights but, as the EU Plan against migrant smuggling shows clearly, at deterrence. In order to deter potential irregular migrants from engaging smugglers, the EU Directive and the EU Plan do not aim only – as the UN Protocol does – at the criminal networks of smugglers but rather at making the risk, the price and their day-to-day life as irregular migrants in Europe not worth their coming at all.

The European Union's database EUR-Lex shows that the Directive has now been transposed into national legislation in almost all Member States.[26] Some recent reports (Provera 2015) show that the legislation passed in transposition of the Directive has been used to prosecute a broader target[27] than the "ruthless networks of smugglers with high returns and low risk" that the European Commission presented as the security threat that justified the norm. Although the 2015 EU Plan against smuggling arrives more than a decade after the deadline for the transposition of the Facilitation Directive, it does not contain a proper evaluation of the implementation of the Facilitation Package. It does acknowledge, however, the risk of expanding criminalisation to those providing humanitarian assistance. A recent study commissioned by the European Commission has indeed found that the Facilitation Directive has had profound unintended consequences for irregular migrants, people and the organisations assisting them, and society in general in terms of social trust and social cohesion.[28]

---

25   EU Action Plan against migrant smuggling (2015-2020) (COM(2015) 285).
26   With the exception of Estonia, Malta and Austria. Denmark did not take part in the adoption of the Directive, and is not bound by it or subject to its application (Incipit 8 of the Directive).
27   Data on the effective implementation of the Directive is scarce and does not disaggregate by type of conduct. However, Provera (2015) reports that in Germany one third of sentences for assistance have been passed against family members.
28   Carrera 2016.

7.3   Breaking the law (1): the protection of religious freedom

A first route to arguing cases in which national legislation deriving from the Facilitation Directive has been violated is that the contested action is a religious practice and, therefore, it is covered by the protection of religious freedom under Article 9 ECHR. These are cases where individuals or groups claim that their faith requires them to welcome and assist the foreigner and that in doing so they are practising their religious beliefs.

7.3.1   Thou shalt love thy neighbour as thyself: caring for others as a religious practice

On a first look, faith-based assistance to migrants can be understood as acts of charity, compassion and mercy mandated by religious sacred texts and religious teachings. Faith based organisations (FBOs) and Church communities have long played a front-line role in the support and integration of migrants, asylum seekers and refugees, as well as other marginalised groups in our society. Religious organisations offer a range of goods and services, such as shelter, food, education, health care, legal counselling, as well as moral support and spiritual comfort. The mission statements of many religious organisations report these activities as direct expression and realisation of their faith. Many mention passages of the Bible, for example, where those activities are required behaviour:

> *Come, blessed of my Father, inherit the Kingdom prepared*
> *for you from the foundation of the world; for I was hungry,*
> *and you gave me food to eat. I was thirsty, and you gave me*
> *drink. I was a stranger, and you took me in. I was naked,*
> *and you clothed me. I was sick, and you visited me. I was in*
> *prison, and you came to me. (...) Most certainly I tell you,*
> *because you did it to one of the least of these my brothers,*
> *you did it to me.*[29]

Also, different denominations' religious teachings include benevolent acts among the expression of faith and the expected behaviour of believers. The Works of Mercy, for example, which are charitable actions through which believers help others both in their spiritual and in their material needs, play a significant role in the Social Doctrine of the Catholic Church as well as for other Christian denominations.[30]

---

29   Matthew 25:31-40.
30   The Works of Mercy might be corporal or spiritual. Corporal works include: to feed the hungry, to give water to the thirsty, to clothe the naked, to shelter the homeless, to visit the sick and the imprisoned, to bury the dead, and to give alms to the poor. The spiritual works include: to instruct the ignorant, to counsel the doubtful, to admonish the sinners, to bear

As we have discussed in the preceding section, under the Facilitation Directive charity work aimed at the support of irregularly residing migrants falls outside the scope of Article 1(1)(b), which requires financial gain.[31] Yet, on a closer look, faith-based assistance to irregular migrants goes beyond charity understood as gratuitous assistance (i.e. giving alms to the poor) to fall under a more complex understanding of charity as love. Based on the second half of the Great Commandment (Thou shalt love thy neighbour as thyself), this understanding of charity and compassion is not limited to providing for those dispossessed or unable to provide for themselves, but more generally is directed at promoting a feeling of solidarity with the others, to reach out and care for our neighbours. The definition of who is the neighbour is contained in the Samaritan Parable in the Bible, which commends the action of the Samaritan who helped a stranger in need but, more to the point, it does so by contrasting the Samaritan's behaviour with the actions of those who "passed by on the other side" and were indifferent. The contrasting conduct is thus not that of the robbers who had inflicted the harm but that of those who did not care and did not offer to help.

Under this understanding of charity, efforts to assist irregular migrants according to the teachings of their faith might include actions which are either not gratuitous (and thus meet the requirement of financial gain) or that are of support for non-gratuitous acts. Believers or faith-based organisations could, for example, either offer jobs to migrants or rent them accommodation or other goods and services or – more frequently – help migrants to find jobs, rented accommodation, transport or any other goods or services. Religious organisations can spend their contacts and influence as intermediaries between the irregular migrants and the wider society (or sympathetic segments of the wider society) in helping the former overcome distance, fears and prejudice created by the social isolation of irregular migrants. In doing so they are thus facilitating irregular migrants to function normally in society, offering them access to work or accommodation, making up for the legal isolation and the vulnerability which immigration law produces. This kind of action by faith-based organisations or their members, even when it does not meet in itself the requirement of financial gain, facilitates an action (the renting of the apartment, the hiring of the migrant person, the provision of goods or services) which does and is therefore punishable, as accomplices, under Article 2(b) of the Directive.

I shall assess, therefore, whether this kind of assistance can fall under the meaning of religious manifestation in Article 9 ECHR and should be protected

---

patiently those who wrong us, to forgive offences, to comfort the afflicted and to pray for the living and the dead.

31 The fact that they cannot be criminally prosecuted does not entail that charitable activities are not affected by the turn to criminalisation of irregular migration and those assisting them. Among the "unintended effects" of the Directive, some organisations have reported the discontinuation of EU funding to support humanitarian assistance to irregular migrants as well as confusion among civil society organisations about how the Facilitation Directive might affect their work (Carrera 2016, 26).

from State interference (through an exemption from criminal liability, for example).

7.3.2 Stretching the argument under Article 9 ECHR beyond charity

Article 9 ECHR protects freedom of thought, conscience and religion. Freedom of religion is traditionally considered a primordial right and the ECtHR has declared this to be its understanding too.[32] Yet, notwithstanding its importance within human rights systems, case-law on freedom of religion has kept a low-profile for a long time[33] and although it has been rapidly expanding lately there are still a number of controversial issues.

This freedom has been traditionally seen from a double angle: the internal forum, which refers to the ideas formed within an individual conscience and the external forum, which consists in the manifestation of those ideas. Article 9 establishes the absolute protection of the internal forum, i.e. the right to have, adopt or change religious beliefs, as well as the right not to have religious beliefs.[34] It establishes also protection for the external forum, for the manifestations of those religious beliefs, although in this case this protection is not absolute and can be limited according to the criteria set out in paragraph 2. In Article 9(1), external manifestations of religion include worship, teaching, practice and observance.

To determine whether the protection of external manifestations under Article 9 cover the cases of assistance to irregular migrants punishable under the Facilitation Directive (and related domestic legislation), there is a "checklist"[35] of five questions that have to be answered. The first two questions refer to the applicability of Article 9(1) to the case at hand.

The first question in our checklist is: *Does our case fall within the scope of Article 9?* Article 9.1 protects external manifestations of religious beliefs both in the private and the public spheres; they are considered an integral part of the

---

32 In its first judgement on freedom of religion, the Court stated that "[F]reedom of thought, conscience and religion is one of the foundations of a 'democratic society' within the meaning of the Convention. (...) The pluralism indissociable from a democratic society, which has been dearly won over the centuries, depends on it". ECtHR 25 May 1993, 14307/88, *Kokkinakis v. Greece*, para. 31.

33 This has been attributed not only to the high level of protection that freedom of religion enjoyed in Europe (as compared to other parts of the world) but also the restrictive approach towards this article taken first by the former European Commission of Human Rights and, later on, by the ECtHR. The first case on freedom of religion was decided in 1993, and case law on Article 9 started to increase (together with scholarly literature on this matter) from the mid-2000s.

34 The absolute protection of the internal forum is, according to the Court, reflected in the wording of Article 9 para. 2: "Unlike the second paragraphs of Articles 8, 10 and 11 which cover all the rights mentioned in the first paragraphs of those Articles, that of Article 9 refers only to 'freedom to manifest one's religion or belief'". *Kokkinakis, cit.*, para. 33.

35 Determined jointly by the wording of Article 9 and the reasoning of the ECtHR, this checklist is the backbone of argumentation in Article 9 cases and constitutes a common layout in guides on the implementation of Article 9 (Murdoch 2007); CoE 2015).

protected right: "bearing witness in words and deeds is bound up with the existence of religious convictions".[36] Moreover, in the determination of whether assistance to irregular migrants punishable under Articles 1(1) or 2(b) of the Facilitation Directive falls within the scope of "religious practice" within the meaning of Article 9, it must be borne in mind that States' religious neutrality excludes any discretion on their part to determine whether religious beliefs or the means used to express such beliefs are legitimate.[37]

For a long time, under the influence of the early restrictive interpretative line of the former Commission (ECmHR), the established understanding was that the term "practice" refers to acts prescribed by religion but did not cover every act motivated or influenced by a religion or belief.[38] Establishing whether a manifestation is prescribed or merely inspired by religion can be less than straightforward and, more often than not, would involve the States' courts (or the ECtHR) in the determination of questions of theological conformity which would exceed the boundaries of the principle of neutrality. Some retreat from this restrictive and troublesome line of argumentation can be observed lately: in *Eweida*, for example, the ECtHR specified that whereas there must be a "sufficiently close and direct nexus between the act and the underlying belief" this is a matter to be determined on the facts of each case: in particular, it cannot be assumed that only recognised acts of worship or devotion or the fulfilment of duties mandated by religion constitute protected manifestations of belief.[39]

In the case at hand, assistance to irregular migrants either as gratuitous provision of basic needs or as support to avoid their being isolated and vulnerable to harm and exploitation in society can be considered a manifestation of religion, commanded in religious texts and practised as such by many people both individually and in faith-based organisations. It is irrelevant to the case, according to *Eweida*, that this manifestation is not considered a rite, that it might not have the strength of a religious obligation, or that it is not a practice undertaken by the majority of believers.

Once we have established that assistance to irregular migrants can be understood as a religious manifestation, we must then answer question number 2 of the checklist: "*Has there been any interference with Article 9 rights?*" It is the combination of an interference with the lack of justification, under the criteria of Article 9.2, which determines the existence of a violation of the rights in Article 9. The ECtHR has maintained that not only the imposition of religious practices upon individuals but also the restrictions placed upon individual action

---

36 *Kokkinakis, cit.*, para. 31.

37 ECtHR 26 September 1996, 18747/91, *Manoussakis a.o. v. Greece*, para. 47; also, ECtHR 26 October 2000, 30985/96, *Hasan and Chaush v. Bulgaria*, para. 78.

38 The leading case on this line of reasoning was *Arrowsmith v. the United Kingdom*, where the distribution of leaflets encouraging soldiers not to go to Northern Ireland was considered inspired by the pacifist beliefs of the applicant, but not a direct manifestation of those beliefs. ECmHR of 16 May 1977, 7050/75, *Pat Arrowsmith v. the United Kingdom* (dec).

39 ECtHR 15 January 2013, 48420/10, 59842/10, 51671/10 & 36516/10, *Eweida a.o. v. the United Kingdom*, para. 82.

or behaviour mandated by belief fall within the scope of Article 9. In the case at hand, following the Facilitation Directive States have put on those actions arguably the harshest restriction possible in a democratic society (i.e. criminal liability).

Over the years, the Convention organs have established that a restriction imposed on the manifestations of religious beliefs does not necessarily amount to interference under Article 9. This was the case, for example, if the persons involved had other means to manifest their religion (by changing jobs or by expressing their religion outside the professional sphere, for example).[40] In *Eweida*, the Court moved away from that line and stated that "rather than holding that the possibility of changing job would negate any interference with the right, the better approach would be to weigh that possibility in the overall balance when considering whether or not the restriction was proportionate".[41]

The Convention organs, especially the ECmHR, have also seemed reluctant to perceive an interference with religious manifestation when the acts do not directly express the belief concerned or are only remotely connected.[42] This has been particularly consistent in the case where religious grounds were pitted against general legislation.[43] However, in this respect it is important to recall that even when general legislation applies "on a neutral basis without any link whatsoever with an applicant's personal beliefs",[44] it may still have a differentiated impact on certain groups and therefore, according to the *Thlimmenos* doctrine, discriminatory interference could result when "States, without an objective and reasonable justification, fail to treat differently persons whose situations are significantly different".[45]

After establishing that a manifestation of religious belief has been interfered with, the checklist continues with three questions which assess whether the interference is justified under the criteria set out in Article 9(2). It is only if the interference with religious manifestation is not justified that we have a violation of freedom of religion. States' interference, to be justified, must comply with three cumulative requirements: the limitation must be prescribed by law, must have a legitimate aim, and must be necessary in a democratic society.

The fourth question is therefore, *"Is the limitation on manifestation of religion prescribed by law?"* In the case at hand, this is an uncontroversial question, since the transposition of the Facilitation Directive required the constitution of criminal offences and these must be provided by law. The fifth question in the checklist is: *"Does the limitation on manifestation of religion*

---

40 ECtHR 13 April 2006, 55170/00, *Kosteski v. the former Yugoslav Republic of Macedonia*; ECtHR 2 October 2001, 49853/99, *Pichon and Sajous v. France* (dec.).
41 *Eweida, cit.*, para. 83.
42 ECtHR 3 December 2009, 40010/04, *Skugar a.o. v. Russia* (dec.).
43 ECtHR 15 December 1983, 10358/83, *C. v. the United Kingdom* (dec.); ECtHR 18 July 1986, 11991/86, *H. and B. v. the United Kingdom* (dec.); ECtHR 18 February 1993, 20747/92, *Bouessel du Bourg v. France* (dec.); *Skugar, cit.*
44 *Skugar, cit.*, p. 8.
45 ECtHR 6 April 2000, 34369/97, *Thlimmenos v. Greece*, para. 44.

have a legitimate aim?" This question aims at determining whether the limitation imposed by the State protects one (or more) of the legitimate aims listed in Article 9.2: "in the interests of public safety, for the protection of public order, health and morals, or for the protection of the rights and freedoms of others". Scholarship recognises that the interpretation that the Court has made of these aims is rather "nebulous"[46] and that respondent States do not find great difficulty in showing that they were pursuing one or more of those, very broad, aims. In the case at hand, it is likely that the Court would accept public safety, public order and the rights of others as aims being pursued by anti-smuggling legislation, notwithstanding the defective legislative technique, already present in the Directive, which hints at all these aims without focusing on any.[47]

So, we reach the last question of the checklist, the test where the real stakes are, "*Is the limitation on manifestation of religion necessary in a democratic society?*" This question must be answered through a triple test: the interference must:

    a) correspond to a pressing social need,

    b) it must be proportionate to the legitimate aim pursued, and

    c) it must be justified.

Stopping the "ruthless networks" of profiteering smugglers and preventing the suffering and exploitation of smuggled migrants are compelling interests. Yet, necessary does not mean simply 'admissible', 'ordinary', 'useful', 'reasonable' or 'desirable',[48] there must be proportionality and justifying reasons to make the interference necessary in a democratic society. In the case under examination, the proportionality test would raise doubts on the Facilitation Directive's lack of exemptions from punishment for those actions which follow religious commands which have the aim of protecting the life and well-being of others.[49]

The lack of determinacy and the incoherence of the aims pursued by the Directive; the lack of concluding evidence on the capacity of these measures to stop criminal networks; the contrasting evidence on the unintended criminalisation of those helping others out of compassion; and the vulnerability of irregular migrants themselves, could all be powerful arguments for maintaining that making a criminal offence out of the religious mandate to love your neighbour is unnecessary in a democratic society and that the Facilitation Directive (and related national regulation) unjustifiably interferes with the religious practices of those who welcome, assist and support irregular migrants to lead decent human lives in European societies.

---

46   Harris *et al.* 2009, p. 436.

47   At the time of writing this, the Court has just issued the judgement in ECtHR 20 June 2017, 67667/09, *Bayev a.o. v. Russia* (request for referral to the Grand Chamber is pending), based almost only on the discussion of the legitimate character of the aims pursued by the anti-gay propaganda law. Maybe in the future the Court will not be so easily convinced by the legitimacy of declared aims and will look further into their plausibility and effectivity.

48   ECtHR 7 December 1976, 5493/72, *Handyside v. the United Kingdom*, para. 48.

49   *Thlimmenos, cit.*

7.4 Breaking the law (2): conscientious objection

The second route for cases of infringement of legislation deriving from the Facilitation Directive is to argue that the contested actions were dictated by conscience. When confronted with the mandate of the legislation, the transgressor felt that complying with it would violate deeply held convictions and therefore the contested action should be protected by an exemption, a right to conscientious objection to the law.

7.4.1 Arguments for conscience and conscientious objection under Article 9 ECHR

There are people who violate national provisions transposing the Facilitation Directive out of a sentiment of human decency, because they are convinced that it is contrary to the very idea of human dignity and human rights to let irregular migrants drown in the sea, or die or suffer in their transit through Europe, or be left in the hedgerows of our societies, prey to criminal networks and heartless individuals that will abuse them and make profit out of their vulnerable condition.[50] These convictions and the impulse to act on them is dictated by their conscience; they think that the indifference towards the suffering of irregular migrants, which is commanded by the law, is contrary to their most deeply held convictions about the relationship with, and the treatment of, others. For our argument here, I shall make no differentiation if that conscience and deeply held convictions have been formed through religious teachings or without any reference to religion. If the former, these conscience cases are different from those we have seen in the previous section because the contested conduct is not considered, by the claimant, as a religious practice.[51]

Notwithstanding the expanding jurisprudence under Article 9 ECHR, arguing these cases in Strasbourg would be an arduous task. Restrictive and limited as the understanding of religious freedom of the ECtHR has been argued to be, the right to freedom of conscience and the protection that individuals might derive from it is even less certain. I shall argue here that these kinds of cases would give the ECtHR a remarkable opportunity both for updating and upgrading the interpretation of freedom of conscience, and developing a substantive right.

---

50 I have argued elsewhere that I do not agree with the conception of vulnerability as a condition of human beings as human, but I rather see it as a condition of certain (groups of) individuals who are left without the forms of protection that society affords to those not seen as vulnerable (Morondo, 2016). The exposure of irregular migrants to abuse and rights violations is a very poignant case of this understanding of vulnerability.

51 For example, one of the applicants in *Eweida*, Ms. Ladele, did not present her refusal to perform ceremonies of or register civil partnerships for homosexual couples as a manifestation of her religious beliefs but rather as a conscientious objection based on her religious convictions regarding homosexuality.

The ECtHR's case law on Article 9 is dominated by cases on religion and it is therefore difficult to find what is distinctive about the other two rights thereby contained: freedom of thought and freedom of conscience.[52] Furthermore, there is no definition of religion either in the text of the Convention or in the case law. The Convention organs have not developed any specific notion to distinguish external manifestations of conscience from external manifestations of religion and the terms "beliefs" and, less frequently, "convictions" are used for expressions of a religious and non-religious nature. I shall address the limitations which this lack of delimitation puts on the protection of conscience in the next section. Here I shall examine first the two paths open for our assistance out of conscience cases: either they could present the contested conduct as a manifestation of conscience which constitutes a belief under Article 9, or they could argue that the dictates of conscience prevent them from acting according to the law and thus present a case f for conscientious objection.

In the first case, the argument is similar to what we have seen in the preceding section in relation to religious practices, since our applicants would argue that their conduct is a manifestation of a philosophical or moral belief within the meaning of Article 9(1). There are, however, some particularities in relation to the first two questions of the checklist, i.e. whether the conduct is a manifestation of a belief and whether it has been interfered with.

Article 9 has a potentially very wide scope of protection[53] since it protects not only the right to manifest one's religion but also one's beliefs. This is a wider safeguard than traditional religious freedom clauses because it encompasses personal, political, philosophical and moral beliefs and convictions. Yet, these personal beliefs and convictions need to demonstrate that they are more than just either opinions or motivations to claim the protection of Article 9. The Court has constantly required that these convictions attain a certain level of cogency, seriousness, cohesion and importance,[54] that they express a coherent view on basic issues, that they denote convictions which are worthy of respect in a democratic society and which are not incompatible with human dignity,[55] and that they have an identifiable formal content.[56] This attempt at distinguishing mere opinions or motivations from the convictions or beliefs covered by Article 9.1 has led, in practice, to uncertainty, especially so in those

---

52 I shall not discuss here freedom of thought. For this right, the scholarship directs us mostly to the case-law of the former ECmHR (Renucci 2005). Freedom of thought is understood as pertaining to the only internal forum and prohibits the State to interfering with it (ECmHR 11 October 1991, 16311/90, 16312/90 and 16313/90, *Hazar, Hazar and Açik v. Turkey* (dec.)). Like freedom of religion, and differently from freedom of conscience, freedom of thought might be claimed by legal entities as well as by individuals (ECmHR 12 October 1988, 11921/86, *Verein "Kontakt-Information-Therapie" (KIT) and Hagen v. Austria* (dec.)). External manifestation of thought may be protected under Article 10 (freedom of expression) and Article 11 (freedom of association).

53 Renucci 2005.

54 ECtHR 25 February 1982, 7511/76, *Campbell and Cosans v. UK.*

55 *Campbell and Cosans v. UK*, para. 36.

56 ECtHR 15 May 1980, 8317/78, *T. McFeeley v. UK.*

cases which cannot count on a religion to work as the supporting coherent system required by the Court.[57]

In the cases under examination, it is more likely than in the cases under the preceding section that the Court does not find that the moral or philosophical convictions of those assisting migrants out of a sentiment of human decency or by virtue of their understanding of human dignity and human rights constitute "convictions or belief" within the meaning of Article 9 or that the expression of these convictions has been interfered with by the adoption of criminal legislation to fight against irregular migration and human smugglers. Applicants, therefore, should highlight human rights as a political philosophy which imposes duties both on the States and on individuals in society (horizontal effect), to try to move the case into the requirements of paragraph 2 of Article 9, which would work as discussed in the previous section, the main argument being that of the disproportionate relationship between a "blanket ban" and the (uncertain) aims of the legislation.

The second path opened in the argument for freedom of conscience is that of conscientious objection. Conscientious objection is raised when the law demands that one acts in a way which is contrary to the dictates of the individual's conscience, to deeply held moral convictions about the rights and the wrongs of one's own behaviour. Generally, conscientious objection consists in the refusal to perform an action commanded by the law (join the army, provide reproductive health services, register homosexual couples, etc.) whereas the cases under examination consist in the realisation of conduct which is prohibited by law. Yet, they can be easily considered from a reverse perspective, more fitting to traditional conscientious objection cases: the law demands abstaining or refraining from certain actions (assisting irregular migrants), but the individual's conscience compels that action. The conscientious objectors in our cases refuse to be indifferent and to not help.

Conscientious objection is, in principle, not protected by Article 9 ECtHR. From the early former Commission case law, the Convention organs have consistently maintained that Article 9 does not guarantee the right to always behave in public in a manner governed by the individual's convictions or beliefs. In particular, "general legislation which applies on a neutral basis without any link whatsoever with an applicant's personal beliefs cannot in principle be regarded as an interference with his or her rights under Article 9".[58] The Convention organs have thus consistently recognised the power of the State to introduce or not exemption clauses on grounds of conscience in particular pieces of legislation.[59]

---

57 Contrast for example, the acceptance of opposition to abortion or to homosexual marriages as convictions within the meaning of Article 9(1) (in *Pinchon and Sajous* and in *Eweida*), with the swift refusal to consider convictions regarding end-of-life situations equally included in Pretty.

58 *Skugar, cit.*

59 *Eweida, cit.* para 105-106.

It is illustrative in this respect the case law on conscientious objection to military service, which has been, since 2011, the only form of conscientious objection recognised by the ECtHR as being protected by Article 9. Yet, the argument of the Court makes it clear that this protection is not enshrined as such in Article 9,[60] but derives from the virtually general consensus which has evolved among the member States of the Council of Europe, along with other relevant international instruments.[61]

In the case at hand, we must also take into account that the Facilitation Directive does not allow for conscientious objections as such. Facilitation of entry and transit might be exempted when it is intended to offer humanitarian assistance, but as we have already noted, humanitarian is not here a synonym for a solidarity conscience but rather a reference to the requirements of humanitarian intervention under international law.

We must also take into account that there are particular cases within the broad conduct of punishable assistance where conscientious objection might be sustained by sectorial or professional deontological codes. As the Facilitation Directive has not taken those into account either, the command not to intervene might create a conflict of obligations for certain actors: fishing or leisure boats' crews and occupants encountering migrants in distress on the high seas, for example, are under an international law obligation to help them to shore; doctors are under a deontological obligation to provide care to anyone without discrimination; and even average citizens might find themselves under the obligation to assist irregular migrants in situations of necessity or when omission of help would also be punishable.

7.4.2   Conscience, conscientious objection and general obedience to the law

It is only prudent to observe that the ECtHR's approach to conscientious objection to legislation enacted by democratic States with internal mechanisms for the protection of fundamental rights is bound to be very cautious. Taking into account the supranational and subsidiary role of the Court and the controversial and highly political nature of migration management it is more likely that the Court will acknowledge the results of domestic or international processes of civil disobedience rather than trigger them.

---

60 In fact, it has taken decades of inadmissible or dismissed military objector cases before arriving at ECtHR 7 July 2011, 23459/03, *Bayatyan v. Armenia*. See, for example: ECmHR 12 December 1966, 2299/64, *Grandrath v. Germany* (dec.); ECmHR 2 April 1973, 5591/72, *G.Z. v. Austria* (dec.); ECmHR 7 March 1977, 7565/76, *Conscientious Objectors v. Denmark* (dec.); ECmHR 11 October 1984, 10410/83, *N. v. Sweden* (dec.); ECmHR 7 March 1996, 20972/92, *Raninen v. Finland* (dec.).

61 *Bayatyan, cit.*, para. 108. Together with the consideration that the Convention is a "living instrument" the Court dissociates itself from the previous reasoning of the ECmHR, whereby the application of Art. 9 was hindered by the wording of Art. 4.3(b), which explicitly excluded military service or the service exacted instead of compulsory military service from the definition of prohibited "forced or compulsory labour".

Yet, even if effective remedy in Strasbourg is still far away, arguing these conscience cases from the point of view of Article 9 not only gives them a human rights backing and recognisable language, but would also improve the Convention – as a living instrument – to meet the requirements of the consciences of today.[62]

It is unclear among the scholarship and in the case law of the ECtHR what is the relationship established between conscience and the notion of protected "religion and beliefs" that the Court has polished over the years. Indeed, several possibilities have been presented. For some authors, freedom of conscience is just a "negative" right as freedom of thought, referring solely to the internal forum. As such, its protection is absolute. The manifestations of conscience could be protected under Articles 8, 10 or 11, for example. This might have been the understanding of the Convention organs, which tended to view Article 9 as protecting the internal forum and was ready to examine violations of manifestations under other Convention Articles.

Others, however, have argued that freedom of conscience would have no significance if its external manifestations were not protected. These external manifestations may amount to beliefs within the meaning of Article 9.1[63] or, for some few authors (and some dissenting opinions of the ECtHR[64]) they are protected by a general right to conscientious objection.[65] Legal theory, more than case law, has sought to clarify the concept of freedom of conscience.[66] Chiassoni has argued convincingly that freedom of conscience is "the legal projection of individuals' moral autonomy" and, as such, is at the very foundation of liberal democratic States.[67] Freedom of conscience is thus protected, first of all, by the delimitation, for every individual, of a private sphere of autonomy. The greater this unregulated sphere of legal permission, the greater

---

62 Notwithstanding the growing role which is attributed to religion in public life (and which is in my opinion caused by xenophobic over-visibility of Islam-related questions and demands), the data suggests that Europeans' consciences, their understanding of themselves and their relationships in society, are ever less ruled by religious norms or dictates. See, for example: ECmHR 12 December 1966, 2299/64, *Grandrath v. Germany* (dec.); ECmHR 2 April 1973, 5591/72, *G.Z. v. Austria* (dec.); ECmHR 7 March 1977, 7565/76, *Conscientious Objectors v. Denmark* (dec.); ECmHR 11 October 1984, 10410/83, *N. v. Sweden* (dec.); ECmHR 7 March 1996, 20972/92, *Raninen v. Finland* (dec.). On the other hand, human rights and related values play an important role in determining behaviour which was shaped by religious norms in the past. See: European Commission (2012), *The values of Europeans*, Standard Eurobarometer 77 spring 2012, Luxembourg: European Commission.

63 For example: *Pretty, cit.*, examined under Article 8, similar to ECtHR 23 June 1993, 12875/87, *Hoffmann v. Austria*, and ECtHR 16 December 2003, 64927/01, *Palau-Martinez v. France*. Also, under Article 10: ECtHR 12 July 2001, 29032/95, *Feldek v. Slovakia,* or Article 11: ECtHR 10 July 1998, 26695/95, *Sidiropoulos and Others v. Greece*, ECtHR 29 April 1999, 25088/94, 28331/95 and 28443/95, *Chassagnou and Others v. France*, and ECtHR 17 February 2004, 39748/98, *Maestri v. Italy*.

64 *Eweida, cit.*, joint partly dissenting opinion of Judges Vučinič and De Gaetano.

65 Chiassoni 2011, 55.

66 Renucci 2005; Chiassoni 2011.

67 Chiassoni 2011, 50.

plurality of views on behaviour will be admitted. Chiassoni reminds, though, that in a liberal democracy these behaviours cannot be imposed on others, they are admitted only in the individuals' reserved sphere of autonomy. Indeed, the case law of the Convention organs shows the development towards this more liberal understanding of freedom of conscience, obliging the States not to interfere and permitting thus greater space for diversity of individual choices.

However, theoretical – as well as jurisprudential – difficulties with freedom of conscience become less clear when individuals' consciences clash with what is sometimes conceived of as a form of "collective conscience".[68] On the one hand, the law brings with it the pretence of being generally obeyed. In fact, to admit that any individual conscience might be the basis for exemptions from compliance with the law would turn it into an ensemble of suggestions.[69] General obedience to the law is, from the perspective of the legal system, a closure norm. In fact, not only a differing opinion but also ignorance does not excuse the individual from complying with the law (*Ignorantia juris non excusat*). Yet, from a moral and a political point of view, there is no general obligation to obey the law (), and thus it has been argued that a general right to conscientious objection might act as a safety relief valve in liberal democratic States.

In the cases under examination, there is the additional particularity that applicants would not be representative of a minority worldview seeking a counter-majority guaranteed from their individual freedom; on the contrary, their conscience is an expression of the fundamental values of the system and what they are objecting to is the limitation of human rights and human dignity operated by the law on the basis of other political aims, not all of them legitimate for the purpose of limiting human rights (border security, labour market stability, electoral calculations).

7.5   Conclusions

It is common parlance that Europe is suffering a "migration crisis" which, combined with the financial crisis and the terrorist attacks in European cities, have created an emergency, a tragic situation which needs order and drastic decisions to return to enjoying peace, security and rights. Independently of how much of all this is empirically true, it is certain, however, that it is a discourse which has produced real effects: European political discourse and policies have offered ever more frequently trade-offs between rights and security.

---

68   Zucca 2013.

69   This point has been made by Courts or governments themselves when called upon an eventual right to conscientious objection. E.g., the English Government in *Pretty*, quoting Dr Johnson, argued that: "[f]irst, laws are not made for particular cases but for men in general. Second, to permit a law to be modified at discretion is to leave the community without law." (*Pretty, cit.*, 29).

The legislation examined in this chapter is an example of this. The Facilitation Directive has directed the Member States to approach and treat questions of irregular migration from a perspective which blatantly ignores human rights. The human rights of irregular migrants, which are rendered more vulnerable by the legal and social isolation to which they are earmarked; but also – and this has been the focus of this chapter – the human rights of those who, out of religious obligation or conscience requirement, refuse to treat irregular migrants as if they were criminals and collaborate in their social isolation.

I have tested the protection (and the limits thereof) that Article 9 ECHR could offer to those who engage in conduct which violates national provisions transposing Articles 1(1) and 1(2) of the Directive, in two distinct cases: when the conduct is commanded by religious texts or teachings and can, therefore, be understood as a religious practice; and when complying with the law would violate the conscience of the transgressor, especially when that conscience is formed by notions of human dignity and human rights.

References

Acosta, D. (2009), 'The Good, the Bad and the Ugly in EU Migration Law: Is the European Parliament Becoming Bad and Ugly?', *European Journal of Migration and Law* 11(1), p. 19-39.

Baldaccini, A. (2009), 'The Return and Removal of Irregular Migrants under EU Law: An Analysis of the Returns Directive', *European Journal of Migration and Law* 11(1), p. 1-17.

Carrera, S., E. Guild, A. Aliverti, J. Allsopp, M.G. Manieri, M. Levoy (2016), *Fit for purpose? The Facilitation Directive and the criminalisation of humanitarian assistance to irregular migrants,* Brussels: European Parliament.

Chiassoni, P. (2011), *Diritti umani, sentenze elusive, clausole ineffabili. Scritti di realismo militante,* Roma: Aracne Editrice.

Council of Europe (2015), *Guide to Article 9 - Freedom of Thought, Conscience and Religion,* Strasbourg: Council of Europe.

Council of Europe Commissioner for Human Rights (2013), *The protection of migrant rights in Europe*, Report of 18 April 2013.

European Commission (2012), *The values of Europeans*, Standard Eurobarometer 77 spring 2012, Luxembourg: European Commission

FRA (European Union Agency for Fundamental Rights) (2011), *Fundamental rights of migrants in an irregular situation in the European Union,* Luxembourg: Publications Office of the European Union.

FRA (2013), *Fundamental rights at Europe's southern sea borders,* Luxembourg: Publications Office of the European Union.

FRA (2014), *Criminalisation of migrants in an irregular situation and of persons*, Luxembourg: Publications Office of the European Union.

Friðriksdóttir, B. (2016), *What Happened to Equality? The Construction of the Right to Equal Treatment of Third-Country Nationals in European Union Law on Labour Migration*, Leiden-Boston: Brill-Nijhoff.

Harris, J.D., M. O'Boyle, E.P. Bates & C.M. Buckley (2009), *Harris, O'Boyle & Warbrick: Law of the European Convention on Human Rights*, 2nd ed. Oxford: Oxford University Press.

Morondo, D. (2016), '¿Un nuevo paradigma para la igualdad? La vulnerabilidad entre condición humana y situación de indefensión', *Cuadernos Electrónicos de Filosofía del Derecho* 34, p. 205-221.

Muñoz Ruiz, J. (2016), 'La ayuda humanitaria: ¿una excusa absolutoria o una causa de justificación?', *Revista Electrónica de Ciencia Penal y Criminología* 18(8).

Murdoch, J. (2007), *Freedom of thought, conscience and religion. A guide to the implementation of Article 9 of the European Convention on Human Rights*, Human Rights Handbooks, no. 9, Strasbourg: Council of Europe.

Peroni, L. (2014), 'Deconstructing 'Legal' Religion in Strasbourg', *Oxford Journal of Law and Religion* 3(3), p. 235-257.

Provera, M. (2015), *The criminalisation of irregular migration in the European Union*, CEPS Papers on Liberty and Security in Europe nr. 80.

Raffaelli, R. (2016), 'Immigration and Criminal Law: Is there a judge in Luxembourg?', in: B. de Witte, J. A. Mayoral, U. Jaremba, M. Wind, & K. Podstawa (eds.), *National Courts and EU Law. New Issues, Theories and Methods*, Cheltenham & Northampton: Edward Elgar Pub, p. 217-238.

Renucci, J.F. (2005), *Article 9 of the European Convention on Human Rights. Fredom of thought, conscience and religion*, Human Rights Files no. 20, Strasbourg: Council of Europe

United Nations, Human Rights Council, Special rapporteur on the Human Rights of Migrants (F. Crépeau) (2013), *Regional study: management of the external borders of the European Union and its impact on the human rights of migrants*, A/HRC/23/46, 24 April 2013.

Zucca, L. (2013), *Prince or Pariah?: The Place of Freedom of Religion in a System of International Human Rights*, Robert Schuman Centre for Advanced Studies, Working Papers 2013/26.

European Court of Human Rights

ECmHR 12 December 1966	2299/64	*Grandrath v. Germany* (dec.)
ECmHR 2 April 1973	5591/72	*G.Z. v. Austria* (dec.)
ECtHR 7 December 1976	5493/72	*Handyside v. the UK*
ECmHR 7 March 1977	7565/76	*Conscientious Objectors v. Denmark* (dec.)
ECmHR 16 May 1977	7050/75	*Pat Arrowsmith v. the UK* (dec)
ECtHR 15 May 1980	8317/78	*T. McFeeley v. UK*

ECtHR 25 February 1982	7511/76	*Campbell and Cosans v. UK*
ECtHR 15 December 1983	10358/83	*C. v. the United Kingdom* (dec.)
ECmHR 11 October 1984	10410/83	*N. v. Sweden* (dec.)
ECtHR 18 July 1986	11991/86	*H. and B. v. the UK* (dec.)
ECmHR 12 October 1988	11921/86	*Verein "Kontakt-Information-Therapie" (KIT) and Hagen v. Austria* (dec.))
ECmHR 11 October 1991	16311/90, 16312/90 and 16313/90,	*Hazar, Hazar and Açik v. Turkey* (dec.)
ECtHR 18 February 1993	20747/92	*Bouessel du Bourg v. France* (dec.)
ECtHR 25 May 1993	14307/88	*Kokkinakis v. Greece*
ECtHR 23 June 1993	12875/87	*Hoffmann v. Austria*
ECmHR 7 March 1996	20972/92	*Raninen v. Finland* (dec.).
ECtHR 26 September 1996	18747/91	*Manoussakis a.o. v. Greece*
ECtHR 10 July 1998	26695/95	*Sidiropoulos and Others v. Greece*
ECtHR 29 April 1999	25088/94, 28331/95 and 28443/95,	*Chassagnou and* Others v. *France,*
ECtHR 6 April 2000	34369/97	*Thlimmenos v. Greece*
ECtHR 26 October 2000	30985/96	*Hasan and Chaush v. Bulgaria*
ECtHR 12 July 2001	29032/95	*Feldek v. Slovakia*
ECtHR 2 October 2001	49853/99	*Pichon and Sajous v. France* (dec.)
ECtHR 16 December 2003	64927/01	*Palau-Martinez v. France.*
ECtHR 17 February 2004	39748/98	*Maestri v. Italy*
ECtHR 13 April 2006	55170/00	*Kosteski v. the former Yugoslav Republic of Macedonia*
ECtHR 3 December 2009	40010/04	*Skugar a.o. v. Russia* (dec.)
ECtHR 7 July 2011	23459/03	*Bayatyan v. Armenia*
ECtHR 15 January 2013	48420/10, 59842/10, 51671/10 & 36516/10,	*Eweida a.o. v. the UK*
ECtHR 20 June 2017	67667/09	*Bayev a.o. v. Russia* (request for referral to the Grand Chamber is pending),

Spanish Supreme Court

Judgement 14 December 2011	1378/2011	RJ 2012/453

Part 3

Religious Freedom Laws

Chapter 8   Belief and Conscience

Can Europe do without a specific guarantee for religion?

Jim Murdoch

8.1   Introduction

The affirmation of freedom of thought, conscience and religion in constitutional charters and human rights instruments is commonplace,[1] the sentiment that individual conscience and belief must be recognised as binding legal norms at domestic and at international level reflecting the need by States to be seen to be displaying a commitment to upholding the values of pluralism and tolerance. Denial of the freedom of thought, conscience and religion involves denial of recognition of an inherent element of personal autonomy as well as an attack upon a central aspect of an individual's identity as a member of a community defined by religious affiliation. Legal recognition of these rights through ratification of treaty obligations or through domestic constitutional charter constitutes a public affirmation by a State of its recognition of these freedoms as a hallmark of liberal democracy.[2]

Legal recognition in turn implies some element of acceptance of adjudication via the domestic courts or supervision by an international mechanism. This

---

1   For international human rights standards, see e.g., International Covenant on Civil and Political Rights, Art. 18, provides that 'everyone has the right to freedom of thought, conscience and religion. This right includes freedom to have or to adopt a religion or belief of his or her choice, and freedom, either individually or in community with others and in public or private, to manifest his or her religion or belief in worship, observance, practice and teaching. No one can be subject to coercion which would impair his or her freedom to have or to adopt a religion or belief of his or her choice. Freedom to manifest one's religion or beliefs may be subject only to such limitations as are prescribed by law and are necessary to protect public safety, order, health, or morals or the fundamental rights and freedoms of others.' This also provides that States must respect for the liberty of parents and, when applicable, legal guardians to ensure the religious and moral education of their children in conformity with their own convictions. See also: International Convention on the Rights of the Child, Art. 14; and American Convention on Human Rights, Art. 12. For discussion of domestic provisions, see: Iliopoulos-Strangas (*ed*) (2005), *Constitution and Religion*; Uitz (2007), *Freedom of Religion in European Constitutional and International Case Law*; Martinez-Torrón & Durham (*eds*) (2010), *Religion and the Secular State: National Reports*; Ferrari & Pastorelli (2012), *Religion in Public Spaces*; Dingemans (2013), *The Protections for Religious Rights: Law and Practice*.

2   ECtHR 25 May 1993, 14307/88, *Kokkinakis v Greece*, para 31.

chapter addresses the question of whether international judicial consideration of domestic protection for freedom of thought, conscience and religion has enhanced the flourishing of permitted religious freedom, but it does so from the narrow standpoint of the regional system of protection for human rights in Europe. In short, what specifically has been the outcome of the inclusion of Article 9 of the European Convention of Human Rights in practical terms, when viewed through the prism of the case law of the European Court of Human Rights? The argument to be made is that freedom of thought, conscience and religion is not indispensable where the overall system for human rights protection is highly-developed as it is on this continent. The argument is specifically not that religious interests may be better protected as aspects of group rights rather than as individual rights (although other European human rights instruments and agencies of the Council of Europe proceed upon the basis of religious freedom as a critical aspect of the protection of minorities),[3] but rather that religious freedom is essentially a concept embracing a number of discrete elements, each of which can be – and to a large extent already is - adequately protected through other legal provisions.

Any thesis that freedom of thought, conscience and religion is essentially superfluous is rightly controversial. At a time when notions of tolerance and equality are under strain across many parts of the globe including Europe, the contemporary relevance of an unambiguous legal guarantee appears self-evident, not least as any proposal to weaken the normative value of the protection of thought, conscience and religion could send an inappropriate message in countries in which intolerance is rising both to members of minorities and to those individuals, groups and political parties seeking to advance that intolerance. Freedom of religious belief has proven in recent years

---

3   The European system for the protection of human rights is much wider than merely judicial protection via the Strasbourg Court: see e.g. Reed & Murdoch (2017), 4th ed., *Human Rights Law*, cap 2. See in particular the Framework Convention for the Protection of National Minorities, Preamble: a pluralist and genuinely democratic society should not only respect the ethnic, cultural, linguistic and religious identity of each person belonging to a national minority, but also create appropriate conditions enabling them to express, preserve and develop this identity. The European Commission against Racism and Intolerance (ECRI)'s mandate is to combat racism, xenophobia, antisemitism and intolerance by combating discrimination and prejudice on grounds of race, colour, language, religion, nationality and national or ethnic origin. For other Council of Europe standards, see e.g. PACE Resolution 2076 (2015) on 'Freedom of religion and living together in a democratic society'. The EU Charter of Fundamental Rights, Art. 10 protects freedom of thought, conscience and religion using the formulation found in the ECHR. Note also that the case law of the European Court of Human Rights ('the Strasbourg Court') is not entirely devoid of recognition of denial of collective religious toleration as a violation of the European Convention on Human Rights: the ECHR, Art. 9 may also be engaged in inter-state cases, and here 'group rights' may be more evident: e.g. ECtHR 10 May 2001, 25781/94, *Cyprus v. Turkey* [GC], paras 245–246 at para 245 (restrictions placed on the freedom of movement of Greek Cypriots in northern Turkey 'considerably curtailed their ability to observe their religious beliefs, in particular their access to places of worship outside their villages and their participation in other aspects of religious life': violation of Art. 9).

to be a somewhat fragile concept, and human rights charters and domestic constitutional guarantees proclaim eternal values that are not necessarily self-evident to all. Nor is the growing sense of a Europe of waning religious faith, of a continent in which religious observance is fading fast and where disapproval of organised religion by emboldened secular fundamentalists is increasingly vocal, a reason to reject the principle of freedom of conscience and belief. Reform of domestic law and policy that appears to favour a particular faith in States not specifically founded upon the principle of *laicite* does not in itself attack the principle that individuals are entitled to freedom of religion. Questioning the inter-connectivity in many domestic arrangements between a dominant religion and national arrangements[4] may indeed promote the value of pluralism in the longer-term. Rather, the thesis is that in a mature legal system providing real protection for human rights in general, a specific conscience and belief guarantee may have little if any practical outcome.

8.2 Freedom of thought, conscience and belief and Strasbourg case law

The formulation of the text of Article 9 of the European Convention on Human Rights calls for some comment. It reads as follows:

> *1. Everyone has the right to freedom of thought, conscience and religion; this right includes freedom to change his religion or belief and freedom, either alone or in community with others and in public or private, to manifest his religion or belief, in worship, teaching, practice and observance.*
>
> *2. Freedom to manifest one's religion or beliefs shall be subject only to such limitations as are prescribed by law and are necessary in a democratic society in the interests of public safety, for the protection of public order, health or morals, or for the protection of the rights and freedoms of others.* [5]

Put in another way, Article 9 involves the rights to hold philosophical or religious convictions, to change these beliefs, and to manifest them individually or in common with others.[6] There is, though, a subtle difference between the first two aspects of the freedom and the third. The text of Article 9 is normally taken to indicate that the right to hold and to change ideas is absolute (the so-

---

4   For a recent audit of the place of religion in Scots domestic law, see: Brown, Green & Mair (2016), *Religion in Scots Law*.
5   This textual formulation is replicated in the Charter of Fundamental Rights of the European Union, Art. 10.
6   ECtHR 25 May 1993, 14307/88, *Kokkinakis v Greece*, para 31.

called 'forum internum') in light of paragraph (2)'s recognition that only *manifestations* of belief may be subject to justifiable interference (that is, provided the State can establish that the interference was proportionate, for a recognised end, and in accordance with domestic law, there will be no violation of the provision).

Use of Article 9 by litigants has been surprisingly limited. By the end of 2016, violations of Article 9 had been established in only 65 instances, a figure constituting around 0.4% of the cases in which at least one violation has occurred. Further, only comparatively recently has the Court begun to engage significantly with the guarantee, for more than half of the Court's judgments in which a violation of Article 9 has been established have only been delivered since 2009. It is not just the paucity of judgments in this area that is remarkable: judgments in which a violation of Article 9 has been established concern only 16 of the 47 Member States of the Council of Europe, and moreover, only six of these States have had more than one adverse judgment made against them. Indeed, the preponderance of adverse judgments involving Article 9 - just over 60% - concern only four countries.[7] Religious tolerance – judged at least in relation to the number of judgments involving Article 9 – appears high. While religious pluralism seems a feature in most European States (or possibly reflective of an increasingly secular European society), these statistics do not tell the whole story, for many aspects of religious freedom have fallen to be considered under related Convention guarantees. Paradoxically, it may well be the *absence* of a significant body of Article 9 case law that has led to this situation. Were there to have been the opportunity for the Court to have considered more cases concerning interferences with manifestation of religious belief and at an earlier stage in the development of the Court's jurisprudence, doubtless Article 9 would have been developed with greater vigour. Instead, case law under Article 8 and Articles 10 and 11 have filled the gap by expanding into the area of the exercise of religious freedom. It is not so much that these related guarantees have in time crowded out the ability of Article 9 to establish its own distinct presence, but rather it has been recognised that there may be real value in approaching challenges to State action (or inaction, where a positive obligation arises) through the prism of principles of general applicability rather than applying specific solutions in cases involving conscience and belief.

Article 9 provides that 'manifestations' of belief may take place in a range of circumstances: that is, in private while alone; in private with others; or in public, alone or with others. The textual formulation of Article 9 thus maps onto the essential elements of what it means to have a belief: we can hold (and revise our own) beliefs, we can express belief, and we can try to live our lives in accordance with our beliefs; we can attempt to try to change others' beliefs through persuasion; we may gain succour and encouragement for our own

---

7   There were 13 adverse judgments in respect of Greece; 11 in respect of Turkey; 9 in respect of Russia; and 7 in respect of Bulgaria: European Court *Annual Report 2016* (2017), p. 204-205.

beliefs through shared deliberation, study and worship. These aspects of 'manifestations' of belief are protected by Article 9. None is an absolute right, but as discussed, the rights to hold and to change belief appear to be so. However, these crucial aspects of what it means to hold religious belief, and to put religious faith or individual conscience into practice (in private or in public, alone or with others) can arguably equally be accommodated elsewhere. In particular, individual and collective manifestation could be disposed of in respect of Article 8's respect for 'private and family life', Article 10 guarantees for free speech, or Article 11's requirement of freedom assembly and association.

Before examining the extent to which this has occurred in actual judgments of the Strasbourg Court, it is necessary to note that the Court itself has observed that there is a close inter-relationship between Article 9 and Articles 10 and 11. These three provisions concern a range of civil and political rights that are linked not only in textual formulation but also in substantive content. They also serve to protect a series of related values. Freedom of thought, conscience and religion, freedom of expression, and freedom of assembly and association are viewed by the Strasbourg Court as inter-dependent and as crucial for the protection of democratic life. There is also a further dimension to freedom of thought, conscience and religion: it is an integral aspect of personal autonomy, a matter also at the heart of Article 8's requirement for protection of private and family life. In short, thought, conscience and belief are closely interconnected with the exercise of *collective* political discourse through expression and protest, and in turn, an individual's ability to engage in meeting and measured deliberation may help shape personal attitude and belief, that is, *individual* self-determination.

The links between Article 9 and these other provisions have been recognised at an early stage in the development of the Court's jurisprudence,[8] but also clearly pose a problem for the Strasbourg Court in that identification of the *lex specialis* has not always been straightforward on account of overlap in the scope of these complementary guarantees. The Court's case law suggests there are three alternative approaches that are adopted. First, the Court may consider one provision (and not necessarily Article 9) as the *lex specialis* at the outset; secondly, it may dispose of a case by examining the facts under only one Article when it can be concluded that the merits of the application can be addressed adequately in this way (and thus while the case may be admissible under one or more additional Articles, the Court will simply conclude that there is no need to determine any additional merits);[9] and thirdly, since the ECHR is to be read as

---

8   The question can be addressed through the link between Arts. 9-11 that was acknowledged in early jurisprudence: ECtHR 13 August 1981, 7601/76 & 7806/77, *Young, James & Webster v. United Kingdom,* para 57: 'the protection of personal opinion afforded by Articles 9 and 10 in the shape of freedom of thought, conscience and religion and of freedom of expression is also one of the purposes of freedom of association as guaranteed by Article 11'.

9   ECtHR 13 July 2012, 16354/06, *Mouvement raëlien suisse v. Switzerland* [GC], paras 79-80 (not necessary to consider religious advertisement under Art. 9).

a whole, the Court may read the substantive content of a particular guarantee 'in the light of' another provision.[10] Each approach has its own advantages, but none of this is conducive to consistent jurisprudence. Further, it cannot be readily said that whichever approach is adopted is likely to have much impact upon the eventual conclusion.

Would anything more be achieved other than greater consistency in case law by jettisoning Article 9? The most obvious risk is that something could be lost, as this could undermine the supposedly-absolute nature of the *forum internum*, the only aspect of the scope of Articles 8-11 that appears absolute. While there is no explicit reference in the text to the prohibition of indoctrination or coercion to hold or to adopt a religion or belief (other than implicitly through the reference to the duty to take into account parental convictions in the provision of state education in Article 2 of Protocol no 1), requiring an individual to act against their conscience or beliefs does clearly fall within the scope of Article 9, for protection of the *forum internum* is inextricably linked to the *negative* aspect of freedom to manifest one's beliefs, that is, the individual's right not to be obliged to manifest religious beliefs and not to be obliged to act in such a way as to enable conclusions to be drawn regarding whether an individual holds – or does not hold – such beliefs.[11] In short, the State cannot require an individual to disclose personal beliefs, except perhaps in a highly restricted set of circumstances where access to a privilege (as opposed to a right) is being sought.[12] Article 9 is thus of significance in defining this critical aspect of belief.

---

10   ECtHR 13 August 1981, 7601/76 & 7806/77, *Young, James & Webster v. United Kingdom*, para 66 (disposal under Art. 11 rather than in terms of Arts. 9 or 10); ECtHR 25 May 1993, 14307/88, *Kokkinakis v. Greece*, para 54 (dissemination of religious beliefs considered under Art. 9 rather than Art. 10); ECtHR 10 June 2010, 302/02, *Jehovah's Witnesses of Moscow v Russia*, paras 106–160 and 170–182 (violation of Art. 9 in the light of Art. 11; and violation of Art. 11 in the light of Art. 9).

11   ECtHR 18 February 1999, 24645/94, *Buscarini a.o. v. San Marino* [GC], paras 34–41 at para 39 (individuals who had been elected to parliament had been required to take a religious oath on the Bible ('I swear on the Holy Gospels ever to be faithful to and obey the Constitution of the Republic.') as a condition of their appointment to office: violation, the Court rejecting the argument that the form of words used was essentially of historical and social rather than religious significance and agreeing with the Commission that it 'would be contradictory to make the exercise of a mandate intended to represent different views of society within Parliament subject to a prior declaration of commitment to a particular set of beliefs'); ECtHR 21 February 2008, 19516/06, *Alexandridis v Greece*, paras 35–41 (requirement for solemn declaration instead of oath involved an obligation to reveal in part religious beliefs, the procedure reflecting a presumption that lawyers were Orthodox Christians: the fact that the applicant had had to reveal to the court that he was not such constituted an interference with the freedom not to have to manifest his religious beliefs); and ECtHR 3 June 2010, 42837/06, *Dimitras a.o. v. Greece*, paras 79–88 (requirement to disclose that an individual was not an Orthodox Christian and in certain cases was Jewish or an atheist to avoid having to take a religious oath in criminal proceedings: violation).

12   ECtHR 13 April 2006, 55170/00, *Kosteski v. FYRO Macedonia*, paras 37–40 at para 39 (penalisation for failing to attend the place of work on the day of a religious holiday: if this involved an interference with Art. 9, it was justified the applicant's freedom of religion, this was not disproportionate, the Court observed that 'while the notion of the State sitting in

Here, though, other alternative protection is arguably readily available. In particular, Article 8 now extends to issues concerning how individuals seek to live out their lives in accordance with personal beliefs in treating matters such as belief in assisted suicide as an aspect of personal autonomy falling within the ambit of Article 8.[13] Approaching a case as a matter of 'personal autonomy' rather than 'religious belief' has also the advantage of effectively neutralising the need to investigate whether the claimed basis for the religious faith does indeed demand of adherents a particular course of action in respect of lifestyle choices and thus removing the risk that the *forum internum* may be invaded through invasive questioning.[14] Belief, and the consequences of belief for any individual, may thus be better considered as issues of self-determination that constitute aspects of private life. Alternatively, even if Article 8 proves to be inadequate in this task, Article 10 could provide protection if there is an obligation to affirm to others a commitment to beliefs that are contrary to conscience.[15] To be sure, Articles 8 and 10 lack the suggestion of absolute protection for the holding and changing of beliefs, a matter of some important symbolism, but it may be difficult to envisage circumstances in which the State could ever establish a compelling reason for requiring an individual to disclose their personal beliefs to others. It is also possible without too much conceptual difficulty to revisit early cases disposed of under Article 9 and to relocate the issues raised (for example, the imposition of religious oaths upon members of the legislature as a precondition for sitting in the legislature[16] could now be examined under Article 3 of Protocol no 1, while a requirement to attend religious ceremonies could be considered under Article 11[17]).

---

judgment on the state of a citizen's inner and personal beliefs is abhorrent and may smack unhappily of past infamous persecutions', it had not been inappropriate for the authorities to seek to ascertain whether the applicant properly could take advantage of legislation allowing Muslims to take holiday on particular days as otherwise unauthorised absences could be treated as disciplinary matters).

13 ECtHR 29 April 2002, 2346/02, *Pretty v. United Kingdom*, para 82. See also the Scottish domestic case of *Whaley v. Lord Advocate* 2008 SC (HL) 107 (Art. 9 not engaged by an interference with hunting). The refusal to recognise marriage with an underage girl as permitted by Islamic law was deemed not to involve an interference with manifestation of belief falling within the scope of Art. 9 but rather as a matter concerning the right to marry under Art. 12: ECtHR 1 July 1986, 11579/85, *Khan v United Kingdom*.

14 ECtHR 29 June 2007, 15472/02, *Folgerø a.o. v. Norway* [GC], paras 85–102, where the Grand Chamber by a bare majority ruled that the introduction of new arrangements for the teaching of religion and philosophy in primary schools had failed to respect the rights of parents as required by Art. 2 of Prot. no 1.

15 ECtHR 8 June 1999, 39511/98, *McGuinness v. United Kingdom* (dec), (elected representatives required to take an oath of allegiance to the monarch; application declared inadmissible under Art. 10 since the oath could be viewed simply as an affirmation of loyalty to the UK's constitutional principles).

16 ECtHR 18 February 1999, 24645/94, *Buscarini a.o. v. San Marino* [GC], para 34.

17 ECtHR 18 December 1996, 21787/93, *Valsamis v Greece*, paras 21–37 (no interference with Art. 9 rights. See the dissenting opinion in the Commission of the President, Stefan Trechsel.

Relocation or relabelling cases involving interferences with religious practice by treating the religious element as merely incidental to the facts rather than as the primary determinant is even more straightforward where the facts suggest 'manifestations' of belief rather than disclosure of belief. The wearing of religious clothing in public[18] could be treated as symbolic speech and disposed of under Article 10, and a similar approach could apply in relation to restrictions on proselytism.[19] A requirement for the registration of religious faith in identity documents could be seen as constituting an interference with private life Article 8,[20] as could the disposal of human remains constituting an integral aspect of religious practice (as already may occur where the question has arisen rather as a matter of family life).[21] Collective manifestation of belief (where the tendency is currently to dispose of the issues under Article 9 read in conjunction with Article 11[22] or - where the issue concerns refusal to re-register a religion - under Article 11 read in the light of Article 9)[23] are readily matters that could be addressed solely by reference to Article 11.

---

18 ECtHR 23 February 2010, 41135/98, *Ahmet Arslan a.o. v. Turkey*, paras 44–52 (conviction for wearing religious clothing in public: violation).

19 ECtHR 25 May 1993, 14307/88, *Kokkinakis v Greece*, paras 31–33.

20 ECtHR 2 February 2010, 21924/05, *Sinan Işik v. Turkey*, paras 37–53 (identity cards carried a 'religion' data field but which could be left blank: violation, as a decision to have a card with the religion field left blank inevitably carried specific connotations).

21 ECtHR 10 March 1981, 8741/79, *X. v. Germany* (com.), (but matter can fall within the scope of Art. 8); ECtHR 13 September 2005, 42639/04, *Jones v United Kingdom* (dec), (refusal to allow photograph on a memorial stone did not prevent manifestation of the applicant's religious beliefs). ECtHR 10 July 2001, 41754/98, *Johannische Kirche & Peters v. Germany* (dec), ('restriction of the right to manifest one's religion ...in so far as the manner of burying the dead and cemetery layout represents an essential aspect of the religious practice of the first applicant and its members'); ECtHR 6 November 2008, 38450/05, *Sabanchiyeva a.o. v. Russia* (dec), (refusal to return bodies of alleged terrorists killed by law-enforcement personnel: admissible under Arts. 3, 8 and 9, taken alone and in conjunction with Arts. 13 and 14); and cf ECtHR 6 June 2013, 38450/05, *Sabanchiyeva a.o. v. Russia* (matter disposed of under Art. 8).

22 ECtHR 12 June 2014, 33203/08, *Biblical Centre of the Chuvash Republic v. Russia*, para 54 (a Pentecostal biblical centre was closed by judicial decision on health and safety grounds, unauthorised issuing of study diplomas and failure to obtain prior approval for its operation); ECtHR 10 June 2010, 302/02, *Jehovah's Witnesses of Moscow v Russia*, paras 170–182 (refusal to re-register a religious association and its dissolution without relevant and sufficient grounds as many court findings had not been substantiated and were not grounded on an acceptable assessment of the relevant facts, or involved normal manifestations that were common to other religious practices and freely chosen by the adherents in the context of their personal autonomy; the grounds for the dissolution included alleged 'brainwashing', 'mind control', undue influence on members' families and upon minors, incitement to refusal to serve in the military or to participate in national celebrations, to suicide or to refusal of medical treatment). See also: ECtHR 14 June 2007, 77703/01, *Svyato-Mykhaïlivska Parafiya v. Ukraine*, paras 137-152 (refusal to grant the status of a legal entity to an association of religious believers: violation of Art. 9 in the light of Arts. 11 and 6).

23 ECtHR 5 October 2006, 72881/01, *Moscow Branch of the Salvation Army v. Russia*, paras 81–98; and *Church of Scientology Moscow v Russia* (5 April 2007), paras 94–98.

The proposition is easier made in relation to particular aspects of the operation of religious organisations. Thus the deprivation of a religious organisation's material resources, for example, has been held not to fall within the scope of Article 9, but rather to give rise to issues under the protection of property in terms of Article 1 of Protocol no 1,[24] and imposition of burdens on owners of property to act in a manner inconsistent with freedom of conscience may likewise be disposed of under this alternative guarantee.[25] Similarly, refusal to grant an individual an exemption from the payment of a church tax on the ground of non-registration was considered in terms of the right to property taken in conjunction with the prohibition on discrimination in the enjoyment of Convention guarantees rather than as a matter of conscience or religion.[26] Fair hearing guarantees under Article 6 may also be of relevance in protecting the civil rights of a religious organisation in relation to property rights.[27] In short, a wide range of issues closely associated with the practice of religious belief or conscience can also be (and already is) disposed of under other guarantees.[28]

The argument can also be advanced that the disposal of complaints alleging interferences under principles of general applicability is preferable to treating the case as calling for specific (or enhanced) protection for any religious dimension that happens to arise. There is still, however, the not inconsiderable risk that to do so further could weaken the normative impact of the principle that religious belief is a crucial value, or that personal autonomy arguments may be insufficiently compelling in particular instances, with the result that conscience and belief may be downgraded. However, application of Article 14 which protects the enjoyment of the exercise of substantive Convention

---

24 ECtHR 9 December 1994, 13092/87, *The Holy Monasteries v. Greece*, paras 74–75 (Prot. 1, Art. 1), and cf paras 86–88 (no breach of Art. 9). But cf ECtHR 21 September 2010, 8916/05, *Association of Jehovah's Witnesses v. France* (dec), (refusal to grant association of Jehovah's Witnesses tax (exemption available to religious organisations following classification as a 'sect' and resulting in €45 million tax liability: admissible under Art. 9).

25 See also: ECtHR 26 June 20112, 9300/07, *Herrmann v. Germany* [GC], paras 81-94, (obligation imposed upon landowners opposed on ethical grounds to hunting to tolerate hunting on their property constituted a disproportionate burden: violation of Prot. 1, Art. 1).

26 ECtHR 23 October 1990, 11581/85, *Darby v Sweden*, paras 30–34.

27 ECtHR 19 November 2013, 26270/04, *Bogdan Vodă Greek-Catholic Parish v. Romania*, paras 42-50 (non-enforcement of final judgment in favour of religious organisation regarding use of church).

28 Thus, freedom of conscience issues may also arise under Art. 3's prohibition of inhuman or degrading treatment or punishment (ECtHR 24 January 2006, 39437/98, *Ülke v. Turkey*). Religious beliefs may also arise in the context of respect for family life in terms of Art. 8 in relation to deportation (ECtHR 28 February 2006, 27034/05, *Z. & T. v. United Kingdom* (dec), (Pakistani Christians facing deportation to Pakistan: while the Court would not rule out the possibility that exceptionally Art. 9 may be engaged in expulsion cases, it was difficult to envisage such circumstances which in any event would not engage Art. 3 responsibility); see also: ECtHR 20 June 2002, 50963/99, *Al-Nashif a.o. v. Bulgaria*, (deportation on account of having taught Islamic religion without proper authorisation: in view of finding that deportation would constitute a violation of Art. 8, no need to consider Art. 9.).

guarantees from discrimination *inter alia* based upon religious discrimination may redress this. Discrimination upon religious grounds is not far removed from discrimination on grounds of race; both are considered by international standards as equally abhorrent.[29] While Article 14 of the European Convention on Human Rights refers to discriminatory treatment in general and irrespective of the ground, the Strasbourg Court has identified a number of high-risk categories of discriminatory treatment (such as sex, sexual orientation and illegitimacy). To this list, discrimination on the grounds of race or ethnic origin has been added with the result that 'very weighty reasons' must be adduced by the State to justify this[30]. Indeed, where a non-discriminatory rule is applied in a discriminatory manner, there may indeed be no need on the part of an applicant to establish any intention to discriminate.[31] The responsibility upon State bodies to avoid the imposition of discrimination on the basis of religious belief may indeed include the imposition of an obligation to treat differently persons whose situations are significantly different on the grounds of belief.[32] Further, national authorities are under a duty to remain neutral when exercising any regulatory power in the sphere of religious freedom: the obligation to remain impartial in their relations with different religions, denominations and beliefs may also extend to situations not strictly falling within the scope of Article 9 but where the unequal treatment of religious faiths has arisen through the conferment of

---

29 The UN Declaration on the Elimination of All Forms of Intolerance and of Discrimination Based on Religion or Belief (1981), Art. 3, thus considers that 'discrimination between human beings on grounds of religion or belief constitutes an affront to human dignity and a disavowal of the principles of the Charter of the United Nations'. See also 1990 Document of the Copenhagen Meeting of the Conference on the Human Dimension of the CSCE which 'clearly and unequivocally condemns totalitarianism, racial and ethnic hatred, anti-Semitism, xenophobia and discrimination against anyone as well as persecution on religious and ideological grounds'.

30 ECtHR 13 November 2007, 57325/00, *DH and Others v. Czech Republic* [GC], at para 196.

31 ECtHR 13 November 2007, 57325/00, *DH and Others v. Czech Republic* [GC], at para 178: 'the level of persuasion necessary for reaching a particular conclusion and, in this connection, the distribution of the burden of proof are intrinsically linked to the specificity of the facts, the nature of the allegation made and the Convention right at stake'. See also at para 91: 'a difference in treatment may take the form of disproportionately prejudicial effects of a general policy or measure which, although couched in neutral terms, discriminates against a group'.

32 ECtHR 6 April 2000, 34369/97, *Thlimmenos v. Greece* [GC], paras 39–49 at para 47 (a person who had been refused admission as a chartered accountant because of a criminal conviction arising from his refusal to wear military uniform owing to his religious beliefs as a Jehovah's Witness. While access to a profession is not covered by the ECHR, the complaint concerned the lack of distinction between convictions based upon religious beliefs and other convictions for criminal offences. In effect, the complaint alleged discrimination on the basis of the exercise of freedom of religion. While states could legitimately exclude certain classes of offenders from various professions, any conviction for refusing to wear military uniform on the basis of religious convictions could not suggest dishonesty or moral turpitude. The disqualification did not therefore have a legitimate objective, and was in the nature of an additional and disproportionate sanction).

certain rights upon some, but not all, religions[33] (although a difference in treatment between religious groups on account of official recognition of a specific legal status resulting in the conferment of privileges is not in itself incompatible with the Convention as long as a framework establishing criteria for conferring legal personality is in place and also providing that each religious group has a fair opportunity to apply for this status).[34] Application of Article 14 in such instances has certainly taken place in conjunction with Article 9,[35] but again Article 14 could readily be employed in conjunction with related guarantees so as to provide protection for religious faith. This has already occurred, for example, in relation to employment cases,[36] in child custody disputes in which religious faith has played a part in determinations,[37] and in access to justice cases.[38] Article 14 is readily-available to help address discriminatory treatment based on religious faith.

---

33 ECtHR 9 December 2010, 7798/08, *Savez crkava 'Riječ života' a.o. v. Croatia*, paras 55–59 and 85– 93 (unequal allocation of criteria for rights to have religious marriages recognised as equal to those of civil marriages and to allow religious education in public schools: violation of Art. 14 in conjunction with Art. 9, for while these rights could not be derived from the ECHR, discriminatory measures were inappropriate).

34 ECtHR 10 December 2009, 33001/03, *Koppi v Austria*, para 33; see also: ECtHR 31 July 2008, 40825/98, *Religionsgemeinschaft der Zeugen Jehovas a.o. v. Austria*, paras 87–99 (substantial time taken to determine question of recognition of Jehovah's Witnesses: violation of Art. 14 with Art. 9)). ECtHR 4 March 2014, 7552/09, *The Church of Jesus Christ of Latter-Day Saints v. United Kingdom*, paras 30–36 (refusal of a request for exemption from local rates as it was considered that Mormon temples did not qualify as 'places of public religious worship' since access was restricted to its most devout followers alone: no violation of Art. 14 in conjunction with Art. 9 as the measure was not disproportionate given that its other places of worship that were open to the public were exempted and the temples benefited from an 80% reduction, and in any case this legislative approach applied to all religious groups.

35 In respect of exemption from military service for those discharging leadership responsibilities in a religious community: ECtHR 19 March 2009, 28648/03, *Lang v Austria*, paras 22–32 (failure to exempt a Jehovah's Witness who served as an elder for his religious community through providing pastoral care and conducting religious services: violation of Art. 14 taken with Art. 9); or in respect of failure to recognise exemption from compulsory courses of education: ECtHR 15 June 2010, 7710/02, *Grzelak v. Poland*, paras 84–101 (failure of education authorities to organise a class in ethics and to give a pupil a mark in his school report, leading to harassment and discrimination for not following religious education classes: violation of Art. 14 taken with Art. 9).

36 In relation to dismissal from employment cf: ECtHR 20 May 1999, 25390/94, *Rekvényi v. Hungary*, paras 63–68 (no violation of Art. 14 taken with Arts. 10 or 11).

37 ECtHR 23 June 1993, 12875/87, *Hoffman v. Austria*, paras 43–47 (the applicant had been denied custody of her child because of her involvement with the Jehovah's Witnesses. The Court held that it was unacceptable for a domestic court to base a decision on the ground of a difference in religion. Although the point at issue was essentially one of religion, the Court considered it under Art. 14 in conjunction with Art. 8 as it concerned the determination of child custody, an aspect of family life. As it had already considered the matter under Arts. 8 and 14, the Court held that there was no need to consider the point under Art. 9).

38 In ECtHR 16 December 1997, 25528/94, *Canea Catholic Church v. Greece*, the Court had to consider a situation where the applicant church could not take legal proceedings in order to protect its property rights, although the Orthodox Church and the Jewish Community were

8.3   The proper 'balancing of competing interests' in cases involving a religious element

Cases in which claims based upon religious belief conflict with other human rights guarantees are by no means frequent, but there are suggestions emerging from case law that a principle of general applicability should be applied in such instances rather than attempting to accord religious belief some exalted status. In *Karaahmed v Bulgaria,* for example, the Court examined the authorities' reactions to violent anti-Muslim demonstration by a political party outside a mosque during a religious service. The judgment refers to 'competing *provisions*' (here, the rights to expression and to peaceful assembly on the one side and to freedom of religion on the other), but it is made clear that no one Convention guarantee takes precedent: rather, domestic authorities are expected to carry out an assessment based upon a sensitive awareness of the values and importance of each freedom. This is because '[t]he Convention does not establish any a priori hierarchy between these rights: as a matter of principle, they deserve equal respect.'[39]

The eventual outcome was never in doubt. The protest had taken place in an atmosphere of menace, and there had also been a positive obligation on the authorities to provide protection against demonstrators engaged in public disorder (in line with established jurisprudence concerning positive obligations on police officers in such circumstances). The expectation as to how the interests of the worshipers were to be weighed against those of the demonstrators was straightforward: balancing must take place 'in a manner which recognises the importance of these rights in a society based on pluralism, tolerance and broad-mindedness.'

This idea is simply a variation of the 'calculus of felicity', and could be styled 'pluralist utilitarianism' – the greatest degree of tolerance and broadmindedness being proposed as the most appropriate means of adjudicating whether the interference was 'necessary in a democratic society'. This approach has been recognised in other cases involving conflicting guarantees, and where the interests of a religious adherent conflict with the communal interest of society as a whole rather than with other groups of adherents. In *Bayatan v Armenia*, for example, a case recognising the right of exemption from military service on the basis of belief, the Court observed:

> *The Court further reiterates that pluralism, tolerance and broadmindedness are hallmarks of a "democratic society".*

---

able to do so. The Court found that there could be no objective and reasonable justification for this discriminatory treatment and that there was a violation of Art. 14 taken in conjunction with Art. 6(1) (ECtHR 16 December 1997, 25528/94, *Canea Catholic Church v. Greece,* paras 44–47).

39   ECtHR 24 February 2015, 30587/13, *Karaahmed v. Bulgaria*, paras 91-96 at para 92.

> *Although individual interests must on occasion be sub-*
> *ordinated to those of a group, democracy does not simply*
> *mean that the views of a majority must always prevail: a*
> *balance must be achieved which ensures the fair and proper*
> *treatment of people from minorities and avoids any abuse of*
> *a dominant position (...). Thus, respect on the part of the*
> *State towards the beliefs of a minority religious group like*
> *the applicant's by providing them with the opportunity to*
> *serve society as dictated by their conscience might, far from*
> *creating unjust inequalities or discrimination as claimed by*
> *the Government, rather ensure cohesive and stable*
> *pluralism and promote religious harmony and tolerance in*
> *society.[40]*

Other case law takes a similar approach, including situations in which the interests of counter-demonstrators motivated by religious faith (or at least, by religious leadership) have given way to the interests of those challenging orthodoxy in societal arrangements, an orthodoxy entrenched by intolerance of deviancy purporting to be based upon religious belief.[41] A guiding principle thus emerges: follow the path of tolerance; maximise pluralism; apply the test of broadmindedness. This also applies where the message being challenged itself proclaims intolerance, whether the message is purportedly-religious or not. Religious intolerance may be attacked through freedom of expression; and freedom of manifestation of belief that involves undermining the values of pluralism and tolerance of others' beliefs (whether religious or otherwise) may be subject to interference.

In any event, there is an important inbuilt restriction upon the scope of Article 9 protection, a restriction also applying under Article 2 of Protocol no 1 in relation to the duty to take into account parental convictions in the education of children. Put simply, only thought, belief or philosophical convictions that are worthy of respect should attract protection.[42] 'Belief' under Article 9 is much more than mere opinion, and beliefs must first 'attain a certain level of cogency, seriousness, cohesion and importance' and secondly also crucially be able to be considered compatible with respect for human dignity. Thus the essential scope of Article 9 is restricted to *acceptable* 'belief', that is, as tested against the somewhat nebulous test of being deemed worthy of protection in European

---

40 ECtHR 7 July 2011, 23459/03, *Bayatyan v. Armenia* [GC], at para 126.
41 ECtHR 21 October 2010, 4916/07, *Alekseyev v. Russia*, paras 71–88 (repeated refusals to permit 'gay pride' parades on public order grounds following receipt of petitions opposing the marches and the making of statements by local officials indicating no such parade would ever be permitted: violation of Art. 11 on account of decisions based upon the basis of prevailing moral values of the majority and in the absence of measures to assess public safety risks or of the prosecution of those making threats of violence, the purpose of the parades being to promote respect for human rights).
42 ECtHR 25 February 1982, 7511/76, *Campbell & Cosans v. United Kingdom*, para 36.

democratic society.[43] This approach certainly rejects the more absolutist approach adopted in the USA under the First Amendment.[44] Critically, it accepts that restrictions upon religious speech that are potentially harmful to society may be justified.[45]

There may be thus an occasional but inescapable need to examine matters of religious doctrine to judge the extent to which the particular belief sought to be advanced is worthy of support in a democratic society.[46] But is this any more difficult than defining 'religion'?[47] Where there is a doubt, an applicant may be expected to attempt to establish that a particular 'religion' indeed exists,[48] and while what may be considered mainstream religions and minority variants of such faiths are readily accepted as falling within the scope of the provision as are religious movements of recent origin,[49] circumstances may exist in which it

---

43   This is taken from Prot. 1, Art. 2 case law: ECtHR 25 February 1982, 7511/76, *Campbell & Cosans v. United Kingdom*, para 36 (re Prot. 1 Art. 2); and ECtHR 7 July 2011, 23459/03, *Bayatyan v. Armenia* [GC], para 110; ECtHR 15 January 2013, 48420/10, *Eweida a.o. v. United Kingdom*, para 81 (re Art. 9). See too ECtHR 29 March 1993, 19459/92, *F.P. v. Germany* (com. dec.) (Art. 9 'is essentially destined to protect religions, or theories on philosophical or ideological universal values'); and ECtHR 31 July 2001, 41340/98, *Refah Partisi (the Welfare Party) a.o. v. Turkey* [GC] (prohibition on a political party which sought to introduce Islamic law contrary to the state's secular constitution upheld, in part since the values of such a legal system were contrary to those of the Convention).

44   Most obviously, and notoriously, illustrated in *Snyder v. Phelps* 562 US 443 (2011). concerning the activities of the so-called Westboro Baptist Church. Tolerance is a crucial aspect of the scope and values inherent in Art. 10: e.g. ECtHR 7 December 1976, 5493/72, *Handyside v. United Kingdom*, para 49 (expression was crucial for promotion of 'pluralism, toleration and broadmindedness').

45   ECtHR 13 July 2012, 16354/06, *Mouvement raëlien suisse v. Switzerland* [GC], paras 52–77, discussed at footnote 46.

46   ECtHR 13 July 2012, 16354/06, *Mouvement raëlien suisse v. Switzerland* [GC], paras 52–77 (no unconditional or unlimited right to the use of public space through advertising which, as commercial speech, is covered by a wide margin of appreciation sufficient to cover a range of interests including the protection of morals, traffic safety and preservation of the landscape; no violation, the association also being able to disseminate ideas through other means and the interference limited to public displays of posters).

47   ECtHR 6 November 2008, 58911/00, *Leela Förderkreis a.o. v. Germany*, para 81 (Osha meditation centres, seminars, work projects, etc. for spiritual development and enlightenment), cf: Harris, O'Boyle & Warbrick (2014), *Law of the European Convention on Human Rights* (3rd ed.), p. 593: '... any definition of "religion" would need to be flexible enough to satisfy a broad cross-section of world faiths, as well as sufficiently precise for practical application in specific cases. Such a balance would be practically impossible to strike.'

48   ECtHR 4 October 1977, 7291/75, *X. v. United Kingdom*, (question whether the Wicca movement qualified left open); and see also: ECtHR 14 July 1987, 12587/86, *Chappell v. United Kingdom*.

49   ECtHR 8 March 1994, 20490/92, *ISKCON a.o. v. United Kingdom* (Krishna); ECtHR 2 February 2010, 21924/05, *Sinan Işýk v. Turkey*, (Alevism). Druidism and its variants are also recognised: ECtHR 14 July 1987, 12587/86, *Chappell v. United Kingdom*; and cf: ECtHR 19 October 1998, 31416/96, *Pendragon v. United Kingdom* (dec) (denial of access to Stonehenge for summer solstice celebrations: disposed of under Art. 11 read in light of Arts. 9 and 10); ECtHR 27 June 2000, 27417/95, *Cha'are Shalom Ve Tsedek v. France* [GC]

will be impossible to avoid adjudicating upon whether particular beliefs are central to a particular faith.[50] This is so despite the recognition that it is 'clearly not the Court's task to decide in abstracto whether or not a body of beliefs and related practices constitutes a "religion"'.[51] Judicial competence in theology is limited. But application of the 'cogency of belief' test is not always easy and also runs the risk of intruding into the *forum internum*. Restricting protected 'belief' to 'worthy' belief also inevitably calls for a value-judgment. This may result in the Court appearing to condone views that may not be entirely compatible with tolerance. Thus sincerely-held views on marriage and sexuality, i.e. views that are increasingly out of kilter with more relaxed and broadminded societal attitudes and indeed with the Court's own characterisation of discrimination based upon sexuality as a high-risk area, may nevertheless fall within the scope of Article 9.[52] There is presumably no principled reason why naturism should also not qualify as a protected belief,[53] since pacifism, atheism and veganism[54] and a political ideology such as communism[55] have been deemed to pass the test. Arguably, though, it is much better for the Court to try to avoid all such questions. It has indeed often attempted to do this, again by 'relocating' issues through determination of an alternative *lex specialis*. Thus, interferences with thought and conscience in respect of political beliefs will normally be treated as giving rise to issues arising within the scope of Article 10's guarantee of freedom of expression or the right of association under Article 11.[56] This could be taken further by revisiting existing case law. Ensuring

---

(minority branch of Judaism); ECtHR 15 October 1981, 8652/79, *X. v. Austria,* (the Moon Sect); ECtHR 19 March 1981, 8118/77, *Omkarananda and the Divine Light Zentrum v. Switzerland.* See further: Gunn (2003), 'The Complexity of Religion and the Definition of "Religion" in International Law', 16 *Harv Hum Rts Jo* 189.

50 ECtHR 31 January 2012, 35021/05, *Kovaļkovs v Latvia* (dec), (Hinduism).

51 ECtHR 5 April 2007, 18147/02, *Church of Scientology Moscow v. Russia*, para 64; ECtHR 1 October 2009, 76836/01, *Kimlya a.o. v. Russia*, paras 79–81 (domestic recognition of 'religious' nature of activities, and thus Art. 9 applied).

52 ECtHR 15 January 2013, 48420/10, *Eweida a.o. v. United Kingdom*, para 108.

53 ECtHR 28 October 2014, 49327/11, *Gough v. United Kingdom*, (issue of convictions and sanctions imposed for public nudity disposed of under Arts. 8 and 10, but note. para 188: 'The applicant failed to make submissions as to the applicability of Article 9 to the case. On the basis of the material before it, the Court finds that he has not shown that his belief met the necessary requirements of cogency, seriousness, cohesion and importance to fall within the scope of Article 9 of the Convention')

54 ECtHR 16 May 1977, 7050/75, *Arrowsmith v. United Kingdom,* (pacifism); ECtHR 3 December 1986, 10491/83, *Angelini v. Sweden* (atheism); 18187/91, ECtHR 10 February 1993, 18187/91, *W. v. United Kingdom*, (dec), (veganism).

55 562 US 443 (2011).

56 ECtHR 11 October 1991, 16311/90, *Hazar, Hazar & Acik v. Turkey*, (offence of belonging to the Communist Party: admissible under ECHR, Art. 9). Cf Harris, O'Boyle and Warbrick Law of the European Convention on Human Rights (1st edn, 1995) at p 357: 'the line between a philosophy and a political programme may yet be hard to draw'. ECtHR 26 September 1995, 17851/91, *Vogt v. Germany*. Cf: ECtHR 28 October 2014, 49327/11, *Gough v. United Kingdom*, paras 182-188) (not established that wish to walk naked in public

respect for a person's sincerely-held views on the 'sinful' nature of homo-sexuality that affect the discharge of employment responsibilities could be deemed an aspect of respect for private life under Article 8 and one calling for some reasonable accommodation where possible.[57]

Avoiding investigation of the content of beliefs is thus desirable: and it is invariably much easier to decide which set of competing interests promotes greater pluralism, tolerance and broadmindedness. Discounting wherever possible the issue of religious faith also promotes neutral judicial deter-minations. In *Otto-Preminger-Institut v Austria*, a seizure order had been made against a film that ridiculed particular beliefs of the Roman Catholic Church, the dominant religious faith. While accepting that those who manifest their religious convictions 'must tolerate and accept the denial by others of their religious beliefs and even the propagation by others of doctrines hostile to their faith', the Court considered that national authorities could consider it necessary to take action to protect believers against 'provocative portrayals of objects of religious veneration' where such constitute 'malicious violation of the spirit of tolerance, which must also be a feature of democratic society'.[58] There was no suggestion that outraged parishioners would engage in public disorder; rather, the Court's judgment affirms the responsibilities associated with exercise of expression, not so much to cause offence but rather to prevent ridicule and promote hostile intolerance of others' beliefs.[59] The 'pluralism-tolerance-

---

on the basis of his belief that such behaviour was socially acceptable met cogency test; but issue determined under Arts. 8 and 10).

57   ECtHR 15 January 2013, 48420/10, *Eweida a.o. v. United Kingdom,* para 188 ('Given the importance in a democratic society of freedom of religion, the Court considers that, where an individual complains of a restriction on freedom of religion in the workplace, rather than holding that the possibility of changing job would negate any interference with the right, the better approach would be to weigh that possibility in the overall balance when considering whether or not the restriction was proportionate', noting that this was the approach already adopted under Art. 8 or Art. 10 in case law.).

58   ECtHR 20 September 1994, 13470/87, *Otto-Preminger-Institut v. Austria,* para 47. A similar approach was adopted in: ECtHR 25 November 1996, 17419/90, *Wingrove v. United Kingdom.* See also: ECtHR 13 September 2005, 42571/98, *I.A. v. Turkey,* paras 21–32 (prosecution for blasphemy for publication of work examining philosophical and theological issues: no violation).

59   See: Martinez-Torron (2007), 'Freedom of Expression versus Freedom of Religion in the European Court of Human Rights', in: Sajo (ed), *Censorial Sensitivities: Free Speech and Religion in a Fundamentalist World,* p. 233–269; Temperman (2008), 'Blasphemy, Defamation of Religions and Human Rights Law', 26 *NQHR* 517; and Tulkens (2010), 'Conflicts between Fundamental Rights: Contrasting Views on Articles 9 and 10 of the ECHR', in: Venice Commission, *Science and Technique of Democracy 47: Blasphemy, Insult and Hatred: Finding Answers in a Democratic Society,* p. 121–131. See also: Parliamentary Assembly Resolution Res 1510 (2006), prompted by the controversy surrounding the publication in Denmark of cartoons featuring the Prophet Mohammed (on which, see Boyle (2006), 'The Danish Cartoons', 24 *NQHR* 185; Nathwani 'Religious Cartoons and Human Rights: a Critical Legal Analysis of the Case Law of the European Court of Human Rights on the Protection of Religious Feelings and its Implications in the Danish Affair concerning Cartoons of the Prophet Muhammad' [2008] EHRLR 488; and

broadmindedness' test is essentially neutral. It could help prevent domestic judicial bodies appearing to favour one religion (normally the dominant religion) over others, and the Strasbourg Court from erring.

For example, in *Murphy v. Ireland,* the refusal to allow the radio broadcast of a religious advertisement was challenged under both Article 9 and Article 10 but disposed of by the Court under the latter guarantee as the interference was considered primarily to concern the regulation of the applicant's means of expression and not manifestation of religious belief. This was not an inappropriate determination of the *lex specialis.* However, thereafter a wide margin of appreciation was recognised as the national authorities were seen as better placed than an international court to decide when action may be necessary to regulate freedom of expression in relation to matters liable to offend intimate personal convictions 'since what is likely to cause substantial offence to persons of a particular religious persuasion will vary significantly from time to time and from place to place, especially in an era characterised by an ever growing array of faiths and denominations'. While this may be true, it does fail to recognise that the dominant religion has clearly been favoured to the detriment of another faith. The reasoning seems weak. Acceptance that the authorities had been justified in determining that the particular religious sensitivities in Irish society were such that the broadcasting of any religious advertising could cause offence was based upon the recognition by the domestic courts that religion had been a divisive issue in society, that Irish people holding religious beliefs tended to belong to one particular church, and that religious advertising from a different church might be considered offensive and open to the interpretation of proselytism. Certainly, it was of some relevance that the medium was broadcasting, a means of communication which has 'a more immediate, invasive and powerful impact' than the press, the Court noting that the applicant could still have advertised via local and national newspapers and retained the same right as any other citizen to participate in programmes on religious matters, public meetings and other assemblies. This judgment hardly promotes the notion of pluralism and broadmindedness, and resentment on the part of television viewers is hardly the most compelling ground for interference with free speech even although an international judicial forum may feel that it should be particularly careful to refrain from interfering with domestic determinations on particularly sensitive issues.[60]

Is the suggested test sufficiently robust? The danger may be that merely offensive pro- or anti-religious speech may be banned. There arguably exists sufficient guidance in the jurisprudence to prevent such an outcome. Thus a sustained campaign of harassment by private individuals or organisations may

---

Cram 'The Danish Cartoons, Offensive Expression, and Democratic Legitimacy' in Hare and Weinstein (eds) *Extreme Speech and Democracy* (2009), pp 311–330).

60   ECtHR 10 July 2003, 44179/98, *Murphy v. Ireland*, paras 73–82. See further: Geddis (2004), 'You Can't Say "God" on Radio: Freedom of Expression, Religious Advertising and the Broadcast Media after *Murphy v. Ireland*', *EHRLR* 181.

engage state responsibility,[61] but on the other hand it is legitimate that individuals are free to criticise religious groups, particularly if the criticism concerns the potentially harmful nature of their activities, and when made in a political forum in which issues of public interest are expected to be debated openly.[62] Furthermore, it is possible to be strongly critical of office-holders within a religious body without denigrating the content of the faith itself.[63] This approach can justify the revision of judgments that appear to be out of kilter with the 'maximising of pluralism and broadmindedness' principle.

A 'pluralism, tolerance and broadmindedness' approach to determining conflicts between believers and non-believers has much to commend it. For example, in *Lautsi and Others v. Italy*, the implicit message in the Grand Chamber's judgment was that outsiders should respect the dominant historic tradition and religious adherence in a State. Tolerance is a two-way process. Here, the requirement for the presence of crucifixes in classrooms, while conferring upon the majority religion in Italy a 'preponderant visibility', could not in itself denote a process of indoctrination as a crucifix is an essentially passive symbol whose influence cannot be deemed comparable to that of didactic speech or participation in religious activities, particularly as the curriculum did not include any compulsory teaching about Christianity and as there were clear attempts to provide an understanding of other faiths and promote tolerance of others' beliefs.[64]

---

61 ECtHR 7 October 2014, 28490/02, *Begheluri v. Georgia*, para 160, (state responsibility to ensure the peaceful enjoyment of Art. 9 rights engaged where religious beliefs are opposed or denied in a manner which inhibits those who hold such beliefs from exercising their freedom to hold or express them).

62 ECtHR 27 February 2001, 26958/95, *Jerusalem v. Austria*, paras 38–47. See also: ECtHR 2 May 2006, 50692/99, *Aydın Tatlav v. Turkey*, paras 21–31 (strong criticism of religion, but not an abusive attack on the Muslim faith).

63 ECtHR 31 October 2006, 72208/01, *Klein v. Slovakia* (31 October 2006), paras 45–55 (conviction of journalist for defamation of a Catholic archbishop, the highest representative of the Roman Catholic Church in Slovakia, and thereby also for having disparaged a group of citizens for their Catholic faith through publication of an article critical of the archbishop's attempts to prevent the distribution of a film on the grounds of its blasphemous nature and strong imagery of sexual connotation and allusions to the archbishop's alleged co-operation with the former communist regime: violation of Art. 10 since the strongly-worded pejorative opinion published in a weekly with rather limited circulation and which the archbishop had pardoned had related exclusively to the archbishop and had not unduly interfered with the right of believers to express and exercise their religion, nor had it denigrated the content of their religious faith). Measured discussion of historical opinion on a matter of public interest free from malicious attack on religious belief similarly attracts protection under Art. 10: ECtHR 31 January 2006, 64016/00, *Giniewski v. France*, paras 43–56 (conviction for defamation of Christians, and particularly Roman Catholics, for publication of an article critical of a papal encyclical and the Roman Catholic Church's role in the Holocaust: violation, as the article was written by a journalist and historian and concerned a matter of indisputable public interest, and did not seek to attack religious belief as such but confined itself to addressing a Pope's position).

64 ECtHR 18 March 2011, 30814/06, *Lautsi v. Italy* [GC], paras 62–77 at para 71 (no violation of Prot. 1, Art. 2), and see further: Landau (2007), 'Reflections on the Right to Education:

Application of the 'pluralism, tolerance and broadmindedness' principle is also possible in the workplace as illustrated by the related cases in *Eweida and Others v. United Kingdom,* two of which concerned dismissal from employment on the basis of refusal to carry out employment responsibilities on account of deeply-held personal religious beliefs concerning homosexuality, and a third the refusal of a private employer to allow religious symbols to be worn with uniform. The first case was examined in terms of Article 14 in conjunction with Article 9, the Court considering that the state's margin of appreciation in determining the relative weight to be given to the authority's interests (that is, the provision of a public service without discrimination) in relation to the applicant's right to freedom of conscience and belief had not been exceeded. In the second case, the applicant had voluntarily enrolled in a training programme in psycho-sexual counselling in the knowledge that the private-sector employer had an equal opportunities policy, and while a decision to enter into an employment contract involving responsibilities in conflict with freedom to manifest religious belief was not determinative, this was certainly a matter to be taken into account.[65] In the third case, the Court indeed emphasised that the positive obligation arising under Article 9 upon state authorities to take steps to ensure that religious belief is respected by private employers calls for reasonable accommodation for that belief, particularly when this was already available to

---

the European Perspective', in: Kohen (*ed*), *Promoting Justice, Human Rights and Conflict Resolution through International Law: Liber Amicorum Lucius Caflisch* (2007), p. 281–305. See also: ECtHR 7 December 2010, 37616/02, *Köse and Others v Turkey* (dec), (foreseeable prohibition on wearing of headscarf had been proportionate in view of constitutional principle of secularism and state's obligations to impart knowledge in an objective, critical and pluralist manner: inadmissible); ECtHR 6 October 2009, 45216/07, *Appel-Irrgang a.o. v. Germany* (dec), (compulsory ethics classes of a secular nature in schools contrary to religious beliefs of parents: inadmissible as the state's margin of appreciation had not been exceeded); ECtHR 13 September 2011, 319/08, *Dojan a.o. v. Germany* (dec), (primary school compulsory sex education delivered through mandatory theatre workshops to raise awareness of sexual abuse of children was consonant with the principles of pluralism and objectivity in meeting a curriculum based on current scientific and educational standards, while attendance at carnival celebrations was not compulsory: inadmissible). Cf: ECtHR 11 September 2006, 35504/03, *Konrad v. Germany* (dec), (denial of right of home education to Christian parents who objected to private or state schooling on account of sex education, study of fairy tales, and inter-pupil violence: inadmissible as parents may not refuse the right of education to children on the basis of their convictions, and the state's assumption that schooling helped integrate children into society and gain social experience was compatible with the promotion of pluralism and fell within a state's margin of appreciation); ECtHR 7 December 2004, 50732/99, *Ciftci v. Turkey* (dec), (statutory restrictions upon enrolment in Koranic study classes: inadmissible as the restriction was intended to prevent possible indoctrination of minors by ensuring that children wishing to receive religious instruction in Koranic study classes had attained a certain maturity through completion of primary school education).

65   ECtHR 15 January 2013, 48420/10, *Eweida a.o. v. United Kingdom*, paras 102–110.

those of other faiths.[66] Live and let live is the clear message. It is an appropriate one in a multicultural society.

8.4   Conclusion

Article 9 of the European Convention on Human Rights ultimately seeks to help ensure that societal stability is enhanced through recognising the rights of individuals to be different in thought, conscience and belief. The Court's jurisprudence acknowledges the principle that diversity matters, and thus there may well be a need for limits to freedom of speech and assembly, of religious belief, and of the exercise of personal autonomy.

However, it has been argued that Article 9 may be superfluous insofar as the essential elements of individual and collective manifestations of belief, and the holding and changing of belief, may be readily protected by treating the issues as falling within the scope of other Convention guarantees. The suggestion that Article 9 is not necessary to protect freedom of thought, conscience and belief in light of case law developments involving these related guarantees is also strengthened when Article 14 considerations are applied. The suggestion is that the specific reference to freedom of religious belief in Article 9 serves little actual purpose *in a system of human rights protection that is highly-developed.* There may additionally be advantages in not specifically applying Article 9 in cases in which competing interests must be balanced: that is, that discounting any element of the exercise of religious belief in favour of the application of the principle that cases are better determined by the simple question of which side better advances pluralism, tolerance and broadmindedness. This may lead to more consistent jurisprudence and avoid the Court assessing the relative value of particular faiths.

From a secular standpoint, the real value of religious freedom is the extent to which that religion can promote a vital aspect of the self-autonomy of adherents (their relationship with their perceived creator) *and* the notion that this quest for self-autonomy calls for mutual tolerance of the rights of others to seek their own answers to this eternal issue, and of the rights of religious bodies to propose (rather than impose) alternative answers. Fresh voices, but voices that respect the inherent right of each individual to be different, to find his own answer to the meaning of life and to what extent a spiritual dimension is to be an integral aspect of that person's mind and soul, constitute the essence of pluralism, tolerance and broadmindedness.

---

66   ECtHR 15 January 2013, 48420/10, *Eweida a.o. v. United Kingdom*, paras 94-95, (in absence of 'evidence of any real encroachment on the interests of others', failure by the domestic authorities to protect the right to manifest religious belief, in breach of the positive obligation under Art. 9).

References

Boyle K. (2006), 'The Danish Cartoons', *Netherlands Quarterly of Human Rights* (24), nr. 2, p. 185.

Brown, C., Th. Green & J. Mair (2016), *Religion in Scots Law*, Edinburgh: Humanist Society Scotland.

Cram, I. (2009), 'The Danish Cartoons, Offensive Expression, and Democratic Legitimacy', in: Hare & Weinstein (eds), *Extreme Speech and Democracy*, Oxford: Oxford University Press, p. 311–330.

Dingemans, J. (*et al.*) (2013), *The Protections for Religious Rights: Law and Practice*, Oxford: Oxford University Press.

Evans, M. (2012), 'From cartoons to cruxifixes: current controversies concerning the freedom of religion and the freedom of expression before the European Court of Human Rights', in: E.D. Reed & M. Dumper (*eds*), *Civil liberties, national security and prospects for consensus: legal, philosophical and religious perspectives*, Cambridge: Cambridge University Press, p. 83-113.

Ferrari, S. & S. Pastorelli (*eds*) (2012), *Religion in Public Spaces*, Abingdon: Routledge.

Geddis, A. (2004), 'You Can't Say "God" on Radio: Freedom of Expression, Religious Advertising and the Broadcast Media after *Murphy v. Ireland*', *European Human Rights Law Review*, p. 181.

Gunn, J. (2003), 'The Complexity of Religion and the Definition of "Religion" in International Law', *Harvard Human Rights Journal*, (16), p. 189.

Harris, O'Boyle & Warbrick (1995), *Law of the European Convention on Human Rights* (1st ed.), Oxford: Oxford University Press.

Harris, O'Boyle & Warbrick (2014), *Law of the European Convention on Human Rights* (3rd ed.), Oxford: Oxford University Press.

Hill, H. (2013), 'Eweida v. United Kingdom: the right to manifest religion under article 9 of the ECHR: case analysis', *European Human Rights Law Review*, p. 187-193.

Iliopoulos-Strangas, J. (*ed*) (2005), *Constitution and Religion*, Athens.

Landau, C.E. (2007), 'Reflections on the Right to Education: the European Perspective', in: Kohen (*ed*), *Promoting Justice, Human Rights and Conflict Resolution through International Law: Liber Amicorum Lucius Caflisch*, Leiden: Brill, p. 281–305.

Lassen, E.M. (2016), 'The EU and religious minorities under pressure', *European yearbook on human rights*, p. 159-172.

Martinez-Torron, J. (2007), 'Freedom of Expression versus Freedom of Religion in the European Court of Human Rights', in: A. Sajo (*ed*), *Censorial Sensitivities: Free Speech and Religion in a Fundamentalist World*, Eleven Int. Pub., p. 233–269

Martinez-Torrón & Durham (*eds*) (2010), *Religion and the Secular State: National Reports*, Provo (UT): Brigham Young University.

Murdoch, J. (2012), *Protecting the right to freedom of thought, conscience and religion under the European Convention on Human Rights,* 2nd ed., Council of Europe.

Nathwani, N. (2008), 'Religious Cartoons and Human Rights: a Critical Legal Analysis of the Case Law of the European Court of Human Rights on the Protection of Religious Feelings and its Implications in the Danish Affair concerning Cartoons of the Prophet Muhammad', *European Human Rights Law Review,* p. 488

Pearson, M. (2013), 'Article 9 at a crossroads', *Human Rights Law Review* (13), p. 580-602.

Portaru, A. (2015), 'The "rights and freedom of others" vs. religious manifestation: who wins at the ECtHR?', *European Yearbook on Human Rights,* p. 367-377.

Ringelheim, J. (2015), 'Rights, religion and the public sphere: the European Court of Human Rights in search of a theory?', in: L. Zucca & C. Ungureanu (*eds*), *Law State and Religion in the New Europe: Debates and Dilemmas,* Cambridge: Cambridge University Press, p. 283-306.

Stavros, S. (2014), 'Combating religious hate speech: lessons learned from five years of country monitoring by the European Commission against Racism and Intolerance (ECRI), *Religion and Human Rights,* (9), p. 139-150.

Temperman, J. (2008), 'Blasphemy, Defamation of Religions and Human Rights Law', *Netherlands Quarterly of Human Rights,* (26), p. 517.

Tulkens, F. (2010), 'Conflicts between Fundamental Rights: Contrasting Views on Articles 9 and 10 of the ECHR', in: Venice Commission, *Science and Technique of Democracy 47: Blasphemy, Insult and Hatred: Finding Answers in a Democratic Society,* p. 121–131.

Uitz, R. (2007), *Freedom of Religion in European Constitutional and International Case Law,* Council of Europe Publisher.

European Court of Human Rights

ECtHR 7 December 1976	5493/72	*Handyside v. UK*
ECtHR 4 October 1977	7291/75	*X. v. UK*
ECtHR 16 May 1977	7050/75	*Arrowsmith v. UK*
ECmHR 10 March 1981	8741/79	*X. v. Germany*
ECtHR 19 March 1981	8118/77	*Omkarananda and the Divine Light Zentrum v. Switzerland*
ECtHR 13 August 1981	7601/76	*Young James & Webster v. UK*
ECtHR 15 October 1981	8652/79	*X. v. Austria*
ECtHR 25 February 1982	7511/76	*Campbell & Cosans v. UK*
ECtHR 1 July 1986	11579/85	*Khan v UK*
ECtHR 3 December 1986	10491/83	*Angelini v. Sweden*
ECtHR 14 July 1987	12587/86	*Chappell v. UK*
ECtHR 23 October 1990	11581/85	*Darby v. Sweden*
ECtHR 11 October 1991	16311/90	*Hazar, Hazar & Acik v. Turkey*

ECtHR 10 February 1993	18187/91	*W. v. UK* (dec)
ECmHR 29 March 1993	19459/92	*F.P. v. Germany* (dec.)
ECtHR 25 May 1993	14307/88	*Kokkinakis v. Greece*
ECtHR 23 June 1993	12875/87	*Hoffman v Austria*
ECtHR 8 March 1994	20490/92	*ISKCON a.o. v. UK*
ECtHR 20 September 1994	13470/87	*Otto-Preminger-Institut v. Austria*
ECtHR 9 December 1994	13092/87	*The Holy Monasteries v. Greece*
ECtHR 26 September 1995	17851/91	*Vogt v. Germany*
ECtHR 25 November 1996	17419/90	*Wingrove v. UK,*
ECtHR 18 December 1996	21787/93	*Valsamis v Greece*
ECtHR 16 December 1997	25528/94	*Canea Catholic Church v. Greece*
ECtHR 19 October 1998	31416/96	*Pendragon v. UK* (dec)
ECtHR 18 February 1999	24645/94	*Buscarini a.o. v. San Marino* [GC]
ECtHR 20 May 1999	25390/94	*Rekvényi v Hungary*
ECtHR 8 June 1999	39511/98	*McGuinness v. UK* (dec)
ECtHR 6 April 2000	34369/97	*Thlimmenos v. Greece* [GC]
ECtHR 27 June 2000	27417/95	*Cha'are Shalom Ve Tsedek v. France* [GC]
ECtHR 27 February 2001	26958/95	*Jerusalem v. Austria*
ECtHR 10 May 2001	25781/94	*Cyprus v. Turkey* [GC]
ECtHR 10 July 2001	41754/98	*Johannische Kirche & Peters v. Germany* (dec)
ECtHR 31 July 2001	41340/98	*Refah Partisi (the Welfare Party) a.o. v. Turkey* [GC]
ECtHR 29 April 2002	2346/02	*Pretty v. UK*
ECtHR 20 June 2002	50963/99	*Al-Nashif a.o. v. Bulgaria*
ECtHR 10 July 2003	44179/98	*Murphy v. Ireland*
ECtHR 7 December 2004	50732/99	*Ciftci v. Turkey* (dec)
ECtHR 2 May 2006	50692/99	*Aydın Tatlav v. Turkey*
ECtHR 11 September 2006	35504/03	*Konrad v. Germany* (dec)
ECtHR 31 October 2006	72208/01	*Klein v. Slovakia*
ECtHR 31 January 2006	64016/00	*Giniewski v. France*
ECtHR 13 September 2005	42639/04	*Jones v UK* (dec)
ECtHR 24 January 2006	39437/98	*Ülke v. Turkey*
ECtHR 28 February 2006	27034/05	*Z. & T. v. UK* (dec)
ECtHR 13 April 2006	55170/00	*Kosteski v. FYRO Macedonia*
ECtHR 5 October 2006	72881/01	*Moscow Branch of the Salvation Army v. Russia*
ECtHR 5 April 2007	18147/02	*Church of Scientology Moscow v. Russia*

ECtHR 14 June 2007	77703/01	*Svyato-Mykhaïlivska Parafiya v. Ukraine*
ECtHR 29 June 2007	15472/02	*Folgerø a.o. v. Norway* [GC]
ECtHR 13 November 2007	57325/00	*DH and Others v. Czech Republic* [GC],
ECtHR 21 February 2008	19516/06	*Alexandridis v Greece*
ECtHR 31 July 2008	40825/98	*Religionsgemeinschaft der Zeugen Jehovas a.o. v. Austria*
ECtHR 6 November 2008	38450/05	*Sabanchiyeva a.o. v. Russia* (dec)
ECtHR 19 March 2009	28648/03	*Lang v Austria*
ECtHR 1 October 2009	76836/01	*Kimlya a.o. v. Russi*
ECtHR 6 October 2009	45216/07	*Appel-Irrgang a.o. v. Germany* (dec)
ECtHR 10 December 2009	33001/03	*Koppi v Austria*
ECtHR 2 February 2010	21924/05	*Sinan Işik v. Turkey*
ECtHR 23 February 2010	41135/98	*Ahmet Arslan a.o. v. Turkey*
ECtHR 3 June 2010	42837/06	*Dimitras a.o. v. Greece*
ECtHR 10 June 2010	302/02	*Jehovah's Witnesses of Moscow v Russia*
ECtHR 15 June 2010	7710/02	*Grzelak v. Poland*
ECtHR 21 September 2010	8916/05	*Association of Jehovah's Witnesses v. France* (dec)
ECtHR 21 October 2010	4916/07	*Alekseyev v. Russia*
ECtHR 7 December 2010	37616/02	*Köse and Others v Turkey* (dec)
ECtHR 9 December 2010	7798/08	*Savez crkava 'Riječ života' a.o. v. Croatia*
ECtHR 18 March 2011	30814/06	*Lautsi v. Italy* [GC]
ECtHR 7 July 2011	23459/03	*Bayatyan v. Armenia* [GC]
ECtHR 13 September 2011	319/08	*Dojan a.o. v. Germany* (dec)
ECtHR 31 January 2012	35021/05	*Kovaļkovs v Latvia* (dec)
ECtHR 26 June 2012	9300/07	*Herrmann v. Germany* [GC]
ECtHR 13 July 2012	16354/06	*Mouvement raëlien suisse v. Switzerland* [GC]
ECtHR 15 January 2013	48420/10	*Eweida a.o. v. UK*
ECtHR 6 June 2013	38450/05	*Sabanchiyeva a.o. v. Russia*
ECtHR 19 November 2013	26270/04	*Bogdan Vodă Greek-Catholic Parish v. Romania*
ECtHR 4 March 2014	7552/09	*The Church of Jesus Christ of Latter-Day Saints v. UK*
ECtHR 12 June 2014	33203/08	*Biblical Centre of the Chuvash Republic v. Russia*
ECtHR 7 October 2014	28490/02	*Begheluri v. Georgia*
ECtHR 28 October 2014	49327/11	*Gough v. UK*
ECtHR 24 February 2015	30587/13	*Karaahmed v. Bulgaria*

House of Lords (UK)
Whaley v. Lord Advocate   2008 SC (HL) 107

Supreme Court (United States of America)
Snyder v. Phelps   562 US 443   2011

Chapter 9   Immigration Law versus Religious Freedom Law

Conflicts and solutions in comparative administrative law

Roberto Scarciglia

9.1 Introduction

The aim of this chapter is to discuss some of the legal problems related to the exercise of freedom of religion and immigration from a comparative law point of view. In particular, we consider the contribution of administrative law in solving (or complicating) some of these problems in some recent experiences of EU countries and the United States. From this point of view, some secondary sources can influence the relationships between immigration and administrative law, and, among these, there are the executive orders issued by US Presidents. The paper focuses specifically on legal issues related to the exercise of freedom of religion in places of immigration detention.[1]

---

1   On 25 January 2017, US President Trump issued an executive order, which suspended the US Refugee Admissions (USRAP) for 120 days (Executive Order No. 13767, Border Security and Immigration Enforcement Improvements). It delayed the entry, regardless of valid non-diplomatic visas of people from seven predominantly Muslim countries: Iraq, Iran, Libya, Somalia, Sudan, Syria, and Yemen for 90 days. Finally, it also suspended the entry of refugees from Syria indefinitely (Executive Order No. 13769, 2017-02281, *Protecting the Nation from Foreign Terrorist Entry into the United States*, revoked by Executive Order No. 13769 of March 6, 2017, on Protecting the Nation from Foreign Terrorist Entry into the United States). See also the Executive Order No. 13767, 2017-02095, *Border Security and Immigration Enforcement Improvements*. A federal judge in Brooklyn, Ann M. Donnelly, came first to the aid of scores of refugees and others trapped at airports across the United States after this executive order: see Sheare, M.D., Kulish, N., Feuer, A., Judge Blocks Trump Order on Refugees Amid Chaos and Outcry Worldwide, *The New York Times*, Jan. 28, 2017. A federal judge in Seattle on February, 3rd, 2017, temporarily blocked President Trump's week-old immigration order from being enforced nationwide, reopening America's door to visa holders from seven predominantly Muslim countries and dealing the administration a humbling defeat. After many other decisions on airport arrest cases, the San Francisco-based 9th US Circuit Court of Appeals declined, on February, 9th, 2017 to block a lower-court ruling that suspended the ban and allowed previously barred travellers to enter the U.S. After some contrary decisions for Trump's Administration by federal judges in Hawaii and Maryland and before U.S. appeals courts in Virginia and California, the Supreme Court puts off a final decision on Trump's new travel ban on September 25, 2017 (E.O. No. 13769 of March 6, 2017):
<www.washingtonpost.com., September 12, 2017>.

As West & Sussman point out:[2]

> *executive orders are most often used to establish agencies in the executive branch, to alter administrative rules or actions, to modify the decision-making process, or to flesh out and enforce laws.*

This presidential order contains some profiles of arbitrariness especially for the extension of the ban to those who are already in possession of a visa.

Concerning immigration law, there are different points of view from which we can analyse this issue. However, the question is which viewing angle has to be chosen. Can we consider immigration law independently from all other areas of law? Alternatively, is immigration law more porous, absorbing features of other closely related areas of law? The relationship with other fields of law, it may seem, is evident when you consider the many legal problems that the immigration issue involves: from constitutional to international law, from criminal to administrative law, to mention only a few. Many scholars have explored the intersections between these different fields of law. The objective of this chapter is to ask what role administrative law plays in the resolution of conflicts and solutions for integration between different cultures. Migrants are now ongoing at the intersection of problems and opportunities, at the centre of clashes and confrontations, between values, cultures, traditions and economies of the various human communities. Events related to pseudo-religious terrorism (i.e. Isis, Al-Qaeda, Boko Aram, etc.) have overshadowed the jurist's reflections on the forms of integration between religions and cultures of migrants with the host communities or in transit to other countries. Religion is a fundamental component of human being.

> *The centrality and power of religious beliefs for the individual and for the state (that intends to maximize control over the person by controlling its belief system) explain why religious practices are endorsed by the state.[3]*

In this regard, legal scholars such as Werner Menski, Patrick Glenn and Andrew Huxley have contributed to the development of studies on the interaction between law and religion.[4] Despite this renewed focus on the cultural traditions of immigrants, developed in university classrooms, the reality looks different, like many measures restricting the rights of immigrants, and adopted by some European governments tend to prove.

We start with the number of migrants arriving in Europe in 2016. According to the data provided by the Italian Interior Ministry, the number of migrants that landed in Europe in 2016 is impressive, and covers mainly three countries: Italy

---

2   West & Sussman 1999, 80.
3   Sajó and Uitz 2012, 912
4   Menski 2000 & 2006; Glenn 2000 & 2004; Huxley 2002.

(181,436), Greece (173,477), and Spain (6,826). In the first part of 2016, there were more than half a million non-EU asylum seekers – mainly Syrians, Afghans, and Iraqis – with 61% of the cases lodged in Germany; and Italy, with over 49 thousand requests, was in second place in Europe. These numbers highlight the drama of the problem, if we consider further that a global economic relationship can produce state policies that "directly violate social and labor rights and indirectly produce social conflicts that lead to state violations of human rights".[5]

Many European countries have declared a state of emergency, such as France, Macedonia, Greece, Hungary, and Austria, adopting extraordinary measures to deal with migration and terrorism. These types of decisions can be contrary to EU legislation and establish principles regarding human and social rights and can strip individuals of their legal identity. There are many criticisms at international level, which call for a necessary revision of principles and rules with the aim of protecting migrants and other vulnerable populations.[6]

The Italian philosopher Giorgio Agamben defines the critical nature of this concept of emergency in his famous book *The State of Exception*.[7] It constitutes a "point of imbalance between public law and political fact".[8] There is no doubt that this state dimension describes the augmentation of government powers during these times when sovereignty is perceived to be under threat. In states of emergency, governments suspend elements of the legal order and strip individuals of the rights that mark politicized life: "a quality of human existence that goes beyond the 'bare life' of biological subsistence".[9] Taking up again Agamben's considerations, we can share his idea that in the form of the state of exception:

> *the status necessitatis appears as an ambiguous and uncertain zone in which de facto proceedings, which are in themselves extra- or anti-juridical, pass over into law, and juridical norms blur with mere fact–that is, a threshold where fact and law seem to become undecidable.*

According to Mathiot, in the state of necessity, the judges elaborate a positive law of crisis.[10] However, governments and public administrations also tend to interpret the gaps in public law to resolve conflicts: in this case, between locals and migrants, new and old migrants, between public administration and migrants and for problems concerning religious freedom. Therefore, it creates a trilateral relationship between these three subjects that requires careful

---

5   Brisk 2002, 10.
6   Ramji-Nogales 2014, 701.
7   Agamben 2005, 1.
8   Saint-Bonnet 2001, 28.
9   Ellermann 2009, 1.
10 Mathiot 1956, 424.

balancing. Plenary powers delegated to one of these can preclude any judicial scrutiny of immigration decisions affecting arriving immigrants.

These migrants engage in processes of globalization of their religious beliefs and practices. According to Plüss, "[m]igrants may use their religion not only as a means to adapt to new surroundings but also as a means to differentiate themselves from these surroundings through stressing what they understand to be 'the essence' of their religion".[11] Although not always related to religious freedom, we can see this attitude in many decisions of the European Courts. For example, when they examine cases in which migrants are sometimes in the hands of the administration, and their rights remain trapped in legal limbo.[12]

The same could be said for other non-European courts: when they judge such issues as clothing, food, sport, prison life or education, when an administrative decision-maker has violated a fundamental right, and a court must choose to apply the standards of constitutional law – such as a proportionality text – or the standards of administrative law, such as reasonableness.

Consequently, through the decisions of the constitutional/supreme and administrative courts, we can investigate the current role of administrative law, and whether the global emergencies, like the dramatic phenomenon of actual migrations, are transforming this field of law. This chapter proceeds as follows. I begin by briefly describing the intersection of immigration and administrative law, delving into the question, is "immigration law administrative law?" Then I discuss how administrative procedures can affect the religious freedom of migrants, and how the administrative courts review a public decision, which has violated a fundamental right of a migrant, applying the standards of administrative law. Finally, I will describe the effects of a possible administrative characterization of freedom and due process for migrants.

9.2   Intersection of immigration law and administrative law

Some scholars argue that legal immigration problems, in essence, fall within administrative law. In the opinion of Jill Family, "[a]s a branch of administrative law, immigration law is about the direct regulation of human beings. In immigration law, administrative law doctrines are applied to determine some of the most fundamental and basic human concerns: where an individual will live and work, and whether that individual will live with family or will be separated from a spouse and children".[13]

From this point of view, I would like to define the intersections of immigration law and administrative law. The concept of *intersection of sets* can help clarify the relationship between these two fields of law. Let us take into

---

11 Plüss 2009, 494.
12 See: Savino 2016; ECHR 1 September 2015, 16483/12, *Khlaifia a.o. v. Italy*; CJEU 7 June 2016, C-47/15, *Affum.*
13 Family 2015, 89.

consideration two sets: e.g. two different fields in a legal system, denoted as A and B. For example, we consider Immigration Law (A) and Administrative Law (B), e.g., with different rules:

- those of field A {r, r1, r2, ⋯, rn} (which belong to set A), and
- those of field B {x, x1, x2, ⋯, xn} (which belong to set B).

Suppose that:

- (a) r, r1, r2, ⋯, rn $\in$ A;
- (b) r, r1, r2, ⋯, rn $\notin$ B;
- (c) x, x1, x2, ⋯, xn $\in$ σ B;
- (d) x, x$_1$, x2, ⋯, xn $\notin$ A".

It is possible to identify one or more element in the two sets (e.g., a rule, a procedure, or a legal format, common to both sets), which could form part of an intersection between the two sets (I = A $\cap$ B), and may contain other elements common to A and B. Consequently, it seems necessary to identify those elements or components of A (immigration law) that may be part of the set B (administrative law).

The first of the elements is given by the sources of immigration law and the extent to which the sources coincide with administrative law. From a comparative point of view, we can examine some problems in immigration law related to the use of legislative and non-legislative rules, defining, at least in part, the essential content of immigration law as administrative law. From this point of view, it is not surprising that migrants most often are detained, during the verification of their identity, in migration centres, or prisons, and administrative law rules predominantly govern them.[14] This reflection postulates the existence of special administration supremacy exercising its power over recipient prisoners.[15] Some legal scholars converge on this position when referring to "penal-administrative law" or "administrative penal law".[16] It allows state or administrative bodies to impose sanctions, which have the character of, or at least are similar to punishment and epitomizes penal regulations outside the penal code.[17] In the following pages, I will try to provide some examples from the experience of the United States and France regarding the relationship between religion and detention in prisons or other similar places.

These examples may help to show that similar problems may find different solutions in Western legal systems.

---

14 Nespoli 1981 p. 35.
15 Ranelletti 1911, p. 452.
16 see Cassese, 2016, p. 13.
17 Goldschmidt 1902, P. 71.

9.2.1   Legislative rules, immigration and administrative law

In general, the sources of immigration law are based – as well as on constitutional, EU and international law – on primary and secondary domestic legislation. However, it may be that measures of administrative law may regulate – or at the same time deny – the concrete realization of a right recognized by hierarchically higher-level sources.

What do the national laws that deal with immigration contain? I will highlight a few examples of recent legislation which by varying degrees, has been affected by the climate that the terrorist attacks in Europe have produced.[18] The same also happened in the United States after the terrorist attack of September 11 on the Twin Towers. The federal government's response to September 11 also demonstrates the close relationship between immigration law and civil rights in the United States. Non-citizens historically have been the most vulnerable to civil rights deprivations, in large part because the law permits, and perhaps even encourages, extreme governmental conduct with minimal protection for the rights of non-citizens.[19] And, it is not accidental that Mr. Trump's executive order No. 13769, 2017-02281, is entitled "*Protecting the Nation from Foreign Terrorist Entry into the United States*".

The laws of the EU countries have different contents that cannot be analyzed in this chapter. Among the more recent ones, we can note the French law on rights and freedoms of aliens, published on March 7, 2016 (*Loi relative au droit des étrangers*). For some profiles, this law represents an important step in ensuring the rights of immigrants. Before examining some of its contents, we can consider that many parts of the measure, both on procedural grounds and through the courts, introduced or amended rules governed by administrative law. In this case, the intersection is very wide and demonstrates that both the administration and the government can increasingly turn to administrative law doctrines to shield their immigration decisions from judicial scrutiny.

On the other hand, the administration can choose to entrust to the judges the choice of detention or expulsion. For example, Article 33 of this law, concerning illegal immigrants, states:

> The alien may request the President of the French Admini-
> strative Court to annul the obligation to leave the French
> territory.

Article 33 thus removes the previous administrative detention during which the French prefect could decide to keep a clandestine in detention, while organizing his/her departure.

The new French law contains specific provisions relating to admission and residence of foreigners, on the issue of a multi-year residence permit, to illegal

---

18   E.g. Paris 1995, 2011 & 2015; Utøya, Norvay 2011; Tolosa 2012; London 2013; Bruxelles, 2014.
19   Akram & Johnson 2002, 1.

aliens, and administrative disputes – the administrative courts have extensive powers – in cases of applications for asylum. The application of this provision cannot be separated from the main sources of French administrative law.[20] Furthermore, before the entry into force of the law of 2016, the French administrative courts had enforced the Return Directive[21] , in accordance with the principle of direct application of a European Directive where the same is compatible with the legal system by virtue of the particular binding force of the EU Treaty.

The new law does not refer to freedom of religion. But it is still within administrative law that we can find a connecting element between the right to immigration and religious freedom. In French administrative law, the Code des relations entre le public et l' administration, which came into force on January 1, 2016, introduced significant changes that, to some extent, may affect the rights of immigrants, including those relating to the exercise of religious freedom.[22] Article L100-2 expressly provides that: "[t]he administration acts in the public interest and respect for the principle of legality. It is bound by the obligation of neutrality and respect for the principle of secularism (French: laicité). It complies with the principle of equality and guarantees fair treatment." If "secularism" is a general rule governing the action of public administration, it is necessary to identify the fields, and the limits, that the (administrative) judge attaches to this principle through legal interpretation.

It has been previously noted that immigration law is part of administrative law. Based on this consideration, all provisions relating to immigration – and the measures which dictate the public authorities in this matter – should be compatible with the laws on administrative procedure, unless the law provides otherwise. Similarly, the applicability of constitutional principles, whether about freedom and rights, or whether they relate to public administration cannot be ruled out. From this point of view, we refer primarily to the US experience with regard to its Administrative Procedure Act (APA), surrounding agency use of these rules through the perspective of immigration law, and also to the laws of these models - European and North-American - which are adopted in many countries of the world.

---

20 See the *Code de l'entrée et du séjour des étrangers et du droit d'asile* <www.legifrance.gouv.fr/affichCode.do?cidTexte =LEGITEXT000006070158>; the Law n° 79-587 du 11 juillet 1979 *modifiée relative à la motivation des actes administratifs et à l'amélioration des relations entre l'administration et le public*; the Law n° 91-647 du 10 juillet 1991 relative à *l'aide juridique*; the Law n°2000-321, 12 April 2000, *relative aux droits des citoyens dans leurs relations avec les administrations*; the *Code of administrative justice*, <www.legifrance.gouv.fr/affichCode.do?cidTexte= LEGITEXT0000 31366350>.
21 Directive 2008/115/EC of 16 December 2008.
22 CAA de Bordeaux, 4ème chambre (formation à 3), 25/02/2016, 15BX02697 <www.legifrance.gouv.fr>.

9.2.2   Non-legislative rules

There are significant immigration law issues that are governed by non-legislative rules. According to Family:

> studying immigration non-legislative rules exemplifies how
> general principles of administrative law manifest in
> immigration law. It also shows how attempts to reform the
> use of non-legislative rules in immigration law must take
> into consideration the challenges that all agencies face
> regarding notice-and-comment rulemaking and also must
> acknowledge a debate that is much larger than immigration
> law itself.[23]

I refer to the role of federal administrative agencies in immigration decisions. We know that these agencies are not a part of the Legislative Branch and when the US Congress delegates power to agencies through a statute, this delegation includes the authority to create all kinds of rules, according to the Administrative Procedure Act.[24] On this point, it must be said that distinguishing between no legislative and legislative rules is one of the most complex tasks in administrative law.[25] It is difficult to decide whether an agency has properly used the policy statement or interpretive rule exemptions. In some cases, a plenary power delegated to agencies could preclude any judicial scrutiny of immigration decisions affecting arriving immigrants (Cox 2007, 1671). Confusion about the source of immigration power creates substantial uncertainty about the distribution of that authority between Congress and the executive.

Attention should also be paid to administrative circulars. In the course of its duties, the administration interprets statutes or regulations, which are imprecise or unclear. Administrative circulars are binding upon civil servants, but not upon citizens, and can create a parallel system of law. Administrative circulars often regulate immigration.[26] In some cases, sources related to detention and repatriation are governed by a "dumb law",[27] as, for example, secret agreements governing simplified expulsion procedures followed by the Italian government and agreed with Tunisia.[28]

---

23 Family 2012, 566.
24 APA, 5 U.S.C. § 551 (4) (2006).
25 US Court of Appeals, District of Columbia Circuit, *Am. Mining Cong* v. *Mine Safety &*
     Health Administration, 995 F.2D 1106, 1108 (D.C. Cir. 1993).
26 Gjergji 2013.
27 Sacco 2015.
28 Savino 2015, 1.

9.2.3   The principle of secularism

The relationship between the principle of secularism and the private beliefs of immigrants feeds a permanent debate in France on the limits that the same principle poses to freedom of religion. The sociologist Gunther Teubner coined the concept of "legal irritant" concerning the fact that "the result of transplantation can be anything" and, consequently, "we should not speak of a legal transplant but a legal irritant".[29] If we consider that in France, the vast majority of immigrants are Muslims, "[f]or many of them the confrontation with Western norms and lifestyles and the ensuing experience of the contingency of one's beliefs and ways of life is deeply disturbing." In many cases, Islamic communities in Europe or the USA "not only remain unaffected by Western modernization, but rather reject it explicitly, and draw the justification for this attitude from their religious beliefs. They are accustomed to a state that proclaims itself as an Islamic state, meaning that no clear distinction is made between religion, politics, and law".[30]

The interpretation of the principle of "secularism" – or "laïcité" in France – by judges and legal scholars can better explain these limits.

We should point out that the principle of secularism emerged in the French legal system with precise characteristics more than a century ago. Although through the years it has undergone significant changes, secularism is still a legal and constitutional element that distinguishes French law from that of other European countries and the United States. Cox points out that "[t]he history of immigration jurisprudence is a history of obsession with judicial deference. The foundational doctrine of constitutional immigration law—the 'plenary power' doctrine—is centrally concerned with such deference".[31] From this point of view, immigration law has long been concerned with separation of powers problems, and this doctrine requires that courts give great deference to political branch decisions about immigration policy and enforcement.

In France, the Council of State defends the principle of "laïcité" (or secularism). It states, "Freedom of expression, guaranteed by Constitution, cannot allow them to wear signs of religious affiliation. It would constitute an act of pressure, provocation, proselytism or propaganda, on other public service users, disrupt teaching activities, or disturb the order in the establishment or the proper functioning of the administrative action. The reason is clear, whereas, in the same way, the wearing of certain religious symbols may be legally prohibited for the sake of security.[32] However, this principle requires equality of all citizens before the law, without distinction as to religion and the respect for all beliefs. This same principle requires that the Republic guarantees the free exercise of worship; whereas, accordingly, the possibility of derogating from the obligation

---

29   Teubner 1998, 61.
30   Grimm 2009, 2370.
31   Cox 2008, 1671.
32   CAA de Paris, 6ème chambre 6/12/2016, 15PA03527 <arianeinternet.conseil-etat.fr>.

of stunning for the practice of ritual slaughter does not infringe the principle of secularism".[33]

The French Council of State defines the limits of the principle, specifically concerning detention in prison, and later briefly reviews the US Court decisions. The Court states that the administration must "respect the right of any person to continue when imprisoned, for the exercise of the religion of their choice, must give accreditation to a sufficient number of chaplains, as soon as such request is formulated." The only conditions are the presence of security requirements and the need to preserve the good order of the prison. Moreover, "whereas it must likewise, to the extent the premises permit and only limited for reasons of good order and security, allow the organization of worship in the institutions; whereas the facilitation alone of ordinary law visits of representatives of the religion cannot meet these obligations."[34]

9.3   Religious freedom and administrative procedure

Classically, administrative decision-makers need only strike a proportionate balance between constitutional values and statutory objectives, a flexible, non-formalistic analysis. Still, if there are global factors – such as e.g. war, terrorism, and immigration – these create complex problems for national governments.

As has been pointed out by some scholars, no one is directly suggesting repeal of Article 18 of the International Covenant on Civil and Political Rights, or the guarantees of religious freedom in most constitutions. Rather, there is a tipping point phenomenon and a pattern of erosion by exceptions. These derogations are in the name of other rights and other state interests, of trans-formed equality norms, or deriving from a lost perspective on the importance of freedom of religion.[35]

A striking feature of the crisis is its incremental character in public behaviour and decisions on the issues relating to immigrants. From this point of view, these decisions could be "arbitrary, unreasoned, irrational, inconsistent and unin-formed" (Cox 2007, 1680) derogating from existing administrative procedures and statutory due process protection. Among the vices of an administrative act, we can include the violation of principles, e.g. reasonableness, proportionality or the duty to give reasons. For example, in remembering the tragic historical episodes of mass deportation for religious reasons, we must ensure that the prohibition of the collective expulsions of migrants is interpreted strictly.

The ratio of the ban is to protect foreigners belonging to a religious group from arbitrary use of the administrative power of expulsion. The prohibition of collective expulsion becomes an enhancement tool for due process, through the

---

33 Conseil d'État, Appeal n. 361441, reading of 5 July 2013 <arianeinternet.conseil-etat.fr>.
34 Conseil d'État, Appeal nn. 351115, 351116, 351152, 351153, 351220, 354484, 354485, 354507, 354508, reading of 16 October 2013, at http://arianeinternet.conseil-etat.fr.
35 See Cole Durham 2011, 1.

application of the adversarial principle and the duty to give reasons. The immigration field lends itself to simplifying and introducing faster procedures for economic reasons, contravening these canons. The identification of migrants is not sufficient to ensure compliance with the principle of due process, without participation in the administrative procedure and a particular reason to justify repatriation.

9.4   Conflicts and solutions: the role of administrative law

The previous observations highlight some of the problems related to the religious freedom of migrants and conflicts with the administrative authorities, which often violate fundamental rights through acts not corresponding to the normal dynamics of the administrative procedure. The plenary powers sometimes attributed to the administration for exceptional situations or the need to guarantee security – or the absence of appeal rules – produce criticism of the rejection of immigrants at sea or unjustified time limits.

In my opinion, domestic legislation and EU regulatory measures should develop common principles of immigration law, reconciling them with the general discipline of administrative law. In particular, the laws on administrative procedure should allow administrative discretion and not just impose binding acts that do not allow adequate participation in these proceedings. From this point of view, comparative law can play an especially, important, role.

The provisions related to religious freedom in detention centres constitute a test for administrative law. As we have noted, identification, first reception, detention centres, and prisons characterize the lives of migrants. How should courts review administrative decisions in violation of this fundamental right?

9.4.1   Religious Freedom in Detention Centres

One of the most important issues affecting the lives of migrants is their detention. From the start, their journey means being locked up in cramped spaces, both on land and at sea, the inability to maintain good personal hygiene and often existing in inhuman conditions, which, in many cases, lead to their death. These tragedies are there for all to see. Even if they manage to reach a ship, or to cross a frontier, there are forms of confinement in detention centres or internment in prison.

In most European countries, the custody of migrants for migration related reasons is defined as "administrative detention". It is a measure that does not formally constitute a punishment and does not require conviction of a crime.[36] Nevertheless, although many scholars use the term "administrative detention" to designate incarceration for the purpose of immigration control, in many

---

36 Leerkes & Broeders 2010.

member states the precise boundary between detention as an administrative or penal measure is not so clear cut.

That is partly due to the interaction between criminal proceedings on the one hand and administrative procedures governing detention and expulsion on the other. In addition, some member states do not make a clear distinction between those detention facilities that form part of the penal system and those that are reserved for individuals falling within immigration proceedings. Thus, where individual member states, such as the UK, restrict immigrant freedom to "detention and removal centres", in other countries including France, Germany, and Greece, migrants are regularly incarcerated in penitentiary institutions, prisons and police custody.[37]

What is the guarantee that religious freedom is respected in places of detention? How can a prison administrator or a judge determine the balance between the principle of security of the state and religious freedom? Above all, how is it possible without denying this second principle? When a subject is in a limiting legal situation or is deprived of liberty, he or she is often the recipient of administrative measures which are broadly discretionary. Against these measures, he or she can only access national or supranational courts, as happens with the European courts.

Firstly, I will try to focus on a few but significant cases decided by the US courts. In *Holt* v. *Hobbs*, a prisoner (*Holt*) motivated by his Muslim faith requested an exception to the Director of the Arkansas Department of Correction (*Hobbs*) prohibiting inmates from growing beards, except for quarter-inch beards for approved dermatological reasons. After refusal by the prison administration, Holt appealed to the federal district court, and the warden of Holt's prison claimed that prisoners could use a short beard to introduce contraband into prisons and possibly avoid identification if they escaped, by shaving off the beard. The district judge and the US Court for the Eighth Circuit had upheld the claim by the prison authorities that in this case the need for security prevailed, rather than the exercise of religious freedom. The US Supreme Court had jurisdiction over the matter and to decide the case in the light of the *Religious Land Use and Institutionalized Persons Act* (RLUIPA) governing the exercise of religious freedom of people held in public institutions.[38]

Holt came before the Supreme Court in a time of increasing interest in the Muslim prison population. As some scholars had argued, "[t]he 'War on Terror' has converted American prisons into battlegrounds, pitting prison officials against 'radical Islam'" (Beydoun). On January 20, 2015, the United States Supreme Court ruled that the Arkansas Department of Correction's grooming policy restricting a Muslim inmate from growing a half-inch beard violated the *Religious Land Use and Institutionalized Persons Act*.[39] In many cases, the

---

37 Cornelisse, 2010.
38 Public Law 106-274 (2000).
39 *Holt* v. *Hobbs*, 574 U.S. 1 (2015).

courts believed prison administration to be beyond their jurisdiction, and thus, seldom questioned let alone overruled the administrative decisions of prison officials.

However, these precedents reproduce the issue of whether in cases involving religious freedom – the *Free Exercise Clause* – the judges must apply the *strict scrutiny test*, or the principle in the case of *Division* v. *Smith*, according to which no one can be exempted from general laws even for religious reasons.[40] These different approaches are present in several decisions but always relate to freedom of religion.[41]

In *O'Lone v. Estate of Shabazz*[42], the US Supreme Court, confirming the parameters of the previous decision in *Turner* v. *Safley*[43], defined the conditions that the prison administration had to respect in its decision to avoid violating the rights guaranteed under the US Constitution (*Turner* factors). The Court established four factors:

(1) Whether there is a rational connection between the prison regulation and the legitimate governmental interest put forward to justify it;
(2) Whether an alternative means of exercising the right exists in spite of what the prison has done;
(3) Whether striking down the prison action would have a significant ripple effect on fellow inmates or staff;
(4) Whether there are alternatives available to the prison, or whether the regulation appears instead to be 'exaggerated response' to the problem it is intended to address.

These administrative rules produced the effect of denying a prisoner of the Muslim faith (*Shabazz*) amendment of the prison regulations to enable him to observe Jumu'ah Friday prayer. The Court also took a restrictive approach in *Thornburgh* v. *Abbott* by excluding publications mailed to inmates that were considered "detrimental to the security, good order, or discipline of the institution or [that] might facilitate criminal activity".[44] Nevertheless, the 1993 Religious Freedom Restoration Act placed a new burden on correctional institutions.[45] In particular, the RLUIPA establishes the illegitimacy of administrative measures that produce a "substantial burden", and that is, a severe limitation to exercising religious freedom if the limit is not motivated by an overriding public interest (*compelling governmental interest*) and there is another less detrimental way to satisfy this interest. One could cite many judgments by US courts in which a kind of *metus* is still visible against the prison authorities, although in many ways the prison is the acid test of administrative law that deals with the rights of immigrants and their integration.

---

40 *Division* v. *Smith*, 494 U.S. 872 (1990).
41 Blischak 1988, p. 456
42 *O'Lone v. Estate of Shabazz*, 494 U.S. 342 (1990).
43 *Turner v. Safley*, 482 U.S. 78 (1987)
44 *Thornburgh v. Abbott*, 490 U.S. 401 (1989).
45 Pub. L. No. 103-141, 107 Stat. 1488 (November 16, 1993).

The most recent cases oscillate between these two positions (*strict scrutiny test* and *Turner* factors). On the one hand, it recognizes that Islamic prisoners are entitled to wear the kufi and let their beards grow, subject to the exercise of religious freedom, although Texas penitentiary regulations prohibit this.[46] On the other hand, they have been denied the right to smoke a pipe during their religious ceremonies or to let their hair grow.[47]

Also with regard to respect for Ramadan, it was decided that a Muslim prisoner was entitled to receive the evening meal after sunset, since a prison administration's refusal would oblige him to dine before sunset, thus violating his religious precepts.[48] Again, a Muslim prisoner had the right to abstain from working in the prison kitchen whenever they prepared or cooked pork chops.[49]

9.5   Conclusions: Towards the administrativization of freedom and due process for migrants?

In concluding this chapter, I will try to answer some of the questions previously raised. One of the main issues indicated is that immigration law is part of administrative law. That is the conclusion reached by some legal scholars, both European and American, whereby most of the immigration rules are covered by administrative law. Principles, procedures, and administrative justice form the backbone, as the experiences of European countries and the United States indicate. On the theoretical level, the framework provided by constitutional law, and international conventions on human rights, in addition to these penalty provisions falling under penal discipline, appears in the background.

Administrations have increasingly turned to administrative law doctrines to shield its immigration decisions from judicial scrutiny. Trump's executive order for an immigration ban – which does not spare the elderly, children, religious Christians, scientists, students, entrepreneurs – leads us to reflect on the exercise of discretion at the highest level of the administration, which, without respect for the Constitution, could have unpredictable side effects. On the European side, on the contrary, the idea that European administrative law is developing, in the light of the basic constitutional principles of the European Union, postulates behaviour opposite to the American model: exclusion v. integration. Thereby it can mitigate religious conflicts and create an atmosphere of mutual consideration. However, balancing does not save the legislator or the judge from deciding which right or interest shall ultimately prevail in which situation.

---

46   US District Court for the Eastern District of Texas, *Rasheed Ali* v. *Stephens*, No. 14-41165 (May 2, 2016).
47   US Court of Appeals, 5th Circuit, *Davis Goodman* v. *Davis*, No. 14-40339 (June 14, 2016).
48   US Court of Appeals, 2th Circuit, *Williams* v. *Correctional Officers*, No. 15-692 (May 16, 2016).
49   US District Court, Arkansas, Eastern Division, *Bragg* v. *Smith*, No. 2-16CV00022 (May 18, 2016).

This means that religious freedom may be on the losing side regardless of the importance of a religious requirement for the believer. There are situations in which the only alternatives are adapting to the secular norm, or emigration.[50] As demonstrated, however, recent political choices (e.g. the United States, Hungary) on the balance between the rights of immigrants and the exercise of religious freedom is increasingly in the hands of the judges, who will be called upon – as demonstrated by the case of Trump's executive order – to intervene with emergency measures.

With regard to comparative law, we can say that the right to immigration can be, in large part, framed within a particular part of administrative law. However, one of the principles and procedures that underlie a common core can be found – in the present historical moment characterized by Trump's executive orders – by comparing the experiences of European Union states. Principles, administrative procedures and appeal procedures can, in fact, find a common basis for general measures on immigration binding on the EU member states. If one thinks about American executive orders, one can also share the view that administrative law is currently regarded as a tool, which is not an instrument of the government, to protect people from the government's actions.[51]

If administrative law has its prerequisites in the Constitution, the same cannot always be said for government measures. Immigration has always been an asset to the regions and receiving states. Religion has often provided the spiritual resources necessary for emigration and resistance in the face of adversity, and the dramatic and inhuman hardships endured by migrants. Respect for religious freedom makes the integration and coexistence of different cultural traditions stronger and lasting. The dialogue between courts in different countries can implement forms of integration based on these values. These courts can play a strategic role - at least in Europe - to promote social and institutional changes in migration policies.

Comparative law can show that a common faith in law among different cultures constitutes:

> *an essential element of a world civil religion. [...] It offers hope for establishing world channels of cooperation and resolving world conflicts when less formal and more amicable means fail.[52]*

---

50 Grimm 2009, p. 2382.
51 Cassese, 2016, 13.
52 Berman 2006, p. 750.

References

Agamben, G. (2005), *The State of Exception*, (trans. by K. Attel), Chicago and London: Chicago University Press.

Akram, S.M. & K.R. Johnson (2002), 'Race, Civil Rights, and Immigration Law after September 11, 2001: The Targeting of Arabs and Muslims', *New York University Annual Survey of American Law*, 58, p. 1-124.

Beydoun, K.A. (2015), 'Islam Incarcerated: Religious Accommodation of Muslim Prisoners Before Holt v. Hobbs', <ssrn.com/abstract=2561845> or <dx.doi.org/10.2139/ssrn.2561845>.

Berman, H.J. (2006), 'Comparative Law and Religion', in: M. Reimann & R. Zimmermann (2006), *The Oxford Handbook of Comparative Law*, Oxford: OUP, p. 739-751.

Blischak, M.P. (1998), 'O'Lone v. Estate of Shabazz: The State of Prisoners' Religions Free Exercise Rights', *The American University Law Review*, 37, p. 456-458.

Brisk, A. (2002), *Globalization and Human Rights*, Berkeley and Los Angeles: University of California Press.

Cassese, S. (2016), 'Verso un nuovo diritto amministrativo?', *Giornale di diritto amministrativo*, 1, p. 12-15.

Clarke, P.B. (2009), *The Oxford Handbook of the Sociology of Religion*, Oxford: OUP.

Clayton, G. (2016), *Textbook of Immigration and Asylum Law*, Oxford: OUP.

Durham, C.W.Jr. (2011), 'Religious Freedom in a Worldwide Setting: Comparative Reflections', *Pontificia Accademia delle scienze sociali*, Plenary Session, Vatican City.

Cox, A.B. (2008), *Delegation and Immigration Law*, Public Law and Legal Theory Working Papers, p. 1681-1687.

Ellermann, A. (2009), 'Undocumented Migrants and Resistance in the State of Exception', Paper presented at *European Union Studies Association*, Los Angeles, p. 1-25.

Family, J.E. (2006), 'The Many Sides of Immigration Law and Policy', *Widener Law*, p. 6-7.

Family, J.E. (2012), 'Administrative Law through the Lenses of Immigration Law', *Administrative Law Review*, 64, 3, p. 565-618.

Family, J.E. (2015-2016), 'DAPA and the Future of Immigration Law as Administrative Law', *Washburn Law Journal*, 55, p. 89-100.

Gjergji, I. (2013), *'Circolari amministrative e immigrazione'*, Milano: Franco Angeli.

Glenn, P.H. (2004), *Legal Traditions of the World: Sustainable Diversity in Law*, 2nd ed., Oxford: OUP.

Goldschmidt, J. (1902), *Das Verwaltungsstrafrecht*, Berlin: Scientia.

Grimm, D. (2009), 'Conflicts between general laws and religious norms', *Cardozo Law Review*, 30, 6, p. 2369-2382.

Huxley, A. (ed.) (2002), *Religion, Law and Tradition: Comparative Studies in Religion and Law,* Oxon: Routledge.

Kuppinger, P. (2015), *Faithfully Urban*: *Pious Muslims in a German City,* New York and Oxford; Berghahn.

Joppke, C. & G. Torpey (2013), *Legal Integration of Islam: A Transatlantic Comparison*, Cambridge MA and London: Harvard University Press.

Leerkes, A. & D. Broeders (2010), 'A Case of Mixed Motives? Formal and Informal Functions of Administrative Immigration Detention', *British Journal of Criminology*, 50, p. 830-850.

Menski, W.R. (2006), *Comparative Law in a Global Context: The Legal Systems of Asia and Africa*, 2nd ed., Oxford: OUP.

Nespoli, G. (1981), 'Rilievi sulla funzione amministrativa nel rapporto di esecuzione penitenziaria', *Rassegna penitenziaria e criminologia*, p. 35-60.

Parkin, J. (2013), 'The Criminalisation of Migration in Europe: A State-of-the-Art of the Academic Literature and Research', *CEPS Paper in Liberty and Security in Europe*, 61, p. 1-27.

Phelan, M., Gillespie J. (2015), *Immigration Law Handbook,* 9th ed., Oxford: OUP.

Plüss, C. (2009), Migration and Globalization of Religion, in: P.B. Clarke, *The Oxford Handbook of the Sociology of Religion*, Oxford: OUP, p. 491-506.

Ramji-Nogales, J. (2014), 'Undocumented Migrants and the Failures of Universal Individualism', *Vanderbilt Journal of Transnational Law*, 477, p. 699-763.

Ranelletti, O. (1911), *Principi di Diritto amministrativo, I,* Napoli: L. Pierro.

Saint-Bonnet, F. (2001), *L'État d'exception*, Paris: PUF.

Sacco, R. (2015), *Il diritto muto. Neuroscienze, conoscenza tacita, valori condivisi*, Bologna: Il MUlino.

Sajó, A. & R. Uitz (2012), 'Freedom of Religion', in: M. Rosenfeld, A. Sajó (eds) (2012), *The Oxford Handbook of Comparative Constitutional Law*, Oxford: OUP.

Savino, M. (2015), 'L'«amministrativizzazione» della libertà personale e del due process dei migranti: il caso Khlaifia', *Diritto, amministrazione, cittadinanza*', 3-4, p. 1-22.

Scarciglia R. (2015), 'Comparative Methodology and Pluralism in Legal Comparison in a Global Age', *Beijing Law Review,* 6, p. 42-48.

Scarciglia, R. & W. Menski (eds.) (2015), *Islamic Symbols in European Courts.* Milano: Kluwer.

West, J.P. & G. Sussman (1999), 'Implementation of Environmental Policy: The Chief Executive', in: D.L. Soden (ed.), *The Environmental Presidency,* Albany (NY): State University of New York Press.

European Court of Human Rights
ECtHR 1 September 2015   16483/12   *Khlaifia a.o. v. Italy*

Court of Justice of the European Union
CJEU 7 June 2016   C-47/15   *Affum*

Cour administrative d'appel (France)
CAA de Bordeaux, 4ème chambre (à 3)   25 Feb. 2016, 15BX02697
CAA de Paris, 6ème chambre   6 Dec. 2016, 15PA03527

Conseil d'Etat (France)
Conseil d'État, Appeal 361441, reading of 5 July 2013
Conseil d'État, Appeal 351115, 351116, 351152, 351153, 351220, 354484,
    354485, 354507, 354508,

Supreme Court (United States of America)
Empl. Division v. Smith   494 U.S. 872   1990
Holt v. Hobbs   574 U.S. 1   2015
O'Lone v. Estate of Shabazz   494 U.S. 342   1990
Thornburgh v. Abbott   490 U.S. 401   1989
Turner v. Safley   482 U.S. 78   1987

Federal Court of Appeals (United States of America)
Davis Goodman v. Davis   5th Cir.   14-40339 June 14, 2016
Williams v. Correctional Officers 2th Cir.   15-692   May 16, 2016

District Court (United States of America)
Bragg v. Smith   E.D. of Arkansas 2-16CV00022 May 18, 2016
Rasheed Ali v. Stephens E.D. of Texas   14-41165   May 2, 2016

Part 4

Practitioners' views

Chapter 10 Christian Perspectives and Practices on Refugee Protection

Amaya Valcarcel

10.1 Introduction

> *At this moment in human history, marked by great movements of migration, identity is not a secondary issue. Those who migrate are forced to change some of their most distinctive characteristics and, whether they like or not, even those who welcome them are also forced to change. How can we experience these changes not as obstacles to genuine development, but rather as opportunities for genuine human, social and spiritual growth, a growth which respects and promotes those values which make us ever more humane and help us to live a balanced relationship with God, others and creation?[1]*

This chapter strives to answer the above question by looking through the lens of those who have been hosted as forcibly displaced persons and of those who have hosted them, as well as from the perspective of those who bring communities together and jointly advocate on behalf of forced migrants. Particular reference is made to faith-based motivations and aspirations from both the host and the person hosted.

10.2 Our world today

War and persecution have driven more people from their homes than at any time since World War II, with over 65 million forcibly displaced persons worldwide, including 40 million internally displaced persons, 21 million refugees, and 3 million asylum-seekers. Children represent a disproportionate number of displaced persons, accounting for nearly half of the displaced population, amounting to 28 million children in total. An additional 20 million child migrants have fled their homes for a variety of reasons including extreme poverty or gang violence. In 2016, around 45 per cent of all child refugees under UNHCR

---

1   Message of His Holiness Pope Francis for the World Day of Migrants and Refugees, 2016.

protection came from Syria and Afghanistan, where child exploitation is endemic, but there are thousands of other displaced children at risk of human rights abuses throughout the world (UNHCR, 2015). Globally, children on the move are at risk of forced military recruitment in Eritrea, of sexual abuse in Democratic Republic of Congo, of human or organ trafficking in Sudan or of exploitative labour in Lebanon.

There are also 10 million stateless people who have been denied a nationality and access to basic rights such as education, healthcare, employment and freedom of movement. In our world, nearly 34,000 people are forcibly displaced every day as a result of conflict or persecution.[2] While for some migration is a positive experience, it is increasingly clear that a lack of human rights-based systems of migration governance at all levels (global, regional and national) is creating a human rights crisis for migrants. Millions of migrants and refugees are being deprived of their basic rights, and the world is depriving itself of the full benefits of what refugees and migrants have to offer.

Since the end of the 19th century we have seen more and more deterrent systems for migrants and the externalisation of borders. The complex interrelationship between migration and human rights – including the right to freedom of religion – is multifaceted, and found at all stages in the migratory cycle: in the country of origin, during transit, and in the country of destination. The criminal profits of the arms and ammunition industry, of human trafficking and smuggling, and political and judicial discrimination against migrants, are amongst the greatest evils of our contemporary world. More than one million refugees arrived in Europe on smuggler boats in 2016, a fourfold increase from 2015, and record numbers also applied for asylum.[3] Yet, around 86 per cent of the world's refugees are hosted in developing countries. Eight countries host more than half the world's refugees and they are struggling to meet the challenge.

10.3   The contribution from Catholic Social Teaching to widen refugee protection

The starting point of Catholic reflection on any social issue, whether it concerns security, the economy, governance, work and pay, or politics, is that it is about human beings. We need to begin our reflection by focusing on the human beings affected, not on abstractions about the economy or security.

The first, and core principle, which is grounded not only in Christian faith but also in many other religious and philosophical traditions, is that each human being is of unique value and is precious. Catholics ground that value in the fact that God loves each of us personally and infinitely. Because each human being

2   UNHCR 2015.
3   UNHCHR 2017

is of unique value, no one may be treated as an object or as a means to some larger end.

People who flee from persecution and cannot return to their homeland must have many needs met if they are to live with dignity. They need, for example, food, shelter, medical care, freedom of association, access to education and the possibility to begin a life's project through work and assured residence. These things, denied in their place of origin, flesh out the meaning of protection.

The central question to ask is whether we have a moral responsibility to offer protection to people who ask it of us. If we accept the premise that all human beings are mutually responsible for one another, especially for those in most need, the *prima facie* conclusion is that we are indeed responsible for them and are held to treat them with respect for their human dignity.

This conclusion presupposes that societies and governments have the same obligations to strangers in need as do individuals. In the Catholic understanding, the State is an expression of the solidarity of citizens with one another. It is responsible for so organizing society that it cares for the flourishing of all citizens, particularly the most marginalized, when other groups are incapable of doing so.

10.4 Who is a refugee? The definition according to International Law and the Catholic definition of a refugee

10.4.1 The 1951 Refugee Convention

Refugees have always existed, but the right to asylum and the legal category of 'refugee' was set out by the United Nations in its 1951 Convention and was originally bound in time and space, as it was created to address the plight of Holocaust victims, other refugees from the Second World War and new refugees from Central and Eastern Europe who faced discriminatory persecution by their own governments. The 1951 Convention defines a refugee as someone who has been persecuted, or has a reasonable fear of persecution, because of race, religion, ethnicity, membership in a particular social group or political views.

Though narrow in its scope, the Convention arose out of a much broader recognition that where States are unable to offer *de facto* or *de jure* protection to their citizens, the international community has an obligation to offer protection. But in practice, the definition does not capture the totality of circumstances under which people are forced to cross an international border and are unable to return as a result of an existential threat faced at home.

10.4.2 People the Convention fails to protect. *De facto* refugees and the response of the Catholic Church

Increasingly, large numbers of people are leaving their country of origin for reasons that fall neither within the 1951 Convention definition nor within the category of voluntary, economic migrant. The International Federation of the Red Cross and Red Crescent Societies (IFRC) has made reference to people moving as a result of severe economic and social distress. The combination of livelihood collapse, environmental disaster, and State failure increasingly contributes to non-refugees leaving their country of origin.

Even the wider definition set in the 1969 Convention governing the specific aspects of refugee problems in Africa by the Organization of African Unity (OAU) needs to be revisited almost 50 years after its coming into force. That the Convention was not perfect and that it had its shortcomings must have been quite clear at the time of its adoption. Even so, it has not undergone any amendment and remains the same document that it was in 1969 even if the times have changed considerably and there have been calls for its review for some time.[4] The same has happened with the 1984 and Cartagena Declaration on Refugees, with a Latin American scope.

In 1992, the Catholic Church expanded its understanding of the term 'refugee' to include *'de facto* refugees', encompassing victims of armed conflicts, erroneous economic policy or natural disasters, as well as internally displaced persons.[5] The Vatican document "Refugees: A Challenge to Solidarity" offered a new definition of refugee:

> *In the categories of the International Convention are not included the victims of armed conflicts, erroneous economic policy or natural disasters. For humanitarian reasons, there is today a growing tendency to recognize such people as de facto refugees, given the involuntary nature of their migration. In the case of the so-called economic migrants, justice and equity demand that appropriate distinctions be made. Those who flee economic conditions that threaten their lives and physical safety must be treated differently from those who emigrate simply to improve their position.*

10.4.3 Refugee status determination

Determining who gains official refugee status has become more and more complex. A person who is recognised as a refugee in Africa may be no more than an asylum-seeker in Europe. The OAU Convention includes protection for those fleeing generalized violence, which would be less relevant outside the

---

4   Okello 2014.
5   Pontifical Council for Justice and Peace 1992.

African context. The same happens with the Cartagena Declaration for Latin America.

In Europe, inconsistencies plague asylum systems. The same case presented in Britain, Italy, Germany and France could yield four different results. Asylum systems in countries like Italy are overwhelmed, and some nations are tightening their requirements. The same case could be presented to four different commissions in Italy, again with four different results. The key issue is that certain cases do not fall under the right categories. Traditionally, people who leave a country because of poverty are deemed "economic migrants" and do not qualify for asylum. But new factors, intertwined with poverty, are pushing people to leave, like weak governance or a lawlessness that invites impunity. In addition, the challenge of climate change and environmental displacement is likely to make a comprehensive framework for addressing *de facto* refugees increasingly necessary.

10.4.4 Survival migrants

Some academics refer to this broader category of refugees – leaving out internally displaced persons – as "survival migrants": people fleeing an existential threat to which they have no domestic remedy. Such was the case of the around two million Zimbabweans who fled to countries in Southern Africa between 2005 and 2009 for a combination of inter-related reasons: mass livelihood collapse, state failure and environmental catastrophe. For many, emigration represented the only available survival strategy. Yet there was a refugee recognition rate of less than 10% in South Africa. This case is not only unresolved, but also not isolated. For example, in the Democratic Republic of Congo, a similar nexus of livelihood collapse, environmental crisis and State failure are making survival migration an increasingly likely strategy for significant proportions of the population. The same happens with the Somalis, Haitians, Afghans and Iraqis.[6]

The consequences of this definition vacuum are serious: these groups of people have been rendered invisible to the international community as a result of being neither refugees nor voluntary, economic migrants, resulting in the absence of a coherent normative framework or institutional response to address their plight.

10.4.5 Internally Displaced Persons (IDPs)

The 1992 Church definition includes in its scope those who flee persecution and conflicts but have not crossed an international border – the 40 million IDPs of today's world:

---

6   Betts 2013.

> *A great number of people are forcibly uprooted from their homes without crossing national frontiers. In fact, during revolutions and counter-revolutions, the civilian population is often caught in the cross-fire of guerrilla and government forces fighting each other for ideological reasons or for the ownership of land and national resources. For humanitarian reasons, these displaced people should be considered as refugees in the same way as those formally recognised by the 1951 Convention because they are victims of the same type of violence.*

The international community has addressed the IDP issue establishing Guiding Principles at the global level, which lead to the negotiation of treaties at the regional level, such as the 2010 Kampala Convention on IDPs. The institutional response has been the application of the 'cluster' approach agreed in the Inter-Agency Standing Committee (IASC): different agencies have responsibility for different aspects of the needs of IDPs. The cluster arrangements have made it easier to identify where there are gaps in the overall humanitarian response, notably regarding the protection of women and children. Working in coordination has reduced duplication of efforts, has encouraged more harmonized standards of delivery and has enabled stronger advocacy. But it remains perhaps too internationally focused, with local actors and national capacities insufficiently tapped or developed. This does not always encourage the necessary government ownership.

The world of displaced persons is rapidly changing. Many new forms of displacement, many new experiences of vulnerability and suffering have emerged. How can organizations serving the forcibly displaced promote both the spirit and the structures of freedom to respond with agility to these new calls upon compassion? How can we build something more lasting, which strengthens the humanity of those for whom we work?

10.5   Rights denied and other protection challenges ahead

The world, for many millions, remains a very insecure place.

10.5.1   Refoulement

Refoulement incidents of high visibility have occurred in a number of regions of the world, including in Europe, Eastern Africa and Asia. Take just the case of the small group of Uighur men, women and children fleeing the aftermath of the worst ethnic violence in decades in China. They sought asylum in Cambodia, where the UNHCR issued "persons of concern" letters on their behalf. In December 2009, Cambodia forcibly repatriated them just as the Chinese vice president, Xi Jinping, arrived on a visit to Phnom Penh to announce a $1.2

billion aid package to Cambodia.[7] The willingness to flout international refugee law and to ignore the entreaties of refugees not to be sent back to their home countries has become the mark of friendly bilateral relations between States. Thailand sends back Hmong refugees, a group with a history of persecution at the hands of the Lao government dating back to the 1960s, citing a secret bilateral agreement with the Lao government's assurances of their safe treatment. In September 2016, the European Union reached an agreement with Afghanistan to send back home tens of thousands of Afghan migrants who had reached Europe.[8]

10.5.2 Statelessness

An estimated 10 million people around the world – probably an underestimation – are struggling to get along without a nationality. This means, in practice, a daily struggle for legitimacy, to establish a legal residence, to find work, to access medical assistance and education for their children. At the current rate of three ratifications every 12 months to one or other of the Statelessness Conventions, we may be looking at another 50 years before we can talk about a truly global assumption of responsibility to reduce the statelessness problem. A September 2016 report published by the UNHCR, addresses new risks of statelessness in the Middle East and North Africa, and examines how conditions in Syria are blocking access to nationality.

10.5.3 Detention

Detention of asylum-seekers continues to create great individual hardship in many countries. The duration can be exceedingly long, the conditions unjustifiably harsh and the possibilities for legal oversight or review very limited. Research reveals that most detainees are likely to suffer from severe depression, anxiety, crippling stress, insomnia, loss of appetite and deterioration of their well-being.[9] In some countries there are more due process safeguards for criminals than for asylum-seekers. Alternatives to detention – such as the community centres for women and children that the Jesuit Refugee Service (JRS) is fostering in Australia and Belgium– can set a precedent.

10.5.4 The new boat people

Another challenge for refugee protection is the arrival of undocumented migrants by boat, which exacerbates the problem of so-called "irregular secondary movements". The Pacific, the Mediterranean and the Caribbean are the scene where "boat people" are regularly intercepted, turned around, ignored

---

7   Richardson 2010.
8   Bjelica 2016.
9   Amaral 2010.

by passing ships, shot at, or denied landing. When they manage to access a territory and asylum processes, a large percentage of asylum-seekers who come by boat are actually found to be refugees.

About 350,000 migrants and refugees arrived in the European Union in 2016, a sharp decline from 2015 when more than 1 million people arrived, according to Frontex, the EU border control agency. About 180,000 people arrived via Turkey and the eastern Mediterranean, while 170,000 reached the continent across the central Mediterranean route from Libya and Egypt. A deal between the EU and Turkey reduced the number of refugees and migrants coming from the east, but migration from northern Africa by boat rose 30 per cent. Boat arrivals can provoke fears and high emotions in citizens, which governments may find difficult to manage. But closing borders and trying to prevent movement is not the answer. Evidence suggests that tough sea policies have not solved, just changed – and indeed complicated – the dynamics of irregular movement.

10.5.5 Dangerous routes

According to the International Organization of Migration (IOM), 7,500 migrants and asylum seekers died *en route* to safer lands in 2016, notably in Central America. That is an average of 20 deaths each day. These are reported deaths, but many more people have died alone, in the deserts and in the oceans. Migrants and refugees travel in a clandestine way, without papers, in small and dangerous boats, which quite often sink without a trace and nobody actually knows about them. The nature of the crisis makes it difficult for any organisation or government to keep an accurate count of the dead and missing. 4,812 people are said to have died in the Mediterranean in 2016 – a record number.

10.5.6 Security and counter-terrorism

Refugee policies in many States are now tinted by security concerns, which can imply literally closing the border to refugees. Legislation is being changed expressly to restrict access to asylum procedures and to reinforce detention regimes. Criminalising the search for asylum has serious protection consequences for refugees, and breeds its own problems for States, including racism and xenophobia.

The influx of more than one million migrants into Germany in 2015 and 2016, mainly Muslims fleeing countries such as Syria, Iraq and Afghanistan, hardened public views on immigration, weakened support for Chancellor Angela Merkel and fuelled xenophobia. 59 attacks on refugee shelters were recorded in Berlin in 2015 and 48 in 2016. After the truck attack on a crowded Berlin Christmas market in December 2016, refugees in Germany pleaded with their host nation to avoid placing migrants under a blanket of suspicion, after police commandos raided their shelter.[10] "My message to the Germans is: Don't suspect everybody, don't generalise. We have nothing to do with this crime", said Ammar Wazzaz, a 45-year-old refugee from the Syrian city of Idlib. Yaser, a 32-year-old refugee from Syria, said he became dejected when he read about the attack on Facebook. "We fled this kind of terrorism and it is following us here", he said.

10.6 The role of faith and faith communities in refugee protection

As Antonio Guterres, former UNHCR High Commissioner and currently UN Secretary-General, once stated:

> *for the vast majority of uprooted people there are few things as powerful as their faiths in helping them cope with fear, loss, separation and destitution. Faith is also central to hope and resilience. Ignoring faith would be to ignore its potential for preserving dignity and for providing solutions to the people we care for.*[11]

Western humanitarianism has been largely shaped by secular values, and has tended to overlook or downplay the influence of faith outside the realm of private belief. While religion has declined in industrialized countries, the vast majority of people affected by conflicts, disasters and displacement are people of faith. For many, their religious beliefs and values play a major role in their lives, helping to shape the way they understand the world and their role and place within it, providing a moral compass as to what is right and wrong, and helping them cope in times of crisis (Thomson, 2014).

A refugee from a Catholic background explains: "Faith plays an important role for displaced persons as we seek answers to the many questions that we have regarding the pain and suffering that we have gone through. For most of us, our faith in God is what keeps us going in the midst of the many challenges that we face. Our faith is constantly tested. In his letter to the Hebrews (chapter 11, verse 1), Saint Paul defines faith as 'the assurance of what we hope for and the certainty of what we do not see.' This faith is what give us the hope for light at the end of the tunnel in which many displaced persons find themselves."[12]

Faith may encourage acts of compassion, tolerance and respect for human dignity, while inspiring social justice, reconciliation and conflict resolution. Faith leaders, faith-based organizations (FBOs) and local faith communities play a major role in the protection of people affected by conflict, disaster and

---

10 Nasr 2016.
11 Guterres 2012.
12 Interview with a refugee in Rome (anonymity requested), December 2016.

displacement. Humanitarians, however, have only recently begun to fully appreciate the depth, scope and variety of protection work being done by faith actors and the complex interrelationships between faith and protection.

Working with religious leaders is an essential element of serving local communities. It is equally important to understand the religious life of local communities and how belief influences decision-making. Because of their local ties and widespread presence, the reach of local FBOs in crisis-affected and host communities often extends well beyond that of humanitarian actors and even State authorities, whose legitimacy in complex and insecure operating environments is often called into question. Local faith leaders and FBOs are usually deeply embedded in – and generally respected by – local communities, and are intimately attuned to local cultural nuances and social and political dynamics. They also tend to inspire a high level of trust within their community, giving them great influence over local norms, culture and behaviour – all of which is vital for community-based protection work. The scope and size of some of these communities, along with their influence and connectedness, often gives them considerable leverage with State authorities and non-State actors. The long-term engagement of faith actors with local communities and government authorities also allows their protection initiatives to take root and sustain efforts to address root causes, change patterns of behaviour or advocate for changes in law and policy.[13]

Schools, churches, temples and mosques are frequently used as safe shelters and for coordinating response efforts. Their presence before, during and after disasters and conflicts, during the difficult journeys most refugees undertake, and in the country of asylum, means that they are well placed to provide protection. Their role as first responders and witness to refugees' plights is often critical. A humanitarian worker in Syria explains:

> *When a family arrives to a village or a neighbourhood, the whole community asks itself: 'What can we do for this particular family in need?' Later on, local grassroots organizations, mosques, parishes, visit them and organize themselves to help them. This is how organizations make contact with displaced people, through families and local communities, including religious communities. As in Northern Iraq, groups associated with the church and mosques have been on the frontlines, providing a practical response and extending their help beyond their primary beneficiaries – Christian or Muslim.*[14]

FBOs' organizational structures and networks, though often disrupted, provide a ready-made local response capacity. Faith leaders and FBOs can also draw on

---

13 Thomson 2014.
14 Interview with a refugee in Rome (anonymity requested), May 2016.

their social capital to launch new protection initiatives, gain community support and mobilize volunteers. Faith constituencies also reach well beyond the affected community and so are well placed to deal with refugee and host community tensions, combat xenophobia and racism, mobilize support from the wider society, and address the causes of insecurity that require wider social and political change.

Where religion is used as a tool to incite conflict and polarize communities, FBOs also potentially have a unique ability to work with and through their faith communities to counteract extremist views, and reconcile the differences and tensions that fuel conflict and drive displacement.

A good practice is the Interfaith Peace Platform in the Central African Republic, which brings together religious leaders of the three denominations (Catholic, Evangelical and Muslim) to promote inter-community dialogue. Created in 2014, it aims to set up over 20 community peace committees in the capital, Bangui, and in the prefectures, to promote dialogue between fractured communities, reconciliation initiatives and dialogue with the authorities.[15]

10.7 The principle of impartiality in the Christian tradition of hospitality

Common questions for people working in FBOs are: "Do you only help Christians? Do you only help Muslims?" A cornerstone of humanitarian law, the principle of impartiality, put into practice, especially by faith-based organizations, can be a source of reconciliation, a sign towards a different way of thinking, even in the midst of war. In Syria, the Jesuit Refugee Service (JRS), whose mission it is to accompany, serve and advocate for refugees worldwide, works with teams of young Syrians, from Muslim and Christian backgrounds, providing aid to those most in need, regardless of religion. In Aleppo, the JRS offers 10,000 meals every day under the noise of the mortars. Isn't this already a powerful sign of reconciliation in the country? In Damascus and Homs, the JRS takes care of children affected by war.

We have much to learn about the principle of impartiality, reflected in hospitality towards people in need in the Christian tradition. The current refugee crisis in Europe presents us with an opportunity to regain Western values of very basic humanity, by welcoming refugees. In doing so, we stand to rediscover traditional values that we have lost. Refugees have something to teach us. As Pope Francis said to a group of refugees at the JRS' Centro Astalli in Rome:

> *Though treated as a burden, a problem, a cost, you are really a gift. For every one of you can be a bridge that unites distant peoples, that makes possible the encounter between*

---

15   Conciliation Resources 2014.

diverse cultures and religions, a way to rediscover our common humanity.[16]

Hospitality and welcome are a model of locally-led protection. But they require individual change. Pope Francis invites Christians and non-Christians alike to accept the challenge:

Too many times have we failed to welcome you! Forgive the narrow mindedness and indifference of our societies who fear the change in life and mentality that your presence requires.[17]

10.8   Experiences and Views

Based on the above context of religious social teaching regarding obligations towards forced migrants, I would like to draw attention to three experiences which can shed light on the rights of forced migrants, including the right to religious freedom.

10.8.1   Hospitality towards refugees by religious communities

Pope Francis spoke of the responsibility to welcome in the summer of 2015, when he invited parishes and faith communities to sponsor one or two refugee families. Not all 60 million forcibly displaced – one or two families. Pope Francis' visit to Lesvos was remarkable not only as a sign to European leaders to honour their international obligations, but also by bringing three Syrian families back to Rome with him: He modelled protection in deeds, not words.

Organizations with national offices that have roots in the community, and religious institutions behind them, may be well positioned to what seems to be a protection priority: to identify the most vulnerable, who often fall through the cracks of bigger international programmes likely to become more and more confined to capacity-building, research, monitoring and evaluation, rather than direct service.

The humanitarian corridor project launched by the Community of Sant'Egidio, the Federation of Evangelical Churches and the Waldensian Table offers a practical model to European governments. Humanitarian corridors allow the safe arrival in Italy of vulnerable Syrian refugees from Lebanon, avoiding the dangerous boat journeys across the Mediterranean and exploitation by human traffickers. Thanks to an agreement with the Italian government, about a thousand vulnerable people (victims of persecution, torture and violence, families with children, elderly, sick and disabled people) have arrived

---

16   Pope Francis 2016.
17   Pope Francis 2016.

in Italy via these corridors. Pope Francis described this project as "a concrete sign of commitment for peace and life that unites solidarity with security". This ecumenical pilot project – which is self-financed by the organisations that launched it – could become an EU-led project, with governments replicating and scaling up resettlement of the most vulnerable refugees throughout Europe and beyond.[18]

We learn about hospitality from other faiths too, collaborating on concrete projects. In Kafar Zabad, a village in Lebanon's Bekaa Valley bordering Syria, the local Mufti offered the JRS the use of a small school near the mosque for Syrian refugee children. The JRS is running a programme to equip the children with the language skills and other knowledge needed to join Lebanese schools. Communities of hospitality have been created by the Jesuit Refugee Service in Italy through a network of parishes and religious communities offering shelter to refugees who are in a semi-autonomous situation. In 2016, 28 religious communities hosted 95 refugees.

10.8.2 The personal experience of Antony Mukui[19]

One of the refugees hosted by a religious community in Italy is Antony Mukui, a refugee who kindly agreed to share his experience:

> *My family and I fled Kenya in January 2014 due to persecution that left my cousin dead and one of my friends in hospital. So, we made the decision to leave the country that we had called home for all our lives.*

When we arrived in Italy on 21st January 2014, the Franciscans hosted us in their college San Lorenzo da Brindisi where they house foreign students who study in Rome. We have been living with them since then. They helped us not only by offering us a roof but also a place to heal our inner wounds by providing us with spiritual counselling and by allowing us to be part of their family. We eat meals together, share discussions, play football, or watch a game together. They are always ready to offer a special mass for us whenever we need it.

The Church, through its various congregations, has been called to help in what Pope Francis has called a *conversion of attitudes*. In his message on the 2014 *World Day of Migrants and Refugees*, Pope Francis said:

> *Infrequently, the arrival of migrants, displaced persons, asylum-seekers and refugees gives rise to suspicion and hostility. There is a fear that society will become less secure, that identity and culture will be lost, that competition for*

---

18 Riccardi 2017.
19 Consent was given by M. Antony Mukui to use his name and publish his testimony, December 2016.

> *jobs will become stiffer and even that criminal activity will increase.*[20]

With the rise of far-right parties all over Europe, the Church is called on to take a proactive role in shaping this debate. Opening up religious houses for refugees will build credibility and can go a long way in fighting some of the prejudices against migrants. We believe that if religious houses open their doors other Christians will in turn follow with courage this example, opening their homes to refugees. As Pope Francis reminds us, the Church must be able first to see and then help others to see that migrants do not represent a problem to be solved but that they are brothers and sisters who need help and should therefore be welcomed and loved. Displaced persons have many needs such as housing, food or education. However, in my experience as a refugee, what refugees need most is love and compassion, which enables them to restore the dignity that has been taken away from them by conflict and sudden displacement. They need to feel that they are human beings so that they can heal their wounds and rebuild their lives again, and hopefully heal others that are likewise wounded.

Is it enough to offer us refugees a place to sleep and a dinner? It is likewise important to listen to us and share our aspirations. Faith plays an important role for displaced persons as we seek answers to the many questions that we have regarding the pain and suffering that we have gone through. For most of us, our faith in God is what keeps us going, in the midst of the many challenges that we face our faith is constantly tested, and therefore welcoming refugees into your religious homes will help them strengthen this important part of their life. This love and compassion is what I believe all refugees deserve. It is not an easy decision to take someone into your home and make them part of your family, to let them into your "private space", but like my family has proven, it is possible to overcome the challenges. In the 10 months that we have lived with the Franciscans I have seen the attitudes of the brothers change from one of fear and suspicion to one of love, affection and brotherhood. I now feel part of that fraternity of brothers.

I encourage all of you to look at your brothers and sisters in need and take a leap of faith just like the Franciscans took a chance with us and show love and compassion to your fellow man.[21]

10.8.3   Church asylum: The Christian tradition of sanctuary in Germany

The early Christian church adopted the principle of a religious right of asylum, protecting those accused of crime from legal action and from exile. Various rules were developed for what the person had to do to qualify for protection.

---

20   <w2.vatican.va/content/francesco/en/messages/migration/documents/papa-francesco_20130805_world-migrants-day.html>.

21   Antony Mukui, Address to Religious Congregations gathered in the international office of the Jesuit Refugee Service, Rome, October 2014.

Nowadays, Church asylum, or sanctuary, is a practice to support, counsel and give shelter to refugees who are threatened with deportation to inhumane living conditions, torture or even death. Giving church asylum is a specific form of benevolence that has a centuries-long tradition. What is known in Germany as 'church asylum' has mostly been inspired by the American Sanctuary Movement and by movements in other European countries, leading to the Charter of Groningen in 1987 and eventually to a common Charter of the New Sanctuary Movement in Europe in 2010[22]. Excerpts from the Charter read:

> *As members of churches, parishes, cloisters, communities and solidarity groups are called to accept responsibility and to take sides, not only with the refugees and asylum seekers living among us, but also with those stranded on Europe's outer borders, whom we do not get to see. The right to asylum is worthless, if those seeking protection are denied entry.*

Therefore, we pledge:

- to use every opportunity to help refugees in need;
- where deportation looms and human dignity and lives are threatened, to grant refugees sanctuary in our churches until an acceptable solution is found for them. Not to shrink back, should open confrontation with civil authorities become necessary;
- to publicize persistently in order to raise social consciousness of the scandalous practices by which refugees are repulsed at Europe's outer borders and harassed within, such as deportation detention and discrimination in almost all areas of life;
- to strive for policies of asylum and immigration which are oriented on human dignity and human rights, and this at all levels, from the local to the European level;
- to help make refugees feel welcome and be able to participate with equal rights in our society;
- to promote this self-commitment and its goals in our churches and among our fellow Christians;
- to seek cooperation with like-minded people, whatever faith community or world view they adhere to;
- to form European and worldwide networks and work together in solidarity to fulfil these commitments.

In 1983 a Berlin parish granted church asylum to three Palestinian families threatened with deportation to Lebanon during the civil war there, and since

---

22 Charta of the New Sanctuary Movement in Europe, Resolution of the Annual Meeting of the German Ecumenical Committee on Church Asylum, Inc. Berlin, October 2010 <www.kirchenasyl.de/wp-content/uploads/ 2013/12/Charta-english1.pdf>.

then church asylum has been established all over Germany and is practised in the Protestant as well as the Catholic Church. Both churches have taken a stand for refugees and their rights in numerous public statements and have used church asylum as an instrument to protect refugees and support them in claiming their rights.[23]

A snapshot: Sherzad, Kovan and Peshtiwan, Yazidis from Iraq, aged 19, 20 and 21, travelled overland from Turkey to Bulgaria and on to Germany. Many of their travel companions were injured on the border between Bulgaria and Serbia, when Bulgarian police opened fire on the refugees who refused to stop. The young men each paid between 9,000 and 11,000 euro upfront to smugglers in Iraq who 'organised' their trip to Germany. Travelling separately, all were caught *en route*, and their fingerprints gave them away. Says Kovan:

> *Bulgarian police stopped me at the border with Serbia. For two days, I stayed in a camp, where I was beaten and not fed. Then I was taken to prison. I stayed eight days. I was threatened that if I did not give my fingerprints, I would stay a long time.*

A few months after reaching Germany, Kovan received one day's notice of his deportation to Bulgaria. A volunteer at the shelter where Kovan was staying advised him to seek church asylum immediately. Much the same happened to the other two.

It was Dieter Müller SJ of the Jesuit Refugee Service in Germany who referred the Yazidis to the parish of St Joseph in Tutzing, an affluent town just outside Munich. They would stay on the parish premises until their deportation order expired, up to six months. Fr Dieter said some 600 refugees sought protection in churches across Germany in 2015, invoking the Christian tradition of sanctuary. He disputes the government's disgruntled claim that church asylum is illegal, although he admits it "stretches the law" for a good cause, "to ensure a fair application of the asylum procedure".

Timely practical support, like that extended by Fr Dieter and Fr Peter Brummer, parish priest in Tutzing, can make or break the future of individuals. There are many Europeans who are eager to lend support in one way or other – the flip side of Europe's much-publicized reluctance to welcome refugees. Fr Peter granted sanctuary to ten refugees facing deportation during 2015. His first experience of church asylum dates back 20 years, when he welcomed a Kurdish family that Germany wanted to deport to Turkey. Fr Peter recalls that the state prosecutor invited him for a meeting back then:

> *He asked me why I was doing this. I opened the Bible and told him to read inside for my answer. We had a very good conversation.*

---

23   Neufert 2014.

For Fr Peter and his parish council, "there is no doubt we have to do this", to welcome and to protect refugees. The encounter impresses him deeply. "You have to meet each other face to face, to hear the story. As we listened, the more we learned, the more our conviction grew." He adds:

> *You have to follow your conscience, there are situations*
> *when you have to say yes or no; no chance to compromise.*

Refugees gamble literally everything in a bid to gain life. They do so knowing that death is also on the cards. But matters of life and death should not depend on luck alone. Solidarity can do much to even out the odds.[24]

10.8.4 Hospitality led by individuals and families in Europe

Since 2009, the Jesuit Refugee Service in France has developed the *Welcome Network*, a programme for individuals and families to welcome refugees into their homes. JRS Europe is now developing this project throughout the continent, inviting European citizens to open their homes.[25]

In offering hospitality, much of the success depends on efforts to involve others. The *Welcome Network* underscores this reality. What started as a small seed of hospitality has grown rapidly, spreading to 34 French cities. In *Ille de France*, the JRS coordinates 150 families hosting asylum seekers. At the end of 2016, 1,200 families hosted 600 asylum seekers. JRS France works with 200 supervisors. "I am discovering the joy of receiving, of knowing that, for a while, my guest will not be hungry or cold," said volunteer Bernadette. "I am discovering the grace of smiling when they welcome me every evening", explains the refugee hosted by Bernadette.

An experience: French couple Jacques and Martine Mercier have been welcoming refugees into their home in Versailles, just outside Paris, for several years. They say that while living with refugees is incredibly rewarding, it is also a responsibility, requiring patience and understanding.[26] Working on hospitality needs a strong advocacy component, to lobby for laws and policies that are more welcoming and just. Based on concrete experiences of hospitality in France, the JRS submitted proposals to the government for improved living conditions for asylum seekers. Marie, a Rwandan refugee who experienced both hospitality and hostility on her long journey towards protection, put it this way:

> *When we talk about hospitality, origin, race and religion*
> *are of little importance. Hospitality is about compassion,*

---

24   Jesuit Refugee Service 2016.
25   Run by the Jesuit Refugee Service in France, the Welcome Network has offered hospitality since 2009 and today is a 150-strong network in 15 cities all over France. <www.jrsfrance.org/reseau-welcome/presentation>.
26   Camilla Schick for BBC: <www.bbc.com/news/world-europe-34472027>.

> *free from pity, and makes you feel at home, free and totally*
> *accepted.*

Another initiative is the *I Get You* campaign, the aim of which is to foster a culture of welcome in Europe, creating inclusive communities where everyone is valued. It was launched by the Jesuit Refugee Service-Europe in Belgium, Germany, France, Spain, Italy, Malta, Portugal, Romania and Croatia, to identify community-building initiatives for local citizens and refugees. The campaign began with some questions: What are the best examples of community-building initiatives? How do they encourage mutual understanding and friendship? How do they counter racism and xenophobia? The research side of the project will enable analysis and comparison of initiatives across Europe.[27] The following testimony by a German woman living in a small village in the Black Forest is an example of how individuals are developing sponta-neous initiatives to accompany refugees in one way or the other:

> *This year, I will spend Christmas at my parent's place,*
> *together with my boyfriend and our friend Henry, an asylum*
> *seeker from the Gambia. In the isolated small town where*
> *we normally live, Henry has become our closest friend, so*
> *we had originally decided to stay in town with him for the*
> *feast days. As my parents, living in another city, very much*
> *wanted to have us over for Christmas, they invited Henry,*
> *too. Then they asked if he was trustworthy to have around*
> *the house, something they have never asked about any of my*
> *friends before. They were worried that he might misbehave,*
> *or steal. Although generally liberal-minded, my parents do*
> *not know a single refugee personally – and so they are*
> *afraid. My mother once said that she found the young*
> *African men shopping at the local supermarket looked a*
> *little frightening. It is true that their unfamiliar features can*
> *sometimes make their facial expressions harder to read for*
> *Europeans. Our friend Henry sometimes wears an*
> *expression that could be interpreted as sullen – but because*
> *I have got to know him well over the months, I know that this*
> *is just what his face sometimes looks like and that he might*
> *be laughing the next second. I am not afraid because I know*
> *him. I am not suspicious of a group of young black men in*
> *the park because they might be just as nice as Henry is.*
> *The region of Germany where I studied is the region*
> *currently behaving most aggressively towards immigrants.*
> *It is also one of the regions with the lowest percentage of*

---

27   JRS Europe is based in Brussels and coordinates a network of JRS offices across 15 European countries. Jrseurope.org

> *foreigners actually living there, compared to the national
> standard. People are afraid of who they do not know.
> My mother has called to ask what they could get Henry for
> Christmas and what he would like to eat, so I guess in her
> case, fear is already being transformed.*"[28]

What if every refugee was accompanied by an individual or a family in their host community? Through friendship and accompaniment of one or two refugees, our perspective of the "global refugee crisis" would change dramatically. Social transformation comes from individual and community responses that value personal interaction. This is a very practical way of protecting refugees.

10.8.5   Inter-faith advocacy on behalf of forced migrants

During 2016, the year of the Jubilee of Mercy, in conjunction with the Islamic pilgrimage to Mecca, and on the occasion of the UN International Day of Peace, Catholic and Muslim leaders united voices calling upon governments, religious institutions, and people of good-will to work together in tackling the root causes of forced migration. As an example, members of the Jesuit Refugee Service and the Religious Islamic Community of Italy (COREIS) called for responsibility-sharing to provide protection for those fleeing from their homes, and to ensure good reception conditions and access, on arrival, to adequate and affordable services. Robust policies, they said, were needed to counter racist and xenophobic tendencies – diversity must be recognized as an opportunity and a gift, not a threat.

In their statement for International Day of Peace, 2016, both faith-based organisations expressed: "The Muslim tradition of protection and hospitality towards the wayfarer, the widow and the orphan is reinforced by the fact that the Prophet Muhammad, peace be upon him, was himself a refugee who fled his home city for safety. Christians are told in their scriptures that every time they welcome a stranger, they make Christ welcome, and the story of the birth of Christ is one of persecution and flight for refuge in a foreign land."[29]

Muslims and Christians strive for a peace that is "beyond all understanding", an experience of intimacy with the mystery of God, and for fraternal harmony with their neighbours. Peace then is neither a vague abstraction nor an unrealistic ideal. It can be achieved when we all recognize that we share a common home, and that we are invited by God to work together for the common good. The pilgrim, the refugee and the migrant are all searching, beyond hearth and home, for a place where they may encounter peace, be free of distress, and

---

28   Testimony provided by Julia Scharfenstein. Germany, November 2016.
29   Excerpts from the *inter-religious statement on behalf of forced migrants*, Jesuit Refugee Service and the Religious Islamic Community of Italy (COREIS), 21 September 2016, <en.jrs.net/news_detail?TN=NEWS-20160919080016>.

enjoy hospitality.[30] Initiatives such as this one, bringing together Muslim and Christian perspectives on behalf of welcoming refugees, are believed to be seeds for further protection and welcome.

10.9   See their faces, listen to their stories

Great traditions, such as the three monotheistic faiths of the Jews, Christians and Muslims, have paid attention to the life of the exile, the refugee, the foreigner, hospitality to strangers being a cornerstone practice in these traditions. Pope Francis calls us to something very basic: to see their faces, to listen to their stories and to do unto others as you would have them do unto you:

> *Our world is facing a refugee crisis of a magnitude not seen since the Second World War. This presents us with great challenges and many hard decisions. On this continent, too, thousands of persons are led to travel north in search of a better life for themselves and for their loved ones, in search of greater opportunities. Is this not what we want for our own children? We must not be taken aback by their numbers, but rather view them as persons, seeing their faces and listening to their stories, trying to respond as best we can to their situation. To respond in a way which is always humane, just and fraternal. We need to avoid a common temptation nowadays: to discard whatever proves trouble-some. Let us remember the Golden Rule: Do unto others as you would have them do unto you (Mt 7:12). This Rule points us in a clear direction. Let us treat others with the same passion and compassion with which we want to be treated. Let us seek for others the same possibilities which we seek for ourselves. Let us help others to grow, as we would like to be helped ourselves. In a word, if we want security, let us give security; if we want life, let us give life; if we want opportunities, let us provide opportunities.[31]*

---

30   *Ibid.*
31   Pope Francis 2015.

References

Amaral, P. (2010, June), Becoming vulnerable in Detention
<www.europarl.europa.eu/document/activities/cont/201110
/20111014ATT29338/20111014ATT29338EN.pdf>

Betts, A. (2013), *Survival Migration, Failed Governance and the Crisis of Displacement,* University Press.

Bjelica, Jelena (2016), *EU and Afghanistan Get Deal on Migrants: Disagreements, pressure and last-minute politics:*
<reliefweb.int/report/afghanistan/eu-and-afghanistan-get-deal-migrants-disagreements-pressure-and-last-minute>.

Cartagena Declaration on Refugees (1984),
<www.unhcr.org/about-us/background/45dc19084/cartagena-declaration-refugees-adopted-colloquium-international-protection.html>

Conciliation Resources (2014), <www.c-r.org/news-and-views/news/faith-leaders-car-launch-national-interfaith-peace-platform> [April].

Guterres, A. (2012), *High Commissioner's Dialogue on Protection Challenges, Faith and Protection.* Opening remarks <www.unhcr.org/high-commissioners-dialogue-on-protection-challenges-2012.html>.

Jesuit Refugee Service (2016), *Journeys of Hope,* 79-80 <www.jrs.net>.

Nasr, J. (2016), *Refugees plead with Germans not to tar them with suspicion,* <www.reuters. com/article/germany-truck-migrants-idUSL5N1EF3F2>.

Neufert, B. (2014), 'Church asylum', *Forced Migration Review* (48), p. 37-38.

Okello, M. (2014), 'The 1969 OAU Convention and the continuing challenge for the African Union', *Forced Migration Review* (48), 70-73.

Organization of African Unity (1969), *Convention governing the specific aspects of refugee problems in Africa,* <www.unhcr.org/45dc1a682.html>.

Pontifical Council for Justice and Peace and Cor Unum (1992), *Refugees: A Challenge to Solidarity,* Vatican City.

Pope Francis (2015), *Address to the US Congress,* 24th September 2015

Pope Francis (2016), *Message* on the occasion of the 35th anniversary of the Jesuit Refugee Service Italy, Centro Astalli (19 April),
<w2.vatican.va/content/francesco/en/messages/pont-messages/2016/documents/papa-francesco_20160419_videomessaggio-centro-astalli-35anniv.html>.

Riccardi, A. (2017), I corridoi umanitari e Papa Francesco (8 March),
<www.santegidio.org/pageID/11676/langID/en/Humanitarian-Corridors.html>.

Richardson, S. (2010), *Uighurs returned to China 'disappear' says rights group,* <news.bbc.co.uk/ 2/hi/asia-pacific/8487724.stm>.

Thomson, J. (2014, November), 'Local faith actors and protection in complex and insecure environments', *Forced Migration Review* (48), p. 5-6.

United Nations High Commissioner for Refugees (2015), *Global Trends.*

United Nations Human Rights Office of the High Commissioner (2017), <www.ohchr.org/EN/Issues/Migration/Pages/MigrationAndHumanRights Index.aspx>.

United Nations High Commissioner for Refugees (2016, September), *In search of solutions: Addressing statelessness in the Middle East and North Africa*, <reliefweb.int/report/syrian-arab-republic/search-solutions-addressing-statelessness-middle-east-and-north-africa>.

Chapter 11 When Denmark Criminalised Kindness

Lisbeth Zornig Andersen

11.1 Introduction

I didn't grow up in an orderly middle-class family with cosy Sunday lunches, people laughing and talking. I was brought up in a shabby cottage outside a remote Danish village, with cold water and a lavatory in the back garden. Hot dogs were a special treat on Sundays. My mum and stepdad were always drunk and didn't work – they lived off benefits. It was not the sort of environment that teaches you universal moral values and ethics.

And yet, I learned – mostly from my three brothers – that people look after one another. We help each other. Even if we don't have much, even if we wear hand-me-downs to school and dig up raw potatoes for dinner, we still help each other. It's when life is tough and your back is to the wall that we matter the most to each other.

When I was introduced to the Bible and Christian teachings as a teenager – nobody ever took me to church as a child – I learned the story about the good Samaritan. I knew what that meant already. Where I grew up, if you saw somebody walking along the road and you were fortunate enough to have a car, you stopped and offered them a lift. That was normal – it's what we all did.

My brothers were removed from our family home one at a time and put into institutions. All three turned to crime and drug abuse. Two are dead, much too young; the third has AIDS. They never had a real chance at life. Not really. The abuse and the beatings they took at home – they protected me from that – crippled their hearts, their minds and their souls.

For some reason, I managed to escape and make it through school. I graduated from the University of Copenhagen as an economist, and got a job at Danske Bank, the largest bank in Denmark. At school, I was lucky enough to meet good people, who understood how to coach the aggressive and emotionally disturbed young girl that I was – believe me, it was no easy task. At one institution for especially difficult girls, I met Karen, who saw through my anger and loathing, and was patient enough that I eventually came to trust her. She became my mentor. Today, thirty-four years later, she still is. She was the person who pushed me on to university – I would never have thought it possible without her.

Some years ago, I received an invitation from the Danish Social Minister. It was strange – I had never been invited to coffee with a member of the government before, but of course I said yes. The minister wanted to know if I would chair the Children's Council in Denmark, the equivalent of the Children's Ombudsman in other countries. I was astounded – I didn't even know what the Children's Council was at the time. So, I called Karen. She wasn't surprised at all. 'Well, I actually thought you'd be perfect as the next CEO of Denmark's Radio and Television (the Danish BBC),' she told me, 'But Children's Ombudsman, that's pretty good too.'

Karen always believed that I could do anything. She's a follower of the developmental psychologist Urie Bronfenbrenner, who writes: 'In order to develop normally, a child requires progressively more complex joint activity with one or more adults who have an irrational emotional relationship with the child. What do I mean by "irrational emotional relationship"? Well, somebody's got to be crazy about that kid.' I think that's Bronfenbrenner's way of saying 'love'. Which is a difficult thing to implement in a professional institution where many children would never have experienced it at home. But Karen managed it for me.

11.2 Helping others

And so, I became the chair of Denmark's Children's Council. It was a chance to make a difference, and took me from an anonymous business career to debating social policy in the national media. I launched a campaign to improve the conditions for socially challenged children in Denmark; wrote a book about my childhood, to share what it's like on the dark side of the welfare society; and even ended up in a documentary: *My Childhood in Hell*. In short, I threw myself into the job, and loved every minute of it.

After three years I decided to establish my own company non-profit, The House of Zornig, dedicated to developing better ways to help troubled families – not just the children, but parents, too. And that's what I still do today. I don't want any more children to end up like my brothers. I don't want anyone to have to live through what I did.

Part of my work is giving presentations around the country, talking about my own experiences, trying to inspire people to do what Karen did for me, and promoting more effective social initiatives. On Monday, 7 September 2015, I was in southern Denmark, close to where I grew up, making one of these presentations. That was the day the great wave of refugees hit Denmark. Thousands of people fleeing the war in Syria had made their way through Europe, many of them heading for Sweden, where the Prime Minister at the time was welcoming them. I heard on the news that hundreds of refugees had entered Danish territory from Puttgarten in Germany on the ferry to Rødbyhavn, and were now walking towards Sweden. It's a long walk: about 160 kilometres. And it was a hot day. To get to Sweden, you need to go to Copenhagen, and cross over from there. I was headed towards Copenhagen already, and I had six empty seats in my car. So?

I went to Rødbyhavn and was met with scenes that I'd never seen before in Denmark. There were refugees everywhere. Complete chaos. Adults, children, single mothers, teenagers, wary people with tired faces, most of them with just small plastic bags containing their belongings; some with nothing but the clothes they wore. Those faces. Not desperate but stern. Weary. Committed. I phoned Mikael, my husband, and said: 'Listen, I'm going to offer some of them a lift.' He said: 'But of course you are. Bring them home, I'll make coffee.'

We weren't sure if it was legal to offer the refugees a lift, so Mikael called the police to ask. They didn't know, they said. Nobody seemed prepared for what was unfolding. At the scene, there were a lot of police. They didn't stop the refugees from walking towards Sweden. So, I parked the car and spotted a group of six, among them two small girls who turned out to be five years old. Sweet children, but very quiet – I wondered what they had seen.

I asked them if they wanted a ride. They did. There was a policeman standing next to my car, and I asked him if he was going to stop me. He said no. While the refugees were climbing into the car a TV journalist came over and filmed us. I explained that I had empty seats, and that I was offering them a lift. And off we went.

We have a house in Solrød Strand, just south of Copenhagen, and I took the family there with me. The girls immediately fell asleep in the car – they had been traveling for forty days: on foot, by train and on bus. They had lost all their belongings when they crossed the Mediterranean to Greece, and had nothing left but the clothes on their back. They were from Damascus. One of them, Younes, had studied pharmacology at university. His brother was a physiotherapist. They were leading a normal life, working and studying, when the bombs started to fall and destroyed their home. Their father was already in Sweden with a brother, living in Helsingborg, and that's where they were headed.

We got to Solrød Strand and Mikael was ready with coffee, soda and cinnamon buns. We talked and offered them a place to rest, dinner and a good night's sleep. They politely declined – they just wanted to get to Sweden as quickly as possible. It had been a long journey and they were very close now. So my husband offered them a lift to the train station on the Danish side of the border. He bought them tickets to Helsingborg and made sure they got on the right train. A few hours later we got a call from their father. He was overjoyed, and grateful.

That was good. But we also felt bad. We had done so little, and yet it had meant so much to these six people. We could see on the news that hundreds of refugees were still on the roads, and more were coming. We thought about driving more people, but we realised that would just be a drop in the ocean. So we turned to Facebook and wrote about what we had done; we wrote about the family, ordinary people in desperate circumstances. And we asked other people to help. Our post was instantly shared by thousands – we later estimated that it had probably reached 300,000 people. Hundreds of cars headed towards Rødbyhavn to help. Our Facebook page was flooded by requests. 'I'm going –

where are they?'; 'We have SUVs, where do we pick them up?'; 'I have housing and food, bring them here'; 'I have a boat, I can take fifty to Sweden'. Even a former Government minister called. He said he'd like to pay for busses to go and pick up refugees, which would be more efficient. Mikael called a bus company and asked if he could rent a number of busses. 'Are they for refugees?' the man in charge asked. Mikael said yes, expecting a no. 'You can have my busses, there's no charge,' he said. That was wonderful, but we had no bus drivers. So, we asked for volunteers on Facebook, and immediately we had more drivers than busses.

11.3 Consequences

All that happened on the Monday. The next day the police issued a statement declaring that giving rides to refugees was illegal. That scrapped the bus idea. Many people continued to drive south to offer people lifts, regardless. The consensus was that we do not accept that refugees from a war, people in distress, have to walk on the highways in Denmark and sleep in the open, when so many of us have cars and beds. Some used the term civil disobedience, infuriated by the statement from the police. On Wednesday, the police again changed their position. Now, it was no longer illegal – now people offering lifts were merely 'leaning towards breaching the law'. And at the same time the police allowed the refugees they had detained in Rødbyhavn, to travel freely. All were let go and picked up by waiting cars to be driven towards Copenhagen. After that, refugees were allowed to travel freely through Denmark to Sweden, where they were welcomed – until it became too much and they closed their borders.

Things calmed down. Instead of offering the refugees a lift, hundreds of civilian volunteers manned the train stations from Hamburg in Germany to Malmö in Sweden to keep the refugees safe, and make sure they had tickets for Sweden. Thousands of people were donating money, time, clothes and food for what came to be known as operation Safe Corridor.

Along the way, the footage of the refugees climbing into my car made the news. I was interviewed and invited to a debate with a member of the *Dansk Folkeparti*, who are vehemently anti-immigration. I was accused of shamelessly publicising myself on Facebook and on TV. Another politician asked how I could know whether the people I helped were carrying bombs. My Facebook page was flooded with hate mail. I was called a traitor, an idiot and a Muslim-lover. People sent pictures of guns, or obscene scenarios of what they would like ten African men to do to me.

This was in September. The following month my husband and I were contacted by the police. They were investigating us on the charge of people smuggling, and wanted us to come in for questioning. Actually, I think the correct term is interrogation. I turned up at the police station and answered a lot of questions about what I had done. It was a strange experience, to be interrogated by the police. It turned out that about fifteen people had filed complaints against me – five or six had filed complaints against my husband. One had even been in our garden and peeked through the windows of the living room to be certain ours was the house where refugees had been sheltered. The police did not initiate the investigation by themselves, they did it because of the number of complaints from Danish citizens.

In judicial terms our crime consisted of aiding, transporting and harboring persons without valid travel documents. That's the lift and the coffee. I had to ask what 'valid travel documents' meant. They explained that it is a valid passport and a valid visa. I was not aware of the law, and the idea of asking the family for valid travel documents never entered my mind. I have never asked anybody for valid travel documents before when offering them a lift. And when we had asked the police at the time – both by phone and at the site – none of them had mentioned anything about valid travel documents. Even if they had presented Syrian passports to me, I wouldn't have been able to judge whether they were valid or not.

Time passed. We visited the Syrian family in Helsingborg just before Christmas. They were doing well and learning Swedish fast in order to commence their studies and find jobs. My husband connected them to a Swedish family who were happy to provide support and help them learn the language. On our visit, they served lots of wonderful Arabic food – and a plate of cinnamon buns. We thought that was sweet and funny. But best of all, for the first time I saw the girls smile.

11.4   In court

On 11 March, we had our day in court. The prosecutor was unable to locate the policeman my husband talked to, while the policeman I talked to did not recollect our conversation. The prosecutor suggested a combined fine of DKK 45,000 (about £4,000), or fourteen days in prison. Our lawyer stressed that what we had done was motivated by humanitarian reasons and that the circumstances were extraordinary – the police had not known what to do and the Government was quiet on the subject. It took the judge about twenty minutes to consider before he passed his verdict, which was in accordance with the prosecutor's suggestion.

I was angry. Outside, the media was waiting, and I told them I was angry. Angry about being criminalized for acting with simple human decency. 'We are not people smugglers,' I told them. 'We are ordinary people helping fellow human beings in distress.' Many other people were angry – astonished, even – and journalists from all over the world were soon in touch: *the Guardian, the Independent, the BBC, Reuters, Associated Press, Al Jazeera, the Washington Post, El Pais, El Mundo* – Swedish, Finnish, Norwegian, German, Dutch and Canadian media outlets all wanted to tell the story of the Danish court order that criminalized ordinary human decency.

We were not surprised by their interest. The judgement challenged universal human values, the simple drive to help people in distress. Most of us, regardless of religion, are brought up with a set of values that underlines the importance of doing just this. Even I, growing up in a socially dysfunctional home on the wrong side of the tracks, had learned that. This is what we teach our children.

When a Danish court punishes people for helping refugees, it contradicts our core human values. This is especially poignant in a country known for its universal welfare system, designed to help everyone in need. I never knew that decency, generosity, charity – whatever you choose to call it – was reserved for people with valid travel documents.

What message does the judgment send to our children? Just hours after the court order was passed, a young man called us about some hungry refugees he had met on the street in Copenhagen. Fearing legal repercussions, he didn't know whether he should help them or not. That's what the judgment teaches our children. We used to teach them that helping Jews flee to Sweden during World War II was a heroic effort. How things have changed.

11.5 Higher Courts

We appealed the judgment, and the case went to the Danish High Court. Our anger was shared by many people. A Danish jazz musician, Benjamin Koppel, set up a fundraiser to cover the fine. Contributions poured in. Within a few days people had donated more than DKK 160,000 (£15,000), far exceeding the target. Most of the donations were small, but there were many of them. We saw this as a public demonstration against the court order – our opponents, however, attacked the fund, claiming that is was illegal. They reported us to the tax authorities. I have never met so much hatred as I have in this period – for helping refugees. The fund was all in good order. We decided to use the money to help pay the fines of others who have been persecuted for doing the same thing we did. There are hundreds – some are young students, some pensioners, some have large families and little to spare. Any surplus is donated to unaccompanied child refugees.

Surprisingly, there was almost no political reaction to our case. One parliamentarian on the far left did criticize the judgment, but otherwise nobody commented. The question of changing the law, or challenging it, was not raised. But anti-Muslim sentiments are very strong in Denmark today, and people vote accordingly. Kindness towards Muslims scares away voters, so there is no room for kindness in government. On the contrary, measure after measure is being taken to make the life of the refugees as miserable as possible. People are housed in tents, even in winter, even though better accommodation is available. The refugees are searched for valuables when they enter Denmark, and met with ludicrous demands when applying for asylum, reunion with their families or permanent citizenship. The Danish government has published ads in Middle Eastern newspapers warning refugees to stay away from our country. To me it seems that we have sacrificed the human decency Danish society is built on.

To put our court order in perspective, a Danish man who spat on refugees passing below a motorway bridge received a fine of DKK 5,000 (£450). While it should be recognized that our legal system still finds it a criminal offense to abuse people in distress – hooray for small victories – it also shows that spitting on refugees is a milder offense than helping them. On 21 September 2016, the Danish High Court ruled on our appeal. The verdict was upheld. We now know that it is a criminal offence to help refugees in distress on Danish highways, even if it's just a lift down the road or a cup of coffee, no matter what the circumstances.

We tried to take our case to the Danish Supreme Court. However, appeals against a high courts' decision are subject to permission from the Appeals Permission Board. This Board turned us down. They considered our case not to be principal enough.

Our last resort was the European Court of Human Rights. Sadly, the Strasbourg Court declared our application inadmissible in the summer of 2017.

11.6   What is next?

We must continue discussing the refugee situation, and how our society and the countries around Europe should react to the human disaster currently unfolding in Syria. How many people are we able to help, and where, and how, should we help them? This is a debate with many questions and seemingly few answers. Refusing to help the people standing right in front of us, needing care and assistance, corrupts our moral values and perceptions about decency and common humanity. It is a dangerous path to choose. It breeds a cynicism that may well poison the remnants of solidarity in Denmark, and actually unravel the social fabric that some of our opponents, in a misguided way, are actually trying to protect. Right now, too many people are quietly looking on while our core values are being undermined, because defending them may prove too expensive in terms of public opinion. I thought we were better than that. Really, I did.

The Danish state church is Protestant, and we call ourselves Christians. We tell our children the story about the good Samaritan who did not turn his back. We demand that immigrants in our country learn, and adopt, our Danish values. So how are they expected to understand that in Denmark we punish people for compassion?

My husband and I could not have acted differently. It would have been a betrayal of everything we hold dear and believe in, including what we teach our children.

Chapter 12 Piety or ulterior motive

*Legal assessment of belief authenticity of Pastafarians
and converted asylum seekers*

Derk Venema

12.1 Introduction

How do Dutch government institutions judge whether someone really has the
religion they say they have? In this contribution, I will compare two cases. The
first case concerns Pastafarians (members of the Church of the Flying Spaghetti
Monster, FSM) who wish to appear in their ID photo wearing their religious
headgear, the colander. The other case involves asylum seekers who claim the
right to asylum based on their conversion to a faith whose adherents are
persecuted in their country of origin. The Pastafarian case also has implications
for the more general question of how governments (should) treat religions that
are new, unknown, weird or small, in short 'NUWS' religions, making this case
also relevant for the theme of migration and religious freedom, because
immigrants sometimes bring NUWS religions with them.

In both cases, private individuals file an application to gain certain rights or
privileges based on their religion. To achieve this, they need recognition of their
religious status from the authorities. In both cases, too, the authorities are
suspicious and reluctant: the conversions and the FSM religion are often deemed
not credible, because they are suspected of being devised as mere instruments
to acquire a residence permit and to publicly express criticism of religion. These
goals are viewed as the 'real' ulterior motives.

After a brief look at the role of religion in society, especially in the
Netherlands, I will discuss the attitudes and actions of civil servants handling
ID renewals for Pastafarians and interviewing converted asylum seekers and
judges in court cases about both topics. In my concluding remarks, I will make
some policy suggestions.

12.2 Religion and society

Religion, like morality is not so much a spiritual instrument for countering biological urges, but itself a product of biological evolution.[1] In a Darwinian

---

1   Dawkins 1992, Boyer 2001, Wilson 2002.

process of group selection, the human brain acquired the capacity to produce artefacts, language and ideas, which led to the formation of many different cultures. Those cultures developed further in an evolutionary process of their own, in interaction with the biological evolution of the human species (gene-culture coevolution)[2].

From that perspective, the main functions of religion are promoting in-group cooperation and procreation, and maintaining group identity. To perform that function, religions need to be sufficiently adaptive to changing circumstances. Over the centuries, some religions have done this very successfully, some have died out, and new ones are constantly being born, whether branching off from a 'parent' religion (e.g., the many forms of Protestantism), composed from elements of several different religions (syncretisms or patchwork religions like Sufism or Unitarianism) or newly 'invented', often inspired by existing religions (like Rastafari, Scientology, UFO-religions, neo-pagan and new age religions).

In the Netherlands, the adaptability of the traditional religions (Catholicism and various factions of Protestantism) to modern society has been diminishing rapidly for half a century and new religious or spiritual movements have filled only a very small part of the gap.[3] Due to immigration since the 1960s, Islam has established itself in the Netherlands as the religion of about 5% of the inhabitants.[4]

Since the Second World War, different kinds of spiritual movements have appeared in the Western world that deviate considerably from traditional forms of religion. Some are inspired by literary of cinematographic fiction, like the Church of All Worlds (1962), Jediism (2000) and Matrixism (2004), some by science fiction, like Scientology (1955), and some have other roots in (post)modern culture, like Discordianism (1963), the Church of the Sub-Genius (1970s), Kopimism (2012) and the Church of the Flying Spaghetti Monster (FSM) or Pastafarianism (2005). All feature at least the elements 'new' and 'weird' of NUWS religions. These movements are variously called 'parody religions', 'fake cults', 'invented religions' or 'hyper-real religions'. Of those mentioned, only Pastafarianism has gained a substantial following in The Netherlands.

Denying them the status of religion might at first glance seem logical, as they have been constructed very recently and appear satirical or dishonest or having a purpose very different from traditional religions. This conclusion would be premature, however, because, although there are many competing functionalist and essentialist definitions, there is nothing near a generally agreed upon scientific definition of religion. Defining religion has even become somewhat

---

2   Richerson & Boyd 2005, Mesoudi 2011.
3   Bernts & Berghuis 2016.
4   Schmeets 2016.

of a power struggle.[5] A very general definition by properties could be: a composition of myths, rituals, holy texts, a concept of history and a vision of the future.[6] Moreover, it is impossible to distinguish the religiousness of adherents to new and weird religions from the religiosity of people who identify as Christians or Muslims. And satirical elements or origins do not necessarily disqualify a movement as a religion.[7] Because of the difficulties in defining religion, the Dutch government (and other Western governments) usually adopt very broad concepts of religion.[8]

Although the social and societal role of organised religion has diminished very much, religious freedom is still held in high regard by politicians and lawyers. Not many endorse the pleas of some jurists who propose deleting freedom of religion from constitutions and treaties because of its purported redundancy. Nonetheless, in many countries, non-religious 'beliefs' (Article 9 European Convention on Human Rights) or 'world views' are now protected on a par with religion, indicating that the difference between religious and non-religious belief systems or opinions is no longer thought of as absolute. In any event, deep personal ethical convictions (religious or not) are still generally considered an important matter, and not the government's business. Expressions of those convictions in actions such as performing rites and stating religious views are often better protected or more facilitated than actions of members of non-religious associations or the expression of non-religious opinions.

12.3   Rule application in people processing organisations

Many procedures involving civilians and civil service institutions can be described as 'people processing'. The way these procedures are conducted is determined by two important institutional characteristics: the institutions have a monopoly on the service rendered, and, as they are not commercial, they do not have anything to lose from unsatisfied 'customers', at least not directly. This means that clients do not have alternative institutions from which to choose and that they are dependent on the benevolence of the civil servants. In this position, clients tend to accept the legitimacy of the civil servants handling their requests. Clients do not interact with the officials on the basis of a utilitarian calculation or trust, but rather out of fear.[9] This makes it very important that those officials are instructed and encouraged to make reasonable decisions awarding due weight to the interests of the applicants.

The organisations relevant here, municipal civil affairs departments, courts of law and the Dutch Immigration and Naturalisation Service (IND), are people

---

5   Possamai 2012.
6   Hammer & Rothstein 2012.
7   Cusack 2010.
8   Bijsterveld & Vermeulen 2016; Broeksteeg 2016.
9   Lipsky 2010, p. 54-57.

processing organisations. In these organisations, the officials dealing with applicants or plaintiffs have the possibility to create locally their own work routines and criteria within the limits of their competence. Although these varying routines and criteria are created in practice in response to the unclear fit between general legal rules and concrete cases, they may create legal uncertainty themselves: civilian parties do not know these unpublished practical criteria that do not necessarily correspond to the official policy objectives of the service organisation, and may not always be observed by the people who created them.[10] Although judges are more highly educated and trained specifically to apply general rules to particular (classes of) cases in uniform ways, they too struggle with this, resulting in the well-known phenomenon of differences in style and policy between different courts or between judges in the same court.

Political pressure and public opinion can be important factors in determining whether street-level bureaucrats in people processing organisations are more or less trusting of applicants/plaintiffs and consequently more or less inclined to approve the application of certain rules.[11] The finding of Bardach & Kagan in their well-known work *Going by the Book*, that administrative agencies are inclined to enforce rules more legalistically and restrictively when the public perceives them as being too permissive and lax,[12] is especially interesting with regard to decision making in asylum procedures.

Hearing similar stories repetitively in different asylum cases can cause civil servants to, 'consciously or unconsciously, categorize applications into generic case profiles and make predetermined assumptions about their credibility and other issues'.[13] Conversely, when being confronted with a new and strange religion for the first time, also tends to make decision makers suspicious rather than merely surprised, intrigued or amused, as will be shown hereafter.

There are two further important factors in the relationship between people processing organisations and their clients. The first is that they expect clients to act rationally and give complete, accurate, plausible, timely, detailed, articulate and consistent statements throughout the procedures, on penalty of losing on the grounds of non-credibility.[14] These are also the standards developed by the International Association of Refugee Law Judges[15] and by the European Court of Human Rights, the UNHCR and the Committee Against Torture.[16] The other, related, factor is the fact that professionals – like municipal civil servants, Immigration Service interviewers and judges – are not better at lie detection than anybody else.[17] Understandably, the UNHCR researchers who investigated the practice of credibility assessment in asylum procedures in the EU were

---

10 Doornbos 2011, p. 102-103.
11 Kagan 2006.
12 Bardach & Kagan 1982.
13 UNHCR 2013, p. 40; Garlick 2013, p. 55-57.
14 Doornbos 2006, p. 39-50.
15 Barnes & Mackey 2013, p. 127-130.
16 Baldinger 2015, p. 471-472.
17 Doornbos 2006, p. 32-37 & p. 282-283.

surprised 'to note that many decision-makers interviewed in this research have stated that the credibility assessment was not one they found particularly difficult and that it was a straightforward task'.[18]

All this needs to be taken into account when assessing the assessments administrative and court decision makers make about the credibility of applicants' religion, in both the Spaghetti Monster and the asylum cases.

12.4   The Church of the Flying Spaghetti Monster

In 2005, Bobby Henderson from Portland, Oregon, sent a letter to the Kansas Board of Education in reaction to their decision to oblige schools to teach intelligent design theory alongside evolution theory in biology class.[19] He wrote that there were different versions of intelligent design, and that the version including an all-powerful flying bunch of spaghetti and meatballs should not be omitted. Henderson also included some mock-scientific evidence. Subsequently, he wrote the *Gospel of the Flying Spaghetti Monster* (2006), and later the *Loose Canon* appeared. The satire is most striking. Through the internet, the FSM became very popular and churches were founded in his name by Pastafarians all over the world; national branches can be found in most Western countries. In Pastafari heaven there are stripper factories and beer volcanos, just like in hell, only there the beer is lukewarm and the strippers have sexually transmittable diseases. Some important rituals are: wearing pirate clothing on certain occasions, wearing a colander on the head, and consuming pasta and beer on Fridays. The most important ethical standards are written in the eight I'd-really-rather-you-didn'ts, received by pirate Mosey on clay tablets on top of mount Salsa from the FSM himself:[20]

1. *I'd really rather you didn't act like a sanctimonious holier-than-thou ass when describing my noodly goodness. If some people don't believe in me, that's okay. Really, I'm not that vain. Besides, this isn't about them so don't change the subject.*
2. *I'd really rather you didn't use my existence as a means to oppress, subjugate, punish, eviscerate, and/or, you know, be mean to others. I don't require sacrifices, and purity is for drinking water, not people.*
3. *I'd really rather you didn't judge people for the way they look, or how they dress, or the way they talk, or, well, just play nice, okay? Oh, and get this in your thick heads: woman = person. man = person. Samey – samey. One is not*

---

18   UNHCR 2013, p. 33.
19   See the official US website: <www.venganza.org>.
20   Henderson 2006, p. 98-101.

> *better than the other, unless we're talking about fashion and I'm sorry, but I gave that to women and some guys who know the difference between teal and fuchsia.*
>
> 4. *I'd really rather you didn't indulge in conduct that offends yourself, or your willing, consenting partner of legal age and mental maturity. As for anyone who might object, I think the expression is go f*** yourself, unless they find that offensive in which case they can turn off the TV for once and go for a walk for a change.*
>
> 5. *I'd really rather you didn't challenge the bigoted, misogynist, hateful ideas of others on an empty stomach. Eat, then go after the b*******.*
>
> 6. *I'd really rather you didn't build multimillion-dollar churches/temples/mosques/shrines to my noodly goodness when the money could be better spent (take your pick):*
>   *(1). Ending poverty*
>   *(2). Curing diseases*
>   *(3). Living in peace, loving with passion, and lowering the cost of cable*
>   *I might be a complex-carbohydrate omniscient being, but I enjoy the simple things in life. I ought to know. I am the creator.*
>
> 7. *I'd really rather you didn't go around telling people I talk to you. You're not that interesting. Get over yourself. And I told you to love your fellow man, can't you take a hint?*
>
> 8. *I'd really rather you didn't do unto others as you would have them do unto you if you are into, um, stuff that uses a lot of leather/lubricant/Las Vegas. If the other person is into it, however (pursuant to #4), then have at it, take pictures, and for the love of mike, wear a condom! Honestly, it's a piece of rubber. If I didn't want it to feel good when you did it I would have added spikes, or something.*

From this it is clear that Pastafarians have an ethic of friendliness, non-violence, tolerance, sobriety (in the intellectual sense), modesty, relativism, critical thinking, joy and humour. Wearing a colander in public is a veritable exercise in humility. The elements of parody or satire together with the critique of certain behaviour of members of other religions have caused many angry reactions from members of more traditional religions who feel mocked.[21]

---

21   <www.venganza.org/category/hate-mail>.

12.5   The Pastafarian colander cases

Inspired by passages from the *Gospel of the FSM* and the *Loose Canon*, and possibly direct communication from His Noodliness, many Pastafarians wear colanders on their head:

> *Then the FSM saw that the wickedness of Man was great on earth, and that every thought of the little midget was ruled by his stomach. Then the FSM said, "Fine, I'll just cook for myself", and He produced a great Colander of Goodness and He did collect water in an enormous pot, (...)'.*[22]
> *But as TV hadn't been invented yet, Penelope put the Holy Colander on her head and grabbed a handy pair of salad tongs. She decided to take a short nap under a meatball tree. Naps had been invented just last week and Penelope was nothing if not a trend setter.*[23]

Some wear them more regularly than others, but over the whole world, Pastafarians have applied for driver's licences and other photo IDs, handing in photos in which they are wearing a colander.

<www.venganza.org/wp-content/uploads/2017/06/azlicense.jpg>

Many applications have been successful, an unknown number have been rejected. I will discuss the arguments of the Dutch mayors (who formally issue IDs) and courts in question that are relevant for the freedom and equal treatment of religion.

---

22   Henderson 2006, p. 73-74.
23   *Loose Canon, Book of Penelope*, Ch. 2, verse 7; Ch. 3, verse 7-8

In the Dutch regulations for photos on IDs there is an exception to the rule that forbids headwear:[24]

> Deviating from section 2 [banning headwear], a photo [with headwear] can be accepted if the applicant has shown that there are religious or world view reasons against not covering the head.[25]

This means that Pastafarians wishing to appear in the ID photo with their colander must convince the court to answer the following questions in the affirmative:

(1) Is Pastafarianism a religion/world view, or not? and
(2) Does the Pastafarian plaintiff have real religious reasons against not wearing the colander in the photograph?

I will explain how four Dutch courts answered these questions in three court cases. Interestingly, the courts all used different approaches to the two questions, but reached the same final conclusion. In the latter two cases, against the mayors of Eindhoven and Nijmegen, I acted as legal counsel for the Pastafarian applicants. I am not a member of the FSM Church myself.

12.5.1 Is Pastafarianism a religion or belief?

In the first case, against the mayor of Emmen, the court neatly avoided judging on the content of Pastafarianism. Concerning the first question, the court merely stated that, 'at the hearing, together with both parties, it has been determined that Pastafarianism is in any case a world view present in Dutch society'. Nevertheless, the Pastafarian plaintiff could not invoke the exception clause, because the court ruled negatively on the second question: the Pastafarian also let non-religious reasons determine when he wore his colander, taking it off when helping clients.[26] He could thus not convince the court that the 'religious reasons against not covering the head' in the ID photo were pressing enough.

The criterion the ECtHR uses to determine whether something is a 'religion or belief' is that it must 'attain a certain level of cogency, seriousness, cohesion and importance'.[27] Movements thus recognized as religions include: Hinduism, Scientology, pacifism, atheism, Buddhism, Druidism, Devine Light Zentrum, and the Osho Movement.[28] In the case against the mayor of Eindhoven, the court used the second element, seriousness, to reach the conclusion that

---

24 Article 28(3) Paspoortuitvoeringsregeling Nederland
25 Article 28(3) (Dutch) Paspoortuitvoeringsregeling: 'In afwijking van het tweede lid kan een pasfoto worden geaccepteerd indien de aanvrager heeft aangetoond dat godsdienstige of levensbeschouwelijke redenen zich verzetten tegen het niet bedekken van het hoofd'.
26 Rechtbank [Dutch District Court] Noord-Nederland 28 July 2016, ECLI:NL:RBMNE :2016:3626.
27 ECtHR 25 February 1982, 7743/76 & 7511/76, *Campbell & Cosans v. United Kingdom*.
28 White & Claire 2010, p. 404-405 and cited cases.

Pastafarianism, as a satirical form of religion criticism, was not itself a religion, citing the eight I'd-really-rather-you-didn'ts and Bobby Henderson's letter to the Kansas Board of Education.[29] The court's reasoning was especially interesting because it might be used more widely to disqualify NUWS religions: the content of the religious beliefs was deemed not credible. The court specifically noted that the eight I'd-really-rather-you-didn'ts were, purportedly, many centuries old, yet they spoke of 'lowering the cost of cable'. This approach is surprising, as courts normally observe 'interpretative restraint' regarding the content and expressions of religions.[30] Furthermore, the court did not, as little as the ECtHR does, specify how high the 'level of seriousness' must be and how this was measured. The court also did not answer the plaintiff's argument that the eight I'd-really-rather-you-didn'ts contained a very serious ethic.

If courts assessed all religions with this not very restrained method, traditional religions would also have to be disqualified, as the website of the FSM church explains:

> *Elements of our religion are sometimes described as satire and there are many members who do not literally believe our scripture, but this isn't unusual in religion. A lot of Christians don't believe the Bible is literally true – but that doesn't mean they aren't True Christians. If you say Pastafarians must believe in a literal Flying Spaghetti Monster to be True Believers, then you can make a similar argument for Christians. There is a lot of outlandish stuff in the Bible that rational Christians choose to ignore.*[31]

If the mayor could show that the FSM was an elaborate expression of an opinion but not a religion or belief, he could make the valid point that an ID photo was not the place to ventilate opinions. Opinions do not fall under the category of 'religion or beliefs' and are not protected by the freedom of religion (Art. 6 Dutch Constitution), but by the freedom of speech (Art. 7 Dutch Constitution). In the scholarship of new religious movements, however, it has been argued that applying humour or having a joking founder does not disqualify the followers of a faith from being real believers.[32]

Finally, the silence of the plaintiff, who left the talking to his counsel, was interpreted as the inability to answer questions about his belief independently, and used as an additional argument for the lack of seriousness.

---

29 Rechtbank [Dutch District Court] Oost-Brabant, 15 February 2016, ECLI:NL:RBOBR :2017:762.
30 Bijsterveld & Vermeulen 2016, par. 4. See also: Hof [Dutch Court of Appeal] Arnhem 11 July 1984, *NJ* 1985/536 and CRvB 17 November 1994, *AB* 1995/322.
31 <www.venganza.org/about>.
32 Cusack 2010, p. 136-137.

12.5.2   Are there religious reasons for wearing the colander?

This argument was used in the case against the mayor of Nijmegen. The two courts involved did not answer the first question: Is Pastafarianism a religion, or world view, or not? But concentrated instead on the second one: does the Pastafarian plaintiff have real religious reasons against not wearing the colander in the photograph? The habit of wearing a colander can be traced back to the passages from the *Gospel of the FSM* quoted above. There is no explicit order in any of the scriptures to wear a colander, but neither is there explicit obligation for women to wear a headscarf in the Quran either, the two surahs most cited in this context being:

> surah 24:30–31:
> *And say to the believing women [...] that they should draw their khimār over their breasts and not display their beauty except to their husband, their fathers, [...]*

> *and surah 33:59:*
> *O Prophet! Enjoin your wives, your daughters, and the wives of true believers that they should cast their outer garments over their persons (when abroad): That is most convenient, that they may be distinguished and not be harassed.*

In a preliminary injunction hearing, in which the plaintiff asked for a remedy for the problem of not having a valid driver's licence, the judge ruled that 'the plaintiff hasn't succeeded in showing that the Flying Spaghetti Monster forbids her to appear on an ID photo without a colander'.[33] At the hearing, the judge said with regard to inconveniences like not having a valid driver's licence anymore: 'maybe that's just the problem of a new religion'.

   In the proceedings on the merits, the court demanded an explicit obligation in holy scriptures, and found none.[34] According to the court, 'Pastafarianism does not know any obligations or restrictions'. First, this presupposes a very specific and narrow interpretation of the exception clause which speaks only of 'religious reasons', not of obligations or explicit commandments. And secondly, by interpreting religious rites and scriptures in this way, the court, just as in the Eindhoven case, did not observe interpretative restraint. The Netherlands Institute for Human Rights has repeatedly ruled that religious behaviour should be accepted as such when declared by the believer: that some Muslim women do not wear headscarves is no reason to doubt the religious obligation of those

---

33   Rechtbank [Dutch District Court] Gelderland, 17 January 2017, ECLI:NL:RBGEL :2017:275.
34   Rechtbank [Dutch District Court] Overijssel, 25 July 2017, not yet published.

that do.[35] The committee even mentioned the social pressure applied to women who wear head scarves, and seemed to suggest that that was the reason for permitting them to wear headscarves in ID photos.

These lines of argument by government institutions are the same as were used in a similar German case where a Pastafarian wished to appear on his ID card with pirate headgear.[36] It reveals not only the common tendency to judge the authenticity of a religion by (consciously or not) comparing it to traditional religions,[37] but also the zealousness to disqualify the FSM church. In this respect, a quasi-legal argument from the mayor of Eindhoven is interesting, because it had no legal basis and apparently was meant to confuse and discourage the applicant. It was argued that it was impossible for the applicant to get his license renewed because the expiry date was still so far away (two years). The court quickly brushed this aside.[38]

12.5.3 No threat to the purpose of the regulation

An important point to note is that wearing a colander in an ID photo does not impair the recognisability of the holder at all. So, the problem for IDs is not really that serious. Colanders can be worn in a way that more of the face is visible than with permitted types of hijab or turban.[39] An interesting comparison can be made with the types of cases in which the behaviour of the suspect (these were criminal cases) *did* impair the goal of the relevant legislation which, moreover, had no exception clause. Nevertheless, several courts have ruled that an exception must be made on the grounds of freedom of religion.[40] These cases concerned members of the Santo Daime Church, an amalgam of Catholicism and indigenous South American religion. In their sacred rituals, the believers drink the hallucinogenic Ayahuasca tea, which contains dimethyltryptamine. This drug is on the list of forbidden drugs together with heroin, cocaine and amphetamine. But because the drug is consumed in small quantities in a controlled setting, freedom of religion could prevail. In these cases the courts readily recognize the religion in question (maybe because it contains a heavy portion of Catholicism?), step over the dangers of breaking the law (public

---

35 College voor de Rechten van de Mens (Netherlands Institute for Human Rights): CRM 26 May 2016, 2016-45, section 4.3; CRM 9 June 2015, 2015-67, section 3.3; CRM 16 October 2014, 2014-125, section 3.6.
36 Wakonigg & Rath 2017.
37 Cusack 2010.
38 Rechtbank [Dutch District Court] Oost-Brabant, 15 February 2016, ECLI:NL:RBOBR:2017 :762.
39 See examples: <www.rijksoverheid.nl/documenten/brochures/2014/02/18/fotomatrix-2007>.
40 Rechtbank [Dutch District Court] Amsterdam 21 May 2001, ECLI:NL:RBAMS:2001: AB1739, *AB* 2001, 342, m.nt. Vermeulen; Rechtbank [Dutch District Court] Haarlem 26 March 2009, ECLI:NL:RBHAA:2009:BH9844; Hof [Dutch Court of Appeal] Amsterdam 24 February 2012, ECLI:NL:GHAMS:2012:BV6888; Rechtbank [Dutch District Court] Noord-Holland 8 September 2016, ECLI:NL:RBNHO:2016:7557.

health risks) and *create* an exception to that law. In all three of these respects, accepting colander photos is less harmful to law and society.

12.5.4 Real fake religions

It is also instructive to compare the Church of the FSM with genuinely fake religions such as the Smokers' Church, founded to find a way around the ban on smoking in cafes and the Sisters of Saint Walburga, who said they were a section of the Church of Satan, only to evade regular police checks in their brothel. These 'religions' were not accepted as such by government institutions in the Netherlands, witness a Supreme Court ruling on the Walburga Sisters,[41] a fine for a café run by a member of the Smokers' Church,[42] and a court ruling on a fellow inhaler in Belgium. The Ghent court even noted that appealing to a membership of the Smokers' Church showed 'arrogance and disdain'.[43]

Contrary to these fake churches, the FSM church was not founded with the purpose of evading certain laws, not even with the purpose of acquiring photo IDs with colander photos. It was the other way around: first, the holy headgear appeared, and subsequently the ID photo problem emerged. After discussing how refugees' religious conversions are judged, I will consider some explanations for the institutional hesitations in both cases.

12.6 Vetting converts

The way Dutch authorities view and treat Pastafarians applying for IDs with colander photos shows similarities with the treatment of asylum seekers who put forward their religious conversion (usually to Christianity) and subsequent risk of persecution in their home country as a basis for their right to asylum. In these cases, refugee status, and subsequently asylum, is awarded to those who succeed in convincing the Immigration and Naturalisation Service (IND), acting on behalf of the Dutch Minister for Migration, that they will probably be persecuted in their home country on the basis of religion.[44] This means that an applicant must show either that he is a member of a religious group which is (known to be) persecuted, or that the authorities in his home country *see* him as a member of such a group. When conversion, and thus the creation of the persecution risk, takes place after arrival in the Netherlands, making the applicant a *refugié sur place*, the refugee has to show that the authorities in his

---

41 HR [Dutch Supreme Court] 31 October 1986, *NJ* 1987/173.
42 <www.nu.nl/algemeen/1694329/rokerskerk-krijgt-eerste-boete.html>.
43 <www.legalworld.be/legalworld/uploadedFiles/Rechtspraak/De_Juristenkrant>.
44 Art. 3.2 Policy Guidelines on the Aliens Act; Art. 29(1a) Aliens Act; Art. 3.37(2) Aliens Regulation.

home country know, or will probably learn about the conversion.[45] After discussing the most important (case) law, I will give some examples of IND interrogations.

12.6.1 Refugee converts: law and case law

The law does not demand that the alien proves the reality of his inner struggle and the sincerity of his new religious convictions – on the contrary:

> *In assessing whether the alien's fear of persecution in the sense of the Refugee Convention 1951 is founded, it is not relevant whether the alien in fact bears the racial, religious, national, social or political qualities causing the persecution, if these qualities are attributed to him by the persecuting agent.[46]*

Nevertheless, the refugee's true religiousness plays a crucial role in the questioning by the IND and in the credibility assessment of the refugee's statements. The IND work instructions specify several 'credibility indicators' for assessing refugees' statements. Relevant here are the indicators 'degree of detail and specificity' and 'internal consistency'.[47] This fits with the widely adhered standards mentioned earlier.[48] In the interviews by the IND with regard to conversions a questionnaire is used containing questions that can be divided into four categories.[49] The first is the motives for and process of the conversion, including a possible baptism. The Minister assumes that a bona fide conversion is always a 'deliberate and well-considered choice'.[50] Secondly, the applicant must explain the personal significance of his conversion or his new faith. Basic knowledge of his new religion is the third category, and, finally, when the convert attends church services, their location, times and the way they proceed are subjects of questioning. The Administrative Jurisdiction Division of the Council of State (ABRvS), the highest appeal court for asylum cases in the Netherlands, has accepted these aspects as relevant for the credibility question and has also accepted that the first category, motives for and process of conversion, is of crucial importance.

This practice is in line with the government's policy, which has been adopted by the ABRvS. This court agreed with the Minister that it is 'the refugee's

---

45 Art. 3.2 Policy Guidelines on the Aliens Act; Art. 3.37b, Aliens Regulation.
46 Art. 3.37(2) Aliens Regulation. A rare application of this rule is Rechtbank [District Court] Den Haag January 18, 2017, ECLI:NL:RBDHA:2017:484, point 23.2.1.
47 Werkinstructie 2014/10 (1 January 2015), par. 3.2.1.1 <ind.nl/Documents /WI_2014_10.pdf>.
48 See above, notes 14-16 and accompanying text
49 ABRvS [Dutch Council of State] 24 May 2013, 201109839/1/V2, ECLI:NL:RVS:2013CA:0955, point 3.2.
50 ABRvS [Dutch Council of State] 24 May 2013, 201109839/1/V2, ECLI:NL:RVS:2013CA :0955, point 6.

responsibility to offer convincing statements to the Minister concerning his conversion and the process leading up to it.' According to the appeal court, courts can therefore leave aside any expert evidence about the conversion, awarding overriding importance to the refugee's statements.[51] In a brochure, the IND explains that files often contain letters from clergy members declaring that the refugee has truly converted to Christianity and/or is active in the church. Nevertheless, the IND explains: 'These letters are written with the best intentions, but are not always motivated by truth finding. We consider these letters in the decision making process, but never as a decisive factor'.[52] What is not mentioned in this brochure, is other assessment reports on conversions sometimes submitted: by the Gave Foundation, advising various churches on converted asylum seekers in their congregation, by the Plaisier Commission, consisting of theologians of the Dutch Protestant Churches, and by professor of psychology of religion Joke van Saane.[53] According to the Minister, all reports and letters are considered 'seriously' in the IND procedures,[54] but in the light of the foregoing this does not give any guarantees.

What makes things worse, is that, based on the ABRvS case law, courts can dismiss any of the reports mentioned. The standard formula is as stated in the IND brochure: any 'report can serve to support the alien's conversion, but doesn't diminish the refugee's responsibility to offer convincing statements to the Minister concerning his conversion and the process leading up to it.'[55] A district court went even further in its interpretation of this characterization of a report by professor Van Saane and disqualified it as an expert report altogether. This means that in these cases any kind of report can be dismissed as 'not expert evidence', so that courts may ignore the findings of these reports without having the obligation to base their dismissal on alternative expert evidence.[56] Not surprisingly, this worries aliens law advocate Frans-Willem Verbaas, who rightly asks: 'Does the ABRvS really think that IND employees are better equipped to judge whether someone has honestly converted than a professor in the psychology of religion or an expert on the religion the refugee says he has converted to?' With this criticism he finds himself in the company of several courts.[57] The UNHCR has criticised the demand for positive persuasiveness of refugee statements, citing cases in which 'one mistake in response to a question

---

51 ABRvS [Dutch Council of State] 5 June 2015, 201410596/1/V2, ECLI:NL:RVS:2015:1911. See also: ABRvS [Dutch Council of State] 24 May 2013, 201109839/1/V2, ECLI:NL:RVS :2013CA:0955, point 1.4.
52 IND 2015.
53 Verbaas 2016, p.25-26.
54 Meeting of the Permanent Parliamentary Justice Commission, 4 June 2015, *Kamerstukken II* 2014/15, 19637, 2025, p. 30.
55 ABRvS 3 July 2015, ECLI:NL:RVS:2015:2187, point 1.4.
56 For example: Rechtbank [Dutch District Court] Den Haag zp Rotterdam, Augustus 19, 2015, AWB 15/5011, ECLI:NL:RBROT:2015:6008, *JV* 2015/303, point 7.9, referring to ABRvS [Dutch Council of State] 3 July 2015, ECLI:NL:RVS:2015:2187.
57 Verbaas 2016, p.27-28.

assessing general knowledge in relation to a material fact [suffices] to determine that the claim is not credible. For example, if an applicant is asked to name three villages in a particular area, and only one named village is correct, according to the Council of State, the determining authority can reasonably conclude that the claim is not positively persuasive.[58] Certificates of baptism may be judged as unimportant as expert evidence or church statements.[59]

More recently, the ABRvS has, in addition to the foregoing, explicitly stated that professor Van Saane's reports are also not decisive because, first, the IND applies the same method as Van Saane, who gives workshops for IND employees, and secondly, her reports only deal with the conversion and do not assess all the refugee's statements in the procedure as a whole.[60] The latter argument is probably meant to render the duty to use alternative expert evidence non-applicable on the grounds of incompleteness.[61] But that would be ironic, or even cynical, because, as mentioned above, the ABRvS agreed with the Minister that *he* does *not* have to consider the other elements mentioned in the IND work instruction besides the conversion itself. Frustrating every possible guarantee of expert evidence being taken seriously is in stark contrast to the great importance attached to equality of arms by the ECtHR in administrative cases in Korošec.[62] I will discuss some of the rejections these criteria allow for in the next section.

12.6.2 Rejected conversions

Asylum lawyer Verbaas feels that sometimes the real reason behind rejecting a conversion as non-credible is that the IND finds it not legitimate because it wasn't necessary: the convert could just as well have chosen a more liberal variant of his own religion (usually Islam). He gives two examples: A woman who said she converted to Christianity because of the more favourable status of women, was told she should have done more research into the other varieties of Christianity besides the Pentecostal church she joined. A 'low point' was the rejection, motivated with bible quotes, of a woman who had had an abortion and stated that she found more forgiveness in the Christian faith than in Islam. The IND pointed out that in both religions abortion was a sin, which rendered the conversion non-credible.[63] In another case the IND specifically asked the refugee: 'Why was it necessary for you to choose a different religion instead of

---

58 UNHCR 2013 citing: ABRvS [Dutch Council of State] 30 May 2011, 201011349/1/V1, ECLI:NL:RVS :2011:BQ7859, point 2.2.3; ABRvS [Dutch Council of State] 4 April 2011, 201008219/1/V1, ECLI:NL:RVS: 2011:BQ0748, *JV* 2011/245; ABRvS [Dutch Council of State] 24 December 2009, 200906274, ECLI:NL:RVS:2009:154.
59 Haar & Douma 2016, p. 23.
60 ABRvS [Dutch Council of State] 30 December 2016, 201505920/1/V2, ECLI:NL:RVS:2016 :3502, point 7-7.5.
61 Battjes 2016, p. 80.
62 De Groot 2017. ECtHR 8 October 2015, 77212/12, *Korosec v. Slovenia*, ECLI:CE:ECHR :2015:1008JUD007721212.
63 Verbaas 2016, p. 33.

practising Islam the way you see it and the way you wish?'[64] It seems as though a refugee cannot legally change faith without an officially approved reason.

Sometimes decisions by the IND on the credibility of statements can be quite incredible themselves. In one Kafkaesque example, the alien applicant had made statements about discussing with his girlfriend their own conversion and the possible consequences, and also statements about his doubts about Islam, his initial disinterest in religion and the gradual process of his conversion. The IND however, following its policy of attaching crucial importance to the statements by the aliens themselves, decided that the applicant 'did not think about the consequences [of his conversion]' and 'did not adequately explain his road to Christianity'. In its decision, the IND stated without explanation that the alien could not explain how he went from being uninterested in religion to becoming a Christian, and that it was incomprehensible that 'someone who is not really involved in religion or looking for one, rather suddenly surrenders to a new religion'. The court understandably quashed the IND's decision as incomprehensible.[65] It almost seems as if it doesn't matter what the alien says for the IND to decide that he hasn't made adequate statements about the relevant issues. Does the IND use a secret blueprint of a 'credible' conversion? Or are the decisions rather random?

Other decisions seem to use a tacit criterion akin to 'Westernisation level' which is used in the 'pardon' of refugee minors: it seems as if a certain level of Christian religiosity is required to acquire an asylum permit. In both cases, persons can be said to be integrated to a degree that will cause enormous trouble (re)adapting to life in, say, Afghanistan or Iran. The more a refugee adopts an identity with which civil servants can identify, the more willing they seem to be to take him in. But the bar is set high. An example is the case of an Afghan refugee who in his seventh (!) application for asylum finally succeeded in getting his conversion confirmed, not by the IND, but by the district court. The court decided that the applicant had shown that he had made progress in his knowledge and practice of the Christian faith and was more and more integrated in the Christian community in which he lived, while the IND in their defence merely stated that 'the plaintiff states that he goes to church, reads the bible and prays. But he stated this in earlier procedures already.' When that is not enough, which is more than most self-declared present-day Christians do, what does it take to be a credible Christian? The IND continued with barely concealed irritation: it is 'not surprising that the plaintiff has gained more knowledge, now that he submits his conversion as motive for asylum for the fourth time.'[66]

The IND also expects applicants to think and act rationally and to be fully aware of their interests and rights and duties at every stage of the procedure. The questions in the interviews 'often assume a high level of education' on the

---

64   IND, Rapport aanvullend gehoor (additional hearing), 28 August 2014 (anonymized).
65   Rechtbank [Dutch District Court] Den Haag, 2 March 2017, ECLI:NL:RBDHA:2017:2808.
66   Rechtbank [Dutch District Court] Den Haag, 2 March 2017, ECLI:NL:RBDHA:2017:2106,
      point 5.2.

part of the asylum seeker.[67] In one case, the Muslim applicant had not mentioned his interest in Christianity in the first hearings, because he was not yet sure about converting: 'my faith was not yet complete'. Failing to mention something so important harmed the credibility of the applicant's story. But the fact that he mentioned it at a later stage, when others had told him that his considering to convert would be relevant in the procedure, was taken as a sign of insincerity as well. Apparently, if you do not act perfectly rationally from the start (even if you are traumatized, homeless, illiterate, culturally different etc.), you run the risk that your statements are labelled as 'insincere'.[68] This is aptly expressed by Dutch author of Afghan origin Rodaan Al Galidi, who in 2011 won the EU Prize for Literature, and subsequently failed his Dutch 'integration test': 'a tidy lie is better than a messy truth.'[69]

I will end this contribution with, first, a brief discussion of the role of rationality in the procedures in both cases and the historical context of conversions and new religions, and, finally, speculate on the real motives underlying institutional reluctance concerning conversions and new religions.

12.7 Character and context of institutional reluctance: rationality and history

It seems as though refugee converts as well as Pastafarian colander wearers have been accused of acting too rationally: using religion as a mere instrument to acquire rights or privileges. Of course, that image does not square with the picture of religion as consisting of deeply personal and very profound convictions about aspects of life that elude rational explanation and choice. But the law, as well as people processing organisations such as the IND, municipal civil service and courts, presuppose the fiction of the rational person: people are rational thinkers and actors with free will who are aware of their objective interests. This leads to contradictory demands, for which I will give some examples.

On the one hand, an asylum seeker must explain his conversion to Christianity as a well thought through and rational decision out of free will. On the other hand, the whole flight history and asylum procedure may not form a part of those rational deliberations, on the penalty of being regarded as not credible. On the one hand, objective evidence is demanded concerning the conversion, while on the other hand, the IND can ignore any scientific reports or other official (church) documents and use only its own judgement based on the refugee's statements in the interviews. The same happens with Pastafarians: on the one hand, the mayor of Nijmegen demands 'objective sources' that show

---

67 Werkman 2017.
68 IND, Voornemen tot afwijzen asielaanvraag (intention of rejecting asylum application), 13 May 2014 (anonymized).
69 Al Galidi 2016, back flap.

Pastafarianism to be a religion. But when those sources are provided – multiple scientific publications, opinions of other Dutch mayors and a Dutch court ruling – the mayor uses the same tactic as the IND and demands credible proof from the Pastafarian herself, of which only the mayor himself is to be the judge.

Rational investigation by courts does not stop at the content of faith, where it should stop in order to respect freedom of religion. The principle of interpretative restraint is clearly violated in both cases: refugees are forced to be completely open about their religious opinions, doubts and changes and to justify their adherence to a certain religion. Pastafarianism is judged on the credibility of its content, and on the existence of explicit written commandments concerning certain rituals (holy headgear).

In history, conversions are abundant. Romans and Germanic tribes were, sometimes by force, converted to Christianity; Portuguese Jews converted to Christianity after the Alhambra Decree; slaves in the colonies converted to Christianity. Does it make any difference when we label these conversions 'not credible'? Maybe motives were pragmatic: humane treatment, escape from poverty and exclusion, respect for human rights and dignity. But if, after conversion, one lives as a Christian, why not recognise the convert as a Christian?

The history of the emergence of new religions is full of examples of more and less success. Let's take a brief look at the Church of Jesus Christ of the Latter Day Saints, or Mormonism. This church is now generally recognised as one of the varieties of Christianity and has millions of followers. However, the circumstances of its foundation were not very dissimilar in terms of credibility to those of the FSM Church: the founder, Joseph Smith, claimed he had received golden plates from an angelic figure called Moroni on which 'reformed Egyptian' characters were written which he translated using a 'seer stone'. The text contained the Book of Mormon. Amongst many other things, it reports that Jesus visited America shortly after his resurrection and that there have been several waves of migration from the Middle East to America starting as early as 2500 BC.[70] Pastafarians have holy headgear, Mormons have religious under-garments. Joseph Smith met with considerable suspicion and resistance, but in the end his church succeeded in attaining official recognition.

12.8   Possible motives for institutional reluctance: policy and authority

Two motives seem to be the most likely candidates for explaining the less than accommodating attitude of government institutions. The first is government policy and the protection of vested interests. In the case of refugees, public opinion as well as government policy is not pro-immigration. The IND is a

---

70   See, for example, Brodie 1995 and Wagoner & Walker 1982.

government agency, executing government policy, which is based on the idea that the people of the Netherlands have to be protected from large numbers of immigrants, especially from non-Western countries. In the Pastafarian case, the Ministry for the Interior sent a letter to all municipal authorities, warning them about applications with colander photos and strongly advising them to reject all such applications.[71] The association for the municipal civil service cheerfully forwarded this message to its members.[72] Although both instructions are not binding for the mayors who formally make the decisions, they are authoritative.

In May 2017, a Pastafarian filed a request under the Government Information (Public Access) Act regarding communication about applications for travel documents by Pastafarians. Quite soon after the first questions in 2014 by municipal civil servants, the Home Office's Identity Data Authority came up with a standard rejection text which it has repeated to civil servants ever since, without reconsidering.[73]

The mayors also argued that religious people might be offended by the Pastafarians' colander photo applications, because they might feel mocked. Also, Muslims might be afraid that the Pastafarians were actually campaigning for the abolishment of the religious exception clause for ID photos, and maybe even for religious privileges altogether. Whether or not this is true, it is not a valid reason for government institutions to restrict the religious freedom of Pastafarians more than the freedom of other believers. It seems that the interests of traditional and traditionally organised religions are still protected very well, although their social relevance is small and rapidly diminishing.

The second possible motive is fear of being tricked into awarding rights and privileges to people who do not really deserve them. Authorities do not like being taken for a ride, which is understandable, because that diminishes their authority in the public eye. The fear of being made a fool of, whether or not justified, was tangible in the procedures I witnessed.

12.9   Conclusion: symbolism or consequences?

To sum up, the suspicious attitude of civil service and courts towards the FSM Church and converted asylum seekers is understandable. But that does not make it justified. In both cases, the consequences of being more lenient and accommodating are not very serious: how many people will want to appear in their photo ID documents with ridiculous headgear just for fun? How many refugees

71 *Nieuwsbrief reisdocumenten*, Nummer 2, 26 juli 2016.
    <abonneren.rijksoverheid.nl/nieuwsbrieven/archief/rijksdienst-voor-identiteitsgegevens---nieuwsbrief-reisdocumenten-caribisch-deel-koninkrijk/716>.
72 <nvvb.nl/nl/communicatie/nieuwsberichten/pastafarians-mogen-niet-met-vergiet-op-id-kaart>.
73 <https://www.rijksoverheid.nl/documenten/wob-verzoeken/2017/09/05/besluit-wob-verzoek-over-aanvragen-reisdocumenten-door-leden-van-de-kerk-van-het-vliegend-spaghettimonster>

will go through the trouble of separating themselves from their religious community and integrating into a new one only for the sake of appearances, to acquire a residence permit? Keeping up appearances seems to be more important in these cases than really addressing the issues and taking a level-headed perspective.

References

Al Galidi, R. (2016), *Hoe ik talent voor het leven kreeg*, Amsterdam: Jurgen Maas.

Baldinger, D. (2015), *Vertical judicial dialogues in asylum cases. Standards on judicial scrutiny and evidence in international and European asylum law,* Immigration and asylum law and policy in Europe, nr. 36, Leiden: Brill Nijhoff.

Bardack, E. & R.A. Kagan (2010), *Going by the Book: The Problem of Regulatory Unreasonableness,* New Brunswick-London: Transaction Publishers.

Barnes & Mackey (2013), 'The Credo Document. Assessment of Credibility in Refugee and Subsidiary Protection Claims under the EU Qualification Directive: Judicial criteria and standards. International Association of Refugee Law Judges (IARLJ)', in: C. Grütters, E. Guild & S. de Groot (eds.), *Assessment of Credibility by Judges in Asylum Cases in the EU,* Oisterwijk: Wolf Legal Publishers, p. 89-216. <www.iarlj.org/general/images/stories/Credo/Credo_Paper_ March2013-rev1.pdf>.

Battjes, H. (2016), 'Wanneer is een bekering geloofwaardig? Het juridische kader voor de beoordeling van de geloofwaardigheid van bekeringen in het Nederlandse asielrecht', *NTKR Tijdschrift voor Recht en Religie* 2016-2, p. 75-83.

Bernts, T. & J. Berghuijs (2016), *God in Nederland 1966-2015,* Ten Have.

Bijsterveld, S.C. van & B.P. Vermeulen (2016), 'Commentaar op artikel 6 van de Grondwet', in: E.M.H. Hirsch Ballin & G. Leenknegt (eds.), *Artikelsgewijs commentaar op de Grondwet,* web-edition.

Boyer, P. (2001), *Religion Explained. The human instincts that fashion gods, spirits and ancestors,* London: William Heinnemann.

Brodie, F.M. (1995), *No Man Knows My History. The life of Joseph Smith,* New York: Vintage Books.

Broeksteeg, J.L.W. (2016), Note with Rechtbank [Dutch District Court] Noord-Holland 8 september 2016, 15/720112-14, ECLI:NL:RBNHO:2016:7557, *JB* 2016/200.

Cusack, C. (2010), *Invented Religions. Imagination, Fiction and Faith,* Ashgate.

Dawkins, R. (1992), *The Selfish Gene,* Oxford: Oxford University Press.

Doornbos, N. (2006), *Op verhaal komen. Institutionele communicatie in de asielprocedure*, Nijmegen: Wolf Legal Publishers.

Doornbos, N. (2011), 'Wat doen ambtenaren als ze regelstoepassen?'. in: *Recht van onderop. Antwoorden uit de rechtssociologie*, Nijmegen: Ars Aequi Libri, p. 99-114.

Garlick, M. (2013), 'Selected aspects of UNHCR's research findings', in: C. Grütters, E. Guild & S. de Groot (eds.), *Assessment of Credibility by Judges in Asylum Cases in the EU*, Oisterwijk: Wolf Legal Publishers, p. 51-66.

Groot, D. de (2017), 'Deskundigenbewijs in het bestuursrecht na het Korošec-arrest', *NJB* 2017/473.

Haar, K. & G. Douma (2016), 'Bekering als asielmotief', *Tijdschrift voor Religie, Recht en Beleid*, 2016-1, p. 19-26.

Hammer, O. & M. Rothstein (2012), 'Introduction to New Religious Movements', in: O. Hammer & M. Rothstein, *The Cambridge Companion to New Religious Movements*, Cambridge: Cambridge University Press.

Henderson, B, (2006), *The Gospel of the Flying Spaghetti Monster*, Villard Books.

IND (2015), *Een uit duizenden. Elf verhalen over de mensen achter de asielaanvraag*, <ind.nl/ Documents/Eenuitduizenden.pdf>.

Kagan, R.A. (2006), *The Organization of Administrative Justice Systems: The Role of Political Mistrust,* JSP/Center for the Study of Law and Society Faculty Working Papers, University of California, Berkeley. <escholarship.org/uc/item/4k20s5zr>.

Lipsky, M. (2010), *Streel-level democracy: dilemmas of the individual in public services*, 30th Anniversary expanded edition, New York: Russel Sage Foundation.

Mesoudi, A. (2011), *Cultural evolution. How Darwinian theory can explain human culture & synthesize the social sciences*, Chicago: The University of Chicago Press.

Possamai, A. (2012), 'Yoda goes to Glastonbury: an introduction to hyper-real religions', in: Adam Possamai (ed.), *Handbook of Hyper-Real Religions*, Leiden: Brill, p. 18-20.

Richerson, P.J. & R. Boyd (2005), *Not by genes alone,* Chicago: University of Chicago Press.

Schmeets, H, (2016), *De religieuze kaart van Nederland, 2010–2015*, Centraal Bureau voor de Statistiek, <www.cbs.nl/nl-nl/publicatie/2016/51/de-religieuze-kaart-van-nederland-2010-2015.

The Loose Canon. A Really Important Collection of Words, <www.loose-canon.info>.

UNHCR (2013), *Beyond Proof. Credibility Assessment in EU Asylum Systems,* <www.unhcr.org/afr/ protection/operations/51a8a08a9/full-report-beyond-proof-credibility-assessment-eu-asylum-systems.htm>.

Verbaas, F.-W. (2016), 'De geloofwaardigheid van het geloof', *Journaal Vreemdelingenrecht,* 2016-1, p. 24-33.

Wagoner, R. van & S. Walker (1982), 'Joseph Smith: The Gift of Seeing', *Dialogue: A Journal of Mormon Thought*, 15(2), p. 48-68.

Wakonigg, D. & W. Rath (2017), *Das Fliegende Spaghettimonster. Religion oder Religionsparodie?*, Aschaffenburg: Alibri.

Werkman, G. (2017), 'Asylum seekers and religion in the Netherlands: Some aspects of the Present situation', unpublished paper presented at the Seminar on Migration and Religion, Radboud University Nijmegen, 9-10 February.

White, R.C.A. & C. Ovey (2010), *Jacobs, White & Ovey. The European Convention on Human Rights*, 5th ed., Oxford: Oxford University Press.

Wilson, D.S. (2002), *Darwin's cathedral. Evolution, religion, and the nature of society*, Chicago: The University of Chicago Press.

Postface

Chapter 13   Concluding Remarks

Elspeth Guild

13.1   Introduction

Romans 13:

> *(1) Let every person be subject to the governing authorities.*
> *For there is no authority except from God, and those that*
> *exist have been instituted by God.*
> *(2) Therefore whoever resists the authorities resists what*
> *God has appointed, and those who resist will incur*
> *judgment.*

or Matthew 25?

> *(35) For I was hungry and you gave me food, I was thirsty*
> *and you gave me drink, I was a stranger and you welcomed*
> *me,*
> *(36) I was naked and you clothed me, I was sick and you*
> *visited me, I was in prison and you came to me.*

The reception of migrants in Europe has become a controversy which leaves no section of society untouched. The arrival in a European Union of over 500 million inhabitants of a couple of million asylum seekers mainly from Syria, Iraq and Afghanistan in 2015 and 2016 has sparked controversies in as disparate areas as social affairs, housing and schooling, employment, integration policies and transport. The activities of charities and non-governmental organizations, mainly in assisting refugees and migrants as they seek protection from war and persecution or better opportunities for themselves and their families (or both) has come under scrutiny, primarily by state authorities (and extreme right groups), regarding whether assisting refugees and migrants is permissible, lawful or illegal. If illegal what sanctions should there be against those who help refugees and migrants?

These controversies about refugees, migrants or possibly simply foreigners are also rending religious communities apart. Even the Catholic church has been riven by differing views on what those who profess a belief in God and the Bible should do when confronted by the distress of the refugee or migrant in the face of state authorities' policies to prevent the assistance of irregular entry and residence in the state. Among Christian religious groups, whether Catholic or Protestant, this controversy seems to express itself most frequently as the

Romans 13 versus Matthew 25 issue: in Romans 13 the faithful are called upon to obey the laws of the state, in Matthew 25 the faithful are called upon to welcome the stranger according to the famous phrase: I was a stranger and you invited me in.

13.2   Scapegoating

There are a number of ways of analyzing the issue and the arrival of religious doctrine into the arena. First, the hardening of law and policy in many European (and North American) countries against migrants and foreigners has sparked substantial controversy about the scapegoating of migrants as the source of other problems such as unemployment et cetera. While state authorities in many countries rely on the argument that the citizens are tired of so many migrants and want them either to leave or to integrate (assimilate), civil society groups in those same states have become increasingly mobilized against the more draconian immigration measures to which authorities have resorted. These civil society actors reject the claims of state authorities that they are acting in accordance with the wishes of the majority; instead, the civil society actors claim both the support of the majority (against a minor extreme right) and an obligation to protect and defend the weak – refugees and migrants. As so often happens, as the arrivals of refugees and migrants in 2015 – 16 increased, there was an escalation in the conflict between state authorities and civil society actors which resulted in an increasing use of criminal law against civil society actors who defied state authorities and welcomed refugees and migrants into their communities.[1] The result has been an increase of criminal sentences being handed down by criminal courts in Europe against people who have and insist on continuing to assist refugees and migrants. Primarily these criminal sentences have been accompanied by fines, but in 2016/17 there was an increase in the use of custodial sentences.[2] Thus, an analysis on the basis of law, resistance, more law and escalation is one framework to understand the changing relationship of Europe and its migrants.

13.3   Justifications

Another analytical framework is through the justifications which European civil society actors give for their actions in defying their own state authorities. Numerous actors facing criminal charges have justified their actions on the basis of the humanitarian crisis which faces migrants and refugees as a result of state

---

1   <picum.org/de/nachrichten/bulletin/52284/#cat_40004> accessed 13 September 2017.
2   <en.rfi.fr/france/20170727-french-press-review-27-july-2017> accessed 13 September 2017.

actions.[3] They claim that the state itself should be providing reception and succour to refugees and migrants who arrive at the borders of their territories. They claim that state authorities are hypocritical when they claim that they comply with their international obligations but leave people in desperate conditions just at the edges of their territory. Still others claim that their faith requires them to provide assistance to refugees and migrants irrespective of the state laws which might prohibit or criminalise these actions. A notable example of this faith based argument is found in the Sanctuary Movement among churches in the USA.[4] However perhaps the most widely reported religious actor calling on the faithful to defy state authority has been the Pope of the Catholic Church.[5]

The Pope's call in 2015 that Catholic religious institutions and the faithful should open their doors and shelter refugees and migrants (irrespective of the prohibition of state authorities)[6] came as a surprise not only to some state authorities but also to many faithfully within the Catholic ranks. Not all bishops and other leaders of the church agreed with the Pope and the controversy spread within the Vatican. The Jesuit Refugee Service has been among the most vocal in support of refugees and migrants[7] while other parts of the faithful are more reluctant.[8] The controversy is frequently expressed in terms of Roman 13 versus Matthew 25 – the language of the Bible, which as is not infrequently the case, appears to point in two directions simultaneously. The fine theological arguments are played out among those who have the specialist training and knowledge for that exercise. It is not here that these will be repeated. Rather it is space which has been chosen by many of the faithful, not only among the Catholic church but also among the Protestant sects, for the debate to take place. Unlike the civil society actors who defy state authorities on the basis of humanitarian grounds, there is no effort in the Romans 13 versus Matthew 25 debate for the state. The language of humanitarian reasons, human rights et cetera, is the language of the 20th century international institutions charged with maintaining peace. This is the field of international conventions, agreements, protocols and other products of international law and diplomacy which is mustered against the claims of state sovereign entitlements of some state authorities to protect their borders against those arriving (albeit on foot and in

---

3   <www.businessinsider.com/r-french-farmer-defiant-despite-suspended-jail-term-for-aiding-illegal-migrants-2017-8?international=true&r=US&IR=T> accessed 13 September 2017.

4   <www.theguardian.com/us-news/2017/feb/08/sanctuary-movement-undocumented-immigrants-america-trump-obama> accessed 13 September 20917.

5   <www.independent.co.uk/news/world/europe/ppeo-francis-refugees-migrants-more-help-politicians-governments-europe-mediterranean-a7904341.html> accessed 13 September 2017.

6   <www.nbcnews.com/storyline/europes-border-crisis/pope-francis-calls-parishes-house-refugee-families-says-vatican-will-n422561> accessed 13 September 2017.

7   <en.jrs.net/> accessed 13 September 2017.

8   <www.theatlantic.com/international/archive/2017/05/catholic-populists-trump-pope-francis-vatican/527766/> accessed 13 September 2017.

need of shelter) and to expel those who have managed to arrive. This is a battle of state sovereignty against the claim that states have ceded competence through international conventions to international organisations regarding how state authorities must behave in respect of refugees and migrants. It is a struggle which takes place before the courts with legal arguments about the meaning, reach and authority of international law in respect of state claims regarding border controls. This is the friction between state sovereignty and international law.

13.4   Religious doctrine and the faithful

But the Romans 13 versus Matthew 25 debate is quite different. It is not founded in law of any form which is still justiciable before the courts of Western states. Instead it takes the language of humanitarianism back to its pre 20th century roots in religious doctrine. Christian and Muslim religions have never ceded ground regarding religious duty to state authorities. Indeed, even the relinquishing of the entitlement to determine the composition of families (birth, marriage and death) has only slowly and some would say partially been relinquished by religious institutions to state authorities (and only for some purposes). That the faithful will find themselves in conflict between the prescriptions of state authorities and their religious obligations is not new. However, the field on which it is currently being carried out is more recent. The arrival of refugees and migrants in Europe and North America in perhaps somewhat larger numbers than state authorities anticipated (though not necessarily in such substantial numbers as to be destabilizing) in 2015 – 16 has opened the debate about the entitlement to obedience.

   For those among the faithful for whom the practice of charity and welcome is an essential element of their doctrine, the Matthew 25 argument is the dominant one. In any discussion about the meaning of Romans 13 and the duty to obey state authorities is always read in a restrictive manner among this group, so as to limit to non-existent the ultimate duty to obey the state and refuse a welcome and shelter to refugees and migrants. For those who find the presence of refugees and migrants disturbing and unsettling, the argument of Romans 13 that obedience to state authorities is a duty of the faithful takes precedence. As the balance of power between religious bodies and state authorities has vacillated towards state authorities in the 20th century, the certainty of the state of its entitlement to determine issue of policy such as border controls, and the refusal of shelter to refugees and migrants has been taken for granted. The arrival of Matthew 25 again in the public sphere as an argument for civil disobedience in support of refugees and migrants is something of a surprise for those authorities. The durability and sustainability of the Matthew 25 arguments in the face of state authorities' power (and eventually violence) is a matter for all religious institutions to reflect upon at this time.

Index